For my Buddy Mike
You probably didn't know I had
a dark side - :) but, alas,
I guess it's all here in print.
Hope you enjoy it!
Phil

BARKERS & BONES

Portrait of an Undercover Narc

Phil Ribera

This book is a memoir—a collection of stories that took place many years ago. As such, the events described herein are subject to the frailties and imperfections of human memory and the differing interpretations of others who were there. My best efforts were made to adhere to factual accuracy of events and situations; however many of the characters in this book are composites. Individual names and identifying characteristics have been changed, as have those of businesses and organizations. Any similarities to actual persons or organizations are strictly coincidental.

ISBN-13: 978-0615462622
ISBN-10: 0615462626

Published by Phil Ribera
Cover design by Terry VanderHeiden
Cover photo taken at The Outpost Sports Bar and Grill in San Ramon, California

Learn more about this book by visiting Phil Ribera on the World Wide Web at:
www.philribera.com

For my dad—

ACKNOWLEDGEMENTS

To my family, friends, and the readers of my first book—I thank you. Your support and encouragement sustained me through this second undertaking. I especially want to thank Sheryl "Scooter" Boykins for her tireless promoting; Margaret Reimche for her editing assistance; all my cousins, their spouses and their kids for their inspiring support; my nephew, Jacob Spillner (cover model); my friend Rob Bilovocky at the Outpost Sports Bar in San Ramon, CA (cover photo location); and once again, Terry VanderHeiden for the photography and layout assistance. Gale and my two wonderful daughters—you are the center of my world. Thank you for always being there. And to my dad, Gil Ribera—a brave and honorable man, a loyal friend, and a thoughtful and loving father.

BARKERS & BONES:

Portrait of an Undercover Narc

Prologue

I sit on the side of the tub—my face buried in my hands. The life I once knew is gone. My entire existence has become an insane carnival ride, spinning and diving, jerking this way and the other. It's both thrilling and terrifying, and it makes me sick to my stomach. Yet, I can't get enough of it. I'm unable to get off the ride. I won't get off.

My hand is balled into a fist and I want to slam it through the wall, but I'm not sure who to blame for all my rage. *Who is it I am I really angry at? My bosses? The feds? Is it the people who are trying to kill me? Is my wife to blame for the position I'm in?*

I walk out of the bathroom to find her sitting alone at the kitchen table. The weathered smile she's fought to keep on her face has all but vanished. The past 3½ years have taken a visible toll. Her trademark optimism has crumbled into bitter disappointment.

I hear the girls whispering in the darkness of their bedroom, and I realize they've suffered too. I'm suddenly struck with a sad reality: In my current state, my family would be much better off without me.

I sit down at the table across from Gale. "We need to talk."

Her soft blue eyes come up to meet mine, but she says nothing.

"I've made a decision . . ."

1

Sweet Dreams

Tuesday, September 6th

Some of them want to use you, and some of them want to get used by you . . .

My thumb raps the dashboard to the beat of the number one song, and I turn the volume up until it's blasting.

I check my new look in the rearview mirror, hoping the long Labor Day weekend has given my beard sufficient time to sprout. All I see is stubble, and it makes my face look a little dirty. I guess that's okay; undercover cops should probably look a little dirty.

The police building is jammed full of employees during the day, something I'm not used to having just come off the night shift. Nobody seems to notice the difference in my appearance. People say hi, ask me if I'm going to court, or pass me by altogether without a word. I walk to the lunchroom where I take the lunch from my duffel bag and put it into the refrigerator.

"Hey, I heard you're going to narcs."

Finally someone acknowledges the thousand pound elephant in the room, or at least the one in my mind. "Yeah," I say, turning to face the voice that finally noticed. "I start today."

The only person I see is Captain Ronald Parks, head of the patrol division. He's sitting by himself, cracking a hard-boiled egg against the sharp edge of the table. I'm suddenly aware that I had answered the captain's question with surly ambivalence, not befitting his status as the number two man in the department. I start into a more engaging response, appropriate and respectful, but he wipes the air with a free hand.

"Save the bullshit." He peels the last of the shell from his egg. "I'm going to give you some advice."

I shut the refrigerator door and walk to his table. I'm awkward in front of him, not knowing if I should take a seat or remain standing. "What's that, sir?"

"I spent some time in the narcotics unit some years back." Parks pauses to sprinkle salt onto the egg, then pepper. "My advice is, never forget who you are." It hangs in the air as he stares at me with egg in hand.

I tap a finger across my lips and nod like I know what he's talking about.

"It's easy to forget who you are when you're a narc." Parks jabs a finger in the air like an exclamation point, then licks the salt off it. "Remember that."

I thank him and walk out of the lunchroom feeling a little insulted. I'm no bum. Does he think I'll go over to the other side? Take payoffs? Steal from people? Use drugs? I've never done drugs in my life—not so much as a single puff of a marijuana joint. I rarely even drink alcohol. I worked hard to get this assignment. As a uniformed cop I had to show I was the best. I spent the last five years proving myself. *Never forget who I am? Christ, I know who I am!*

I swing by to check my mail slot, but stop short when I see my nametag is gone. I locate it upstairs on the wall behind the secretary's desk. Wow. I guess I'm officially in the investigation division. A couple of my former squad partners walk past on their way back from court. They give me a bad time about my appearance, but I know they're envious. I've finally made it to the most coveted position in the police department.

I meander through the maze of inspectors' desks hoping one of them stops to wish me well or tell me how different I look. Nobody does. I pause in front of the door to my new office and savor the moment. I suddenly hear yelling from inside, and the door flies open.

"What in the fuck were you two idiots thinking?" Sergeant Roberts nearly tramples me as he storms out. "Do you know how stupid you made us look?" He glances at me with a half nod and continues into his private office next door.

I wait there for a second, debating whether to greet him or continue into my new office. Something tells me this isn't a good time, so I elect to avoid the sergeant for now. I go in and find my three new coworkers sitting solemnly at their desks. Van Kirk, a guy with whom I worked patrol, gives me a nod. He's been assigned to narcs for all of six months. Miller is eating a sandwich that looks as if it's come apart. Between bites, he carefully fishes pieces of it from his typewriter.

"Pheasant," he says. "My wife made me a sandwich with it after I shot the fucker." I'm not really sure what an appropriate response is to a statement like that. I assume "*the fucker*" he shot is the bird and not his wife. I'm smiling at him like a fellow sportsman, when in reality I have never gone hunting, I've never shot anything, and my wife would never make me a sandwich out of something I killed.

"That's your desk," Cad says. [He's a detective who fills a position in narcotics. Van Kirk, Miller and I are all still patrol officers on a temporary three-year rotation; unless we screw up, in which case it can be a much briefer stay.] It occurs to me that the captain who offered me his sage advice downstairs had his tour cut short. Rumor around the department was that he was kicked out after he had some kind of blowup with one of his bosses. Strangely enough, he later managed to promote to lieutenant and then captain, all with that black mark on his record.

I set my duffel bag on the desk, noting that my new space is in an awkward location. Wedged between the door and a row of file cabinets, the desk has the unit's answering machine taking up one end of it and a giant map of the city plastered to the wall above it. I assume that's why they gave it to *the new guy*, but I'll survive. I'm just glad to be here. I absentmindedly run a hand over the top of my new workstation.

A quick look flashes between the three of them and I think I detect a chuckle. Miller stares back at his sandwich and Van Kirk looks away. Cad grunts himself out of his seat and his behemoth frame wallows over to me. "Your desk has some history," he says with a slight laugh. "Those marks."

I look down and notice a discolored, crusty stain on the upper right side of the desk.

"That's from Skip, the guy you're replacing."

"What is it?" I ask.

"It's from him and a clerk who used to work up here. Her name was Layla, we called her the cadaver because she looked like she was dead."

"Oh yeah, I remember her."

"Yeah well, Skip banged her one night on your desk." Cad's words are matter of fact, punctuating the end of his sentence as if there's simply no more to say about it. He turns and slumps back into his seat, leaving me to examine the stain with an odd mixture of shock, disgust, and titillating imagery.

"Who was getting yelled at by the sergeant when I came in?" I swing my chair around to face the guys.

Miller points his sandwich in Van Kirk's direction. "That dumbshit and Skip etched their names in the wet cement outside the jail back when they remodeled it."

"We wrote our undercover names, not our real names." Van Kirk's counterpoint comes out as a lame commentary on his thought process. "Anyway, the police chief saw it and found out it was us."

The conversation drifts to my undercover name, and they explain that all undercover narcs need to have one. A special driver's license will be issued by the DMV, under the fictitious identity. Van Kirk shows me his license, a bearded face with the name Mike Brown below it. He couldn't do any better than *Brown?*

"You always want to keep your real first name so you don't get confused when someone's talking to you." He slips the license back into an Italian leather wallet.

Note to self: A scroungy drug user probably shouldn't have such a nice wallet. I sit at my desk and pull out my handheld police radio. I turn it on and set it next to me. The other three guys immediately start laughing.

"Turn that shit off," barks Van Kirk. They're all leaning back with their hands behind their heads like they're on Waikiki beach.

The door opens and Sergeant Roberts blows in like a guy who's got to take a leak. "Pick out a UC name yet, Philly?"

I'm on my feet before the last word, and I'm not sure if I should salute, shake hands, or sit back down. He looks at the other guys and they all laugh. "Relax," he says. "First order of business: we gotta get you a fake license with your undercover name. Go ahead, pick one."

I glance at the city map over my desk and my eyes zero in on the snake-like roadway that threads north to south through my old beat.

"Soto Road," I blurt out before I can even think.

"Your undercover name is going to be Soto Road?" Roberts acts like he's writing it down, and the other guys are wetting their pants.

"I meant Phil Soto." They all laugh some more as they repeat the name.

I show up the next day with my new UC driver's license in a cheap Velcro wallet with a marijuana leaf on it. I've gotten my ear pierced, my beard trimmed into a goatee, and I'm wearing stained Levis and a Big Ben work shirt. *The transformation has begun.*

When I step into the office they all look at me in silence. Van Kirk finally blasts out a hardy laugh and the sergeant comes in behind me to see what's so funny.

"Soto Road!" The sergeant grins as he circles me, inspecting the whole ensemble. "We need to get you out there buying dope."

Miller claps his hands together. "I got a new CI who's into a bunch of heroin dealers over off Sonoma Street. He can intro you in, no problem."

A wave of reality slaps me like a wet rag. "Heroin dealers?" *What if they recognize me? What if they ask me something that I should know, but don't? And what the hell is a CI?*

Miller tells me that a CI is a confidential informant—someone who's proven his or her reliability with verifiable information. They have to be kept confidential to protect them from getting killed by the people they're setting up. I find myself wondering what will protect *me* from getting killed by the people they're setting up.

"He's coming in here for some money in a little while," Miller says. "Come in and I'll introduce you to him. See if he's comfortable with you." *Comfortable with me?* What if I'm not *comfortable* with him?

Around lunchtime a short Mexican kid shows up in the parking lot and Miller hustles him up the back stairs. I come in to the interview room where they're waiting, and the kid eyes me with a goofy smile.

"Alberto, this is Phil Soto. Soto, meet The Big A." I reach across the table and shake Alberto's hand, then wonder if drug addicts even shake hands. There's probably some secret thing they do, and I've just blown it.

"He'll work," Alberto says, still sporting the grin. He turns to Miller. "But don't bust anyone while I'm still there, or I'm as good as dead."

Miller tells him not to worry. He says that the plan is to get me introduced to the sellers so they'll trust me enough to do business without Alberto. I'll then go back on my own and make more drug purchases over an extended period of time, long enough for them to forget who introduced me to them in the first place.

It sounds a little risky, but more so for Alberto. I'm wondering if these dealers are really likely to forget something like that.

I sit uncomfortably across from Alberto while Miller goes next door to get some money out of the safe. He pays Alberto forty bucks before showing him out of the building.

"Was the money for setting up an introduction for me?" I ask Miller. He shakes his head. "We only pay after they deliver. That was for a search warrant I wrote behind his information last week. Got a little bit of dope, not much. I figure forty bucks will keep that little fish on the stringer."

I nod, thinking that *The Big A* is more than likely on his way down to Sonoma Street to buy some for himself.

I feel a slap on my shoulder as Sergeant Roberts follows us into the office. "C'mon Philly, let's lose your cherry."

"I'm going to do a buy right now?"

"Nah," Roberts grabs a set of keys from the board. "We'll start you off with a whore. They're easier."

Van Kirk jumps up and the three of us go down to the surveillance van in the back lot. It's just after dark and my old shift is breaking lineup. I can see them checking us out as they load up their cars. A few minutes later we're trolling up and down the main streets of the downtown district. Sergeant Roberts is driving, Van Kirk is in the passenger seat and I'm kneeling on the floor between them, holding onto the door that separates the cab from the back of the van.

"I didn't know the narcs did prostitution cases." I shift my weight to my other knee.

Roberts' eyes pan back and forth at each intersection. "Our vice unit was cut back to only one guy, so we gotta help him out. Besides, these girls know a lot of drug people, and they don't mind snitching."

"Roberts would drive past an armed robbery in progress just to do a whore case," Van Kirk adds.

"There's one." Roberts throws on a pair of thick-rimmed glasses. "Quick, get in the back." Van Kirk climbs back with me and eases the door closed, confining us to the cargo area.

"He's going to pick her up with us in here?" I whisper to Van Kirk.

"Yeah, this is going to be great. Roberts can talk his way around anything. Just watch."

The engine slows and I can hear the sergeant's muffled voice. I can't make out his words, but they're light and relaxed. There's a higher pitched giggle and then the passenger door opens and closes. Now I can hear both of them.

"So, you looking for a date tonight?" the woman says in a friendly, singsong tone.

"A date?" Roberts asks. "Well, yeah, I guess. We could get a frozen yogurt or . . ."

"No, you idiot. Sex!"

"But I've never done anything like this before," whines Roberts. "I don't know what I'm supposed to . . ."

"You're not a cop, are you?"

I feel my heart stop as I wait for Roberts' answer.

"A cop? Most certainly not!" Roberts slaps the steering wheel for added effect. "My wife is out of town, and sure, maybe I've been a little lonely. But if you think that I'm . . ." I feel the van suddenly swerve to the curb.

"No," she cries out. "I just have to ask that question. It's nothing personal."

"Well, alright then." Roberts pulls back into traffic.

"I know a place we could park," she says. "We could do it right here in the back of your van." She turns the knob and suddenly the door between us starts to open. I shrink into a dark corner, knowing all she has to do is turn her head and she'll see us. Meanwhile, Van Kirk is grinning like a kid on his birthday, almost as if he's inviting her to look.

"Oh don't open that," Roberts says calmly. "I don't want my little doggie to get out."

Van Kirk immediately starts yapping like a Chihuahua and the door eases shut. Roberts and the girl talk a little about the dog, and then it sounds as if they're negotiating for sex. Van Kirk is barking so loud I can't hear anything they're saying. Finally, Roberts flips the door open a crack and sticks his hand back with a signal to knock it off.

Van Kirk crawls up and sniffs Roberts' hand, and then starts licking it. Roberts starts laughing and the girl is twisting in her seat to get a glimpse of the cute little puppy. I'm frozen in the corner, watching the whole show in amazement.

Roberts pats Van Kirk on the head. "Now be a nice doggie and shut the hell up."

I pull the curtain back and peek out the side window, noting that we're about a block from the police department. The girl hasn't picked up on our location yet. Instead, she lets out a smoker's cough and then jauntily describes her *specialties* to the sarge.

Roberts picks up speed and takes a sharp and sudden turn into the police lot, tossing both Van Kirk and me across the floor into the cabinet. I hear the girl scream, and Roberts yells something out. I straighten up, unsure of what is happening.

"She jumped out!" Roberts yells. "Get her!"

I throw the sliding door open, and me and Van Kirk take off down the block after the escaping hooker. It's now that I'm finally able to view the woman. Her sandy colored hair is in a long braid, plopping back and forth as she runs. She's wearing flat sandals, which isn't helping her stride, and she's got a fat ass that's packed tightly into denim jeans, which isn't helping her either. We catch up to the woman in front of the post office about a half block away, and walk her back.

Roberts has parked the van in the secured lot and is waiting for us there. "I tried to time the gate opening so I could shoot right in," he says. "But it didn't retract fast enough, and she bailed out before I could grab her."

The hooker mumbles something about thinking she was being kidnapped, but she doesn't seem all that upset by her arrest. Roberts starts pumping her for information before we even get inside the jail. By the time they're finished fingerprinting the woman, she's agreed to set someone up in return for us dropping the solicitation charges.

We leave her in the jail, and I'm left confused. "Isn't that what we wanted?"

Roberts nods. "Sure it is. Any time you can flip someone to be an informant, do it. Just make sure you don't drop their case until after they've given you someone, otherwise you'll never see them again. Besides, the district attorney has to sign off on it."

"You think she'll carry through on the promise to do something for us?"

"She told me about another gal working the streets close to where I picked her up." Roberts says with a shrug, "We'll see if it pans out."

"Gotta keep the hammer on them snitches," Van Kirk says as we walk down the ramp. "Hey look, there's where we wrote our names." We're standing over a new concrete curb alongside the jail sally port. The sergeant pushes him toward the cars with a frown that's already lost its consequence.

We stop in front of an unmarked car parked at the very back of the lot, and Sergeant Roberts hands me a set of keys. "Take this one," he says.

The huge white Cadillac doesn't seem to fit me, but at least it doesn't look like a cop's car. "Is this one of ours?"

"Rental," says Roberts. "We rotate them in and out so they don't get made. When they start to get heated up, we turn them back in."

"It's Cad's car," Van Kirk says with a laugh. "He got the nickname when he started driving it. *The Big White Cad.*"

"We installed a foot mic," Roberts says, pointing to a small black button next to the brake pedal. "All you have to do is press the button and talk. It's dialed into the private narc channel, so you can keep your foot on it the whole time and we'll hear everything."

I don't want to look like a dumbshit, but I have no idea what exactly we're going to do. *Are we going to follow someone, or am I supposed to approach the prostitute, or what?*

"Just cruise around downtown and we'll see what's out there." The sergeant's plan does little to address my concerns. I get the feeling he's much more into improvisation than I'm used to. Uniformed patrol doesn't leave much room for creativity.

Roberts and Van Kirk get into the van and follow me out the gate. We drive around the area where the sergeant made his earlier arrest, and we find a tall, thin, older woman with gray hair, sitting at a bus stop. Van Kirk pulls the van next to me so I'm face to face with the sergeant.

"I've never seen her before," Roberts says. "Want to give it a try?"

I nod, taking a gulp of air into my dry mouth.

"Just pull to the curb and let her approach you," he continues. "She'll probably ask if you're looking for a date. Just let her do the talking. When she solicits you for a sex act, just pull over and we'll move in to make the arrest. As long as you keep your foot on the mic, we'll hear everything."

"What if she doesn't solicit me?"

They both laugh. "What the hell else is she going to do?" Van Kirk says.

"It's all about money," says Roberts. "If you're having trouble getting a solicitation out of her, just mention that you don't have a lot to spend. That'll get her talking about money, and what she'll do and for how much. There isn't a whore in the world that would ever give it away for free."

I pull to a stop right in front of the woman and she gives me a crooked smile. "Want to party?"

"Sure," I say, even though it wasn't the words I had prepared for. My mind fumbles with thoughts of what to say when she asks if I'm a cop. "Let's party." I smile, proud of my spontaneous little improv. *Hope the sergeant and Van Kirk caught it.*

Instead of getting into the car, the woman waves a hand over her head signaling a guy across the street. I had noticed him standing in front of the bar when I pulled up. The emaciated guy limps across the street, tucking his greasy shirt into his greasy pants. For a minute I wonder if it's some kind of rip-off, but I get no threatening vibes from him.

"You looking to get high?" he says, surveying up and down the street as he's talking.

"Sure," I say, using the same lame word I already used on her.

"You're not a cop, are you?"

"No. I mean, hell no! My wife's out of town and . . ."

The guy looks at the girl. She shrugs, like *who gives a shit?* "Okay," he says. "I got some good coke. How much do you want?"

Uh oh . . . we didn't go over this. I haven't got a real good handle on the measurements or street value of cocaine yet, and I'm not all that confident with the terminology. I'm trying to quickly replay things I've heard on patrol—finally pulling a term out of my ass. "I'll take an eight-ball."

The dealer's eyes get wide and he looks at the hooker. Her expression confirms that whatever I said was wrong. "Sure," he says, stealing my own useful expression. "I can get it for you in ten minutes. Give me three hundred, fifty bucks. My man is right inside the bar."

Three fifty? Oops. "I'll need to make a stop to pick up the cash," I say, fumbling the words a bit. "I'll be back in ten minutes." The hooker looks like she wants to get in with me, but I take off and leave her standing at the curb with him. I peel around the corner, followed closely by the undercover van. They pass by and motion me to follow. We stop at an ATM up the street, and Roberts jumps out with card in hand.

"How much coke do I want?" Roberts says, mimicking me. "A quarter-gram, maybe a half-gram, oh what the fuck I'll take a kilo." He and Van Kirk break into laughter and give each other a high five. The sergeant maxes his card and Van Kirk has to use his. They slap the wad of twenties into my hand and jump back into the van, still laughing.

I head back toward the bar shaking my head in disbelief. The way this unit operates is beyond bizarre. Certainly I'm now in a universe far beyond the policy and procedure-driven uniformed patrol division. The van passes by and Roberts yells to me from the window. "Don't front the money, Soto. We'll never see it again."

I pull up to find the old guy standing limply in front of the bar, and the hooker nowhere in sight. Even though he's about as threatening as a Halloween pumpkin, I'm on edge—hyper alert for any sign of trouble during my first drug deal.

I'm second guessing my ability to use street slang convincingly, so I simply say, "Got the stuff?" My question ends up sounding like something from a Starsky and Hutch episode. In any case, the guy shakes his head.

"My guy was dry," he says. I watch as he saunters back into the bar, in what feels like the most anti-climatic ending I could have ever imagined to my first drug buy. *Shit!*

I cringe as I pull away from the curb, afraid of what I'm going to hear over the radio. I see the van behind me, and I assume we're just going to head back to the police station. As soon as we turn onto Mission Boulevard, the sergeant's voice chirps over the radio. "Soto! On the corner, to your right. She's working."

Another woman loiters under a streetlight. "What do I do?"

There's a long pause, and I'm sure they're both laughing at me . . . again. "Meet us in the mortuary lot down the street."

I pull the big white car into the empty mortuary lot and the van screeches up behind me. I walk back to the passenger window where Roberts sits wearing an odd fishing hat. I hand him back the cash he gave me, as if I want nothing more to do with it. He tells me that the woman I just passed is a known prostitute, and he's arrested her downtown before. "Just do like you did with the last one," he says. "Only this time, don't order up anything more than pussy."

I get back in the car and pull onto the street. My heart is racing, and I'm trying to remember everything they told me. *Calm down*, I tell myself. You don't want her to think you're a cop. I check the mirror to make sure my backup is right there, but they're hanging several cars behind. The corner is empty now, and I almost feel a sense of relief.

Van Kirk pulls the van next to me and rolls down his window. "Across the street, Soto."

I glance over and see the woman next to a phone booth. She's a scraggly looking blond girl with a red bandanna on her head. I notice she's wearing a halter-top, denim bell-bottom pants, and has bare feet.

I flip a U-turn and pull to the curb a few feet ahead of her. She quickly jogs up to the passenger window, cradling a pair of shoes under one arm.

I'm all prepared for the "dating" dialog, when without a word she flings the door open and jumps in. I sit dumbly staring at her for a second, trying to figure out what to do.

"Go!" she says, letting out a sigh and rolling her eyes. "There are cops all around here."

I'm about to pull the car over and act all indignant just like Roberts did, and then I realize she hadn't asked me if I was one.

"Go that way." She points to a side street.

I take the turn and scan the mirror for any sign of Roberts and Van Kirk. I see the van make the turn, and notice they're flashing their headlights. *Son of a bitch, I forgot to step on the mic.*

"There's a good spot at the top of this hill," she says.

I try to depress the floor button, but my leg is quivering so much I can barely hold it down. Before I know it she's directing me into the parking lot of a church. The building and the lot are dark and there are no other cars in sight. I circle around the barren lot, hoping she'll just come out with a solicitation and we can get this whole thing over with.

"What's wrong with you?" she finally says. "You look like you're trying to find a good parking space or something. Just stop anywhere."

I tell her I've never done anything like this before and I'm just a little nervous. I put the car in park, but leave the engine running. I know as soon as I turn the key, the radio will shut off and my backup won't be able to monitor anything.

"Well . . ." I say, hoping to generate some useful response.

"Well what?" With a smirk, she dives over the seat into the back of the Cadillac, leaving me sitting at the wheel. I feel like I'm driving Miss Daisy as I try to converse via the rearview mirror. I feel her tugging on my shirt, but I'm clamped down on the floor mic for dear life. She pulls harder and I resist even more. It's a tug-of-war that is beginning to border on ridiculous. I finally take my foot off the floor and climb awkwardly into the back seat with her. As soon as I do, I see that she's broken free of her top. She's on her back and I'm scrunched hard against the door. She playfully whips me across the face with her top—her small white boobs jiggling with each swipe.

My parched mouth can't seem to get a word out. *Why hasn't she solicited me yet?* I begin to panic, and then I remember the sergeant's advice. Nearly screaming the words, I blurt out, "I have no money!"

"What?"

"I'm flat broke." I pull out my wallet and hold it open for her. "See? No money." I now realize that I blew it. Having no money isn't the same as not having a lot to spend. I don't really care at this point, as I would prefer that this whole thing was over and done with. I twist around to see if the van is anywhere in sight, but the lot is empty. *Where the hell are they?*

Expecting the so-called hooker to be dressed and out of the car by now, I'm thrown yet another curve. She's now kicked her pants off and is lying naked in front of me. I must have gasped, because she starts laughing.

She reclines back. "No money? What the hell, you can have it for free."

Free! She didn't just say that, did she?

I'm starting to think that the sergeant and Van Kirk set this up intentionally, when suddenly she leans up and grabs me with both her hands around the back of my head. She throws open her legs and starts pulling me. "Come on," she says. "It's your lucky day."

I rear back like a skittish horse, flailing for the handle behind me. The door springs open and I tumble onto the asphalt, sprawled there like a turtle on his back.

"What's wrong?" the girl's sweet voice calls out from the darkness beyond her bent knees and grinning crotch.

I stagger to my feet. "I . . . I'm sorry. I just can't do it here, in a church parking lot. The priest might see us."

She lets out a frustrated grunt and quickly slips back into her clothes. I stand like a dork with my hands in my pockets as she steps into her shoes and storms past me. No sooner does she get out the driveway and around the corner when I hear hysterical laughter from behind a stand of trees. Van Kirk and Roberts stumble out, doubled over and gasping.

"What happened, Soto?" Sergeant Roberts throws a hand over my shoulder.

I explain the whole conversation and it propels them into another convulsive round of hysteria.

Back in the office I find Miller typing a search warrant. Cad has already left for the night. "Hey Soto," Miller says without looking up. "How did your first case go?"

"Not good." I toss the keys on Cad's desk. "Couldn't make the drug buy and couldn't get either girl to solicit me."

Van Kirk and Roberts walk in and divide up their money while listening half heartedly as I replay my failures. Van Kirk falls into his chair and kicks his feet onto the desk. "Well Soto, at least you buffed her out in your car."

"Yeah, that's not too bad for your first time," says the sergeant. "When Miller gets The Big A back in pocket, we'll get you buying some dope."

I'm stuck on the term, *buffed out*. I can only assume it means that I got the girl out of her clothes. Though it was never my intent to do so, I interpret it as a noteworthy accomplishment among my new peers.

"What do we got for tomorrow?" Roberts asks, checking the grease board on the wall. "Search warrant on E Street. Is that yours, Miller?"

"Yeah, I'm finishing it up now and I'll have it signed by the judge first thing in the morning. Alberto also gave me some info on a guy up off of Foothill who's dealing weed. I can give that search warrant to Soto, to help him get rolling."

Miller hands me the file and I thank him. Although I appreciate the help, I'd really rather kick start my own narc career. I see Miller has already written some of the search warrant himself. I spend the next hour looking over his notes and reading what he's written thus far. I try to line it up in my circa 1950's typewriter, and realize I'm going to have to start the whole thing from scratch. Roberts leaves, and then Van Kirk. Miller and I are the last to go. Miller wants me to meet him at 10 a.m. so he can introduce me to one of the judges and I can see the process for getting a warrant signed. I thank him again for all the help.

As I leave for the night, I stroll around downstairs. I peek into the patrol sergeants' office and walk past the lineup room where the midnight shift is preparing for their watch. I was at the top of my game when I transferred out of uniform, and now I feel almost as if I'm starting over again in a whole new world. But I know I'm equal to the task. Somewhere down deep I feel like this job was meant for me.

I drive home imagining what it would feel like to really master this undercover stuff. I'm an actor by nature and I'm a pretty good cop. For once in my life I just need to play the part of someone other than the *good guy*.

The radio plays softly in the background, permeating my thoughts.

Sweet dreams are made of these . . .

2

Beauty Queen

I wake up early and stare around the room at all the boxes. We moved into the new house over the long weekend, and much of it still needs to be unpacked. Buying a place right now was probably ill timed, given that I began my new assignment the next day. But it's larger than where we lived before and it has a great backyard.

I come out to find my two girls eating breakfast on a blanket in front of the TV. My wife, Gale, is lining the cabinets with shelf paper and stacking them full of dishes. She sits with me while I eat, and though I'm trying to maintain the serenity of the morning, my leg is bouncing anxiously the whole time. My mind is already at work. I give Gale an abbreviated rundown of my failures on the job thus far, but tell her not to worry.

"I think I'm going to make my first successful drug buy today."

"Is it dangerous?" she asks as she clears the table.

"Oh no," I follow her as I gulp the last of my milk. "They'll have me wear a wire, and they'll be right there to cover me." Although the assurances I'm giving to Gale are sincere, I'm really just repeating what the guys told me. In truth, I haven't any idea how dangerous it will be. I change into a grubby outfit, and kiss each of the girls on the head. They turn away from Burt and Ernie momentarily to give me an adoring wave. Amazingly, they don't seem to notice my worsening look.

I meet Miller in the office and we walk across the parking lot to the courthouse. He introduces me to one of the court bailiffs who brings us into a hallway that runs behind the courtrooms. The bailiff tells us that Judge Daniels isn't feeling well, so keep it short. He taps lightly at the open door and the judge looks up from his papers. He's a red-faced guy who looks and smells like he's sweating out last night's hangover. I would bet he's not wearing much beneath that black robe.

Miller introduces us, and the old judge skims over Miller's search warrant the way I breeze through the obituary page: a quick glance at the names in case I know any of them, and beyond that I couldn't care less. The judge, however, is supposed to care. At least that's what I learned in a search warrant writing class I took when I was on patrol. After all, his stamp of approval on a document authorizes us to kick down someone's door and basically ransack their home.

The judge signs the warrant and we're out of there within ten minutes. As we leave the court building Miller says, "I always try to take my warrants to Daniels because he never reads them. The other judges ask a bunch of questions, and sometimes even make you rewrite the thing."

The sergeant is sitting in his office counting money when we come in. "Here, Soto," he says, holding up a bulging envelope and a notebook. "It's your UC funds. Each guy is budgeted two grand a month."

"For what?" I'm staring into the wad of bills.

"Whatever undercover expenses you have; buying dope, paying informants, whatever. Just keep your receipts and log everything in this ledger."

He follows me into our office where Miller is busy at the file cabinet and Van Kirk and Cad are on phone calls.

"I'd like to hit my place as soon as possible," Miller says to the sergeant. "The guy goes to work around three o'clock, and I want to catch him at home before he leaves."

The sarge writes 11 a.m. on the grease board next to the search warrant address. Cad hangs up the phone. "Smitty's on his way over for the briefing," he tells the sarge.

Doug Smitty is technically part of our unit, but handles vice and criminal intelligence out of a private office on the other side of the floor. He's a cantankerous older guy, with a belly that boasts a lifetime of big lunches and long naps. He's got a reputation as a solo operator, but he definitely knows his stuff.

Smitty comes in and takes his first look at me since I transferred in. He ambles over to my desk, sucking on his pipe. "Who are you trying to impersonate, the Frito Bandito?" Without waiting for an answer, he grabs a seat for the briefing. Apparently the guy whose place we're hitting is also part of a biker gang, and Smitty is interested in any names or photos we can collect for his intelligence files.

Van Kirk hangs up the phone. "Okay, I got a buy all set up for today." He swings around to face the rest of us. "One of my CI's just made a three-way call and set up a heroin deal with Marty English. It's supposed to go down at four o'clock this afternoon."

"Who's the buyer?" I ask.

"You." Van Kirk points to the board. "Write it down, boss." Roberts puts down *4 p.m. - Soto - buy/bust.*

"I've heard English's name before," I say to the group. "What's he all about?"

"Small time dope fiend." Van Kirk pulls a photo from his file folder. "He's so stupid that he'll sell to you without an intro."

The rest of them chuckle, but I'm trying to comprehend the whole thing. "He's going to sell heroin to a guy he's never met?"

"My CI told English to meet Phil Soto at the 7-11 store on Harder Road at four," Van Kirk says, slipping the photo back into the file. "She told him that you were a friend of hers."

"Don't worry about all that now," says Roberts. "We'll get Miller's search warrant out of the way first, then deal with English this afternoon.

"You guys sound like a bunch of little girls." Smitty lights his pipe again. "Let's get going. I got work to do."

Roberts asks what he's working on that's so pressing, and Smitty says something about an auto dealership. I have a momentary fantasy that it's a guy who once fired me when I worked as a janitor, but it turns out to be another place. Smitty tells us it's a Harley Davidson dealership with Hells Angels connections.

Miller takes the floor and passes out a two-page op plan. It lists the address we're going to hit, a photo of the suspect and his criminal history. The second page is a copy of the warrant itself, signed by the honorable Angus Daniels. The way things work, as Miller explains mostly to me, is that Miller is the *case agent*, since it's his warrant. He manages the operation, decides on strategies, and makes assignments regarding the case. Of course, the sergeant can overrule him at any time, but it's rare. During the search, we'll collect evidence and bring it to Miller, and he'll write out a receipt to the residents. *Sounds simple enough.*

In the back lot, I fasten my gunbelt, velcro my bulletproof vests into place, and put on a blue windbreaker with POLICE emblazoned across it in bright yellow letters. We all pile into the van—Miller is driving and the sarge in the passenger seat. "Soto, you and Van Kirk will be on the key," Miller says.

"Got it," I say, already familiar with the heavy steel battering ram from having assisted on a few of their entries while on patrol.

The tightly clustered homes give way to larger, more rural lots as we leave the city and head into the hills. The van slows as we pass a cute white cottage set on a deep lot, back from the street. Miller says, "That's the place, and the suspect's car is parked in the driveway."

He asks if we're ready, but doesn't wait for a response. The van jerks to the left and bounces onto the long dirt driveway. Cad slides the door open before we're stopped. I follow suit, feeling strong resistance from the *key* as I get my footing. Van Kirk takes the other side and we wobble up to the porch. Miller pushes past us yelling, "Police, search warrant, open the door!"

"Go!" I hear someone yell, though I can't tell whom. Van Kirk and I swing the heavy cylinder in unison, and then forward with shoulder popping zeal. The doorknob flies in one direction while the flimsy door swings open, bouncing off the wall inside. We pull the ram back out of the way as Miller, Cad, and the sergeant careen past us into the house. Van Kirk and I follow, while Smitty and his pipe take up the rear.

By the time I step into the room, Miller has got the suspect in handcuffs. The guy had been watching TV on the living room couch. His bowl of cereal is now overturned on the floor. I hear a weak scream from the kitchen, and a second later Cad walks the wife out in handcuffs. He sits her on the couch next to the husband, and they both stare up at us with the same expressions. I try to interpret the look, which doesn't strike me as either surprised or particularly angry. It's more like, *I know selling drugs is illegal, but I don't sell enough to justify all this.*

The guy is wearing Levis and no shirt, and his wiry frame bears a few crude tattoos. He's got one of those long narrow pieces of beard growing only on his chin, creating a goat-like look. The woman is blond, with a pretty face and a curvy, Marilyn Monroe figure. Other than both appearing to be in their early twenties, they don't seem to fit together.

Miller assigns the sergeant the easy job of babysitting the two detainees. Cad, Van Kirk and I are each given a room to search, and Smitty is left to probe around on his own. I'm in the master bedroom, which has an unmade, king-size waterbed and a couple of large wooden dressers. It takes me a solid half hour to search through all of it, but I find nothing of interest.

I take a break and wander into the dining room where Miller is logging the evidence collected by the others. He shows me about half a sandwich bag full of white powder, which he estimates is a half-ounce. Van Kirk apparently found it in a toolbox in the garage. I wonder if I would have found it had I been assigned the garage. I go back into the bedroom with renewed vigor. I go through everything again, and still find nothing.

I'm about to give up when I spot a drawer in the pedestal beneath the bed. I hadn't noticed it before, probably because it was covered by blankets. I slide it open and find an unmarked videotape and a couple of biker magazines. I call Smitty into the room, hoping I found some worthy intelligence for him.

He thumbs through the magazines and tosses them back in the drawer. "I already subscribe to these," he says with a condescending smirk. "And the tape is probably just a titty video." I notice he takes it with him anyway.

Having enough evidence to formally arrest both of the residents, Miller has already summoned a patrol unit to come take them to jail. They're just pulling away when I follow Smitty out of the room. With the house now empty, we all remove our gunbelts, windbreakers, and vests, tossing them in a pile by the door.

Smitty strolls over and slides the tape into the VCR and then flips on the TV. Everyone's eyes light up as the recording flickers to life. Their mouths drop open, yet nobody speaks. I move around to where I can see, and I'm paralyzed as well. The video shows the woman who has just been taken to jail. She's posing on the bed, wearing only a skimpy silk thing. She says something about a zucchini, and the husband hustles outside to the garden—camera in hand. He returns with a quite large zucchini. The woman proceeds to pleasure herself with it on camera.

Miller abandons his evidence and races into the room to see. There's no room on the couch, which is now crammed with Cad, Van Kirk, Smitty and Sergeant Roberts. Miller lets out a wild hoot and gives me a high five. "Good find, Soto!"

Smitty later locates a photograph of the girl posing on the bed with the zucchini. The videotape and the photo are both seized as evidence, presumably because they depict ownership and control over the residence—hence possession of the methamphetamine. They're all still talking about it when we get back to the office.

"What do you think, Sarge?" Miller says to Roberts. "Should we put Soto in charge of *Beauty Queen of the Month*?" There is enthusiastic agreement among the group.

I look next to the grease board where a crudely constructed frame has been cut out of construction paper. The words *Beauty Queen of the Month* are penned across the top, and a Polaroid photograph of another naked woman is tacked to it.

"She came out of a search warrant I had two weeks ago," Van Kirk says proudly. That photograph is removed, and replaced with the Zucchini Girl.

The sound of a loud knock on the office door causes the group to grow quiet. Since I'm at the desk closest to the door, I open it. Captain Parks stands there with a serious expression on his face. Roberts hops to his feet and the others try to look busy.

"What can we help you with, Captain?" Roberts maneuvers his way between me and the door.

"I understand your boys seized a video," he says.

Damn! Word travels fast around this place.

Roberts looks as if he's trying to think of something to say, but the captain doesn't seem interested.

"I'd like you to get it for me." Parks' words leave no room for negotiation. Roberts grabs the video from the bag on Miller's desk and hands it to the captain. The door closes and everybody just looks at each other. Maybe I could plead ignorant when internal affairs comes sniffing around—pull the rookie narc card and say I didn't know any better. I'm thinking that I sure enjoyed my few days in the unit. Too bad it didn't last longer.

The office is like a morgue after that, and I feel terrible. I leave the group and walk across the detective's floor toward the bathroom, scurrying past the captain's office to avoid being questioned about it. I pass the police chief's office and private conference room adjacent to the bathroom. I'm washing my hands and thinking as I regard my new look in the mirror. *Damn it, I went to all that trouble getting my ear pierced, and my goatee was just starting to grow in nicely.*

I suddenly hear a burst of laughter coming from the other side of the wall. I dry my face and step into the hallway outside the chief's conference room. The drapes are pulled closed, but it sounds like one hell of a rowdy meeting is taking place inside. I hear more laughing, and someone says, "Look at her take that whole zucchini!"

Holy shit! I'm nearly running as I weave my way through the detectives' desks. I motion to Roberts, who's next door in his office. "You gotta come in here." He follows me through the narc door. My three coworkers are still slumped at their desks.

"You guys want to know why the captain took the video?" I can barely conceal my grin.

"So he could give it to IA?" Miller says.

I shake my head. "The Chief wanted to show it to the commanders at his staff meeting."

"Bullshit!" they all say in chorus. I tell them what I heard from the hallway and they're still dubious.

Another knock on the door and everyone quiets down again. Captain Parks hands the tape back to the sarge. "Thanks," is all he says. We're all pretty relieved until twenty minutes later when an attorney shows up at the front counter with a court order to release the tape. Apparently the suspect and his wife were more concerned about getting it back than they were about getting out of jail. I wonder if the attorney will take a peek at it.

With all the optimism of an acquitted defendant, Sergeant Roberts claps his hands together and sings out, “C’mon Soto, you already got your feet wet. Now it’s time to jump in the pool.” The clock over the door says 3:40 and I suddenly feel like I can’t swallow.

Miller jumps up, grabbing a cloth harness and wire transmitter from the file cabinet. Cad picks up a spool of medical tape and Van Kirk flips open his Marty English case file.

“Okay,” says Van Kirk. “Now this guy thinks you’re a friend of my informant, Marquita. She lives off of Tampa Avenue. Marquita only knows small time users and dealers, so all you need to do is buy a twenty bag from this guy—enough for one hit.

“Yeah,” Roberts laughs. “We don’t want to make another trip to the ATM in the middle of your deal.”

“Street names for heroin are *stuff* or *shit*,” says Van Kirk. “He’ll probably sell it to you in powder form, packaged in a balloon.”

“Okay.” I’ve got my shirt off and my arms raised as Miller and Cad sling the harness over my shoulder, leaving the transmitter to dangle under my armpit. “Twenty bag. Stuff or shit. Marquita who lives off of Tampa. I think I got it.”

“Try not to sweat a lot or you’ll get burned by the battery,” Cad says as he tapes the thing in place against my chest. *Try not to sweat?*

Van Kirk leaves and returns a minute later with a photocopy of the twenty-dollar bill I’m supposed to use. He says it’s so we can prove in court that the bill in English’s pocket when he’s arrested is the same one I gave him for the drugs.

“Speaking of that,” I say. “Do I just arrest him after he hands me the dope?”

“No!” They all yell at once.

Roberts places a fatherly hand on my shoulder. “The UC buyer never makes the arrest. If English were to resist, or shoot you, or whatever, when you’re trying to arrest him, he’s got a built in defense: he didn’t know you were a cop and thought you were ripping him off.”

“Shouldn’t I carry my duty weapon, just in case something goes wrong?”

Cad shakes his head. “He sees it on you and he'll know you're a cop for sure. Don't worry about it, we'll be right there.”

Miller tosses my shirt to me. “You just give the bust signal and we'll move up and make the arrest. We'll hear the whole thing over the wire.”

“Okay, then what's the bust signal?”

Miller looks at Cad, Cad looks at Van Kirk, and Van Kirk looks at the sergeant. “Oh for Christ sake!” Smitty throws his hands in the air. “Just use my name so we can get this goddamn thing over with.”

We do a quick test of the wire in the back lot, and then Miller gives me the keys to his little Toyota coupe. He says we really don't have any UC cars that look good for a heroin buy, but his will have to do. I'm wondering what kind of car an addict like me would have, and then I realize I probably wouldn't have a car at all. It would have already been sold for drug money.

I do a last check of the wire just to be sure, and I see a thumbs-up come from the van's window. I check my mirror a final time to make sure the van is behind me, and then I turn in to the 7-11 lot.

“Pulling in now,” I say, hoping the wire is picking it up. “English is on foot in front of the store, wearing a red plaid shirt and . . .” I stop talking when I see English look in my direction. I drive slowly through the lot, making eye contact with him before pulling into a space. I look up and see I've parked in a handicapped stall. English watches me curiously as I back out and re-park the car in a space facing the street, away from him. *Dammit!*

I've probably muffed this whole thing, and I know I'm going to catch hell from the guys in the van. I quickly come up with a reasoning that I'll use to make like it was intentional: I will now have a better view of English in the mirror as he crosses the lot to me, and he'll now be facing away from the approaching cops when they come up to arrest him.

English keeps his position in front of the store for a few seconds, just checking out the cars in the area and watching to see who's coming or going. I finish giving my audible description of English, including my location in the lot and the fact that he's doing a lot of looking around. For some reason, however, I'm not as nervous as I was with the prostitute. I'm in the moment now, trying to feel as if I'm not a cop. I tell myself, you're not acting a part; you really are the dope fiend, Phil Soto. I feel a rush as I see the guy in my mirror starting to cross the lot. "Here he comes."

"You Marquita's friend?" A voice asks through my open passenger window. I study him for a second before nodding. I turn in my seat to look around the parking lot, just as he had done, and then I tell him, "You can get in."

He sits down next to me, arching his hips forward as he digs into his pants pocket. "Just a twenty, right?"

"I could use more if you have it," I give him a pleading look. "But I only have twenty bucks on me right now."

He looks like he's thinking it over. "Nah," he finally says with a slight smile, "I don't know you good enough to front you any."

Good enough? You don't know me at all! He hands me a knotted red balloon, about the size of a wad of gum. I do another paranoid look around the lot before handing him the twenty. "The last time I came here that cop, Smitty, hassled me. I better get my ass out of here."

"Alright, later." English opens the door and sets one foot on the ground. I hear what sounds like a herd of cattle rumbling across the lot behind us. I glance in the mirror in time to see Van Kirk trip over a parking block and go down. There's a raspy sliding sound and Van Kirk's pistol skids to a stop on the pavement next to English's foot. I turn in my seat and see Miller, running at a full sprint, leap in the air in an attempt to hurdle over the fallen Van Kirk.

"You outta there!" Miller hollers like a baseball umpire, as he flies through the air over Van Kirk.

I'm ready to grab English by the back of the shirt if he reaches for Van Kirk's gun, but it isn't necessary. English is so stunned by what's going on that he just stares at the gun and then back at the heap of cops tumbling toward him. Suddenly a medley of screaming voices wallop us from all directions, "Freeze! Put your hands up! Don't move! Get on the ground! You're under arrest."

The cops pull English out of one side of the car and me out the other. English and I are both put in handcuffs and tossed against the trunk like hams on a butcher block. They quickly load English into a marked patrol car, and then they unhandcuff me as soon as he's out of sight. It was a part of the plan that was never communicated to me, but I kind of liked it. Made me feel even more into the role.

"Did good, Soto." Miller slaps me on the back. Cad picks up the runaway gun and returns it to Van Kirk, who's nursing a couple of raw palms and a skinned knee. Roberts is searching under the passenger seat of the Toyota, in case English dumped anything. Smitty looks like he's disgusted with the whole group of us. I, on the other hand, am thrilled. I just made my first UC buy, and feel pretty good about it.

I pull into the police lot a few seconds ahead of the other guys, bursting with excitement and wanting to tell somebody, anybody, how the deal went down. I'm in the hallway outside the report writing room about to take the stairs to the second floor when I see an older cop whom I've always respected as a solid, no-nonsense guy. I nod to him as we pass one another, and he stops. His sour lemon expression hints of something he wants to say, but he's just standing there studying me from head to foot.

"What's going on?" I ask, still not catching on to the chill.

"You're a disgrace," he says, ignoring my attempt at a greeting. In the fleeting seconds that follow, I'm thinking he heard about my drug buy and he's giving me a bad time. I allow a guarded chuckle as I await the punch line, but it never comes.

"Look at that faggot earring." He flicks my ear with his hand. "That shit growing on your chin, and those greasy clothes. You're no cop, you're a fucking disgrace to the uniform."

It takes a second for my brain to make sense of it. When I get my bearings, I'm surprised to find I'm not pissed off. His words were a direct assault on me and my integrity, and normally would have engendered a sharp, confrontational, and profanity-laden response. What I feel instead is hurt and embarrassment. I consider for the moment, explaining my role to him, and how my success and my safety depend on a convincing appearance, but I'm only able to shrug my shoulders and continue up the stairs. I don't even have the wind to answer him. I had built a reputation as one of the hardest working and most dependable officers in the department, but he's made me feel as if it has counted for nothing.

"Nice work, Soto." Van Kirk's paw swipes across the back of my head, but the fervor of the moment has grown cold. I tell him thanks, and then pull out a report form to begin typing my supplement. I give it to Miller when I'm finished, and he says it looks good. I realize that the other guys are already gone for the night. I mull over the idea of telling Miller about my hallway conversation with the older cop, but I decide not to. Miller is nearly the same age as the guy, and it's likely the two of them are closer than Miller and I.

My house is dark, except for the dim light of the television flickering through the drapes. I find the girls already in bed and Gale sitting cross-legged on the couch. She smiles at me with studying eyes as I come in.

"Everything alright?" she asks.

I tell her about my first drug buy, emphasizing all the security precautions. She chuckles at the part where Van Kirk took a header during the arrest, and even though she doesn't care for the guy, she asks if he hurt himself. It's something I never thought to ask him.

I get myself a bowl of ice cream and join Gale on the couch. I let out a long sigh before taking my first bite, and I can see she's still checking me out.

"There's something else." She doesn't say it like a question. "What's bothering you?"

I start with the usual, "Oh nothing really," and end up spilling the whole story about the old cop. As I talk, I realize the depth of the wound. "It's not as if I really give a shit," I say. "It's just that I've always thought of him as . . ."

"A guy you admired." Gale puts her hand on mine and gives me a squeeze. We sit for a while and then she asks, "Has he ever worked an undercover assignment?"

"No, I don't think so."

"Didn't he serve in Viet Nam?"

"Right," I say. "With the Marines."

"Didn't you tell me he had problems adjusting when he got back?"

"Yeah." I reflect back to the stories I've heard. "It was during the height of the demonstrations and protests, and they threw stuff at his unit when they got off the bus."

Gale nods thoughtfully. "Probably protesters who looked a lot like you."

"I guess." I slide the last of my ice cream off the spoon with my lips.

"What he said probably wasn't meant for you personally," she says. "Most likely he still isn't able to separate the way you look from the emotions of the day he got off that bus."

We get into bed and I lie there imagining what it was like for him. There's a certain symmetry to it, not unlike abusive relationships. The abused often becomes the abuser—repeating on someone else what was done to him. I imagine that after doing my job the best I could, his comments hurt that much worse. It's probably similar to what he felt after doing the best job he could during the war.

In the darkness, my mind rambles onto what lies ahead for me: the upcoming search warrant that I, at least partially, wrote; my introduction to a heroin dealer by The Big A, and hopefully buying drugs from him. I wonder how those cases will go. I wonder if I have what it takes to pull it off. And I wonder if there will ever come a time when the old cop will look at me differently.

3

Jimmy the Gimp

It's been nearly a week since Alberto said he would set something up. I'm anxious, but Miller doesn't seem too concerned. "He'll come around when he needs money," he says.

We're working a later shift today, but I came in at ten instead of noon. I'm still typing the search warrant Miller gave me, and hope to get it wrapped up by the end of the day. I feel as if it's taken me longer than it should, but it's my first one and I want to get it right. One step I'm going to take, although Van Kirk says it's a waste of time, is to physically view the house and confirm the address numbers. Even if it seems excessive, I'd hate to kick in the door of the wrong house.

By 12:30 p.m. everybody else has straggled in. I'm just about to take a drive to check the house when Sergeant Roberts comes in. "I just got a call from the San Leandro narcs." He turns and writes on the grease board: *1 P.M. SLPD WARRANT*. "They're coming into our city to do a search warrant, and want our help."

The sarge tells us we're supposed to meet up with them in thirty minutes, behind the Mexican bar a few blocks from the house they're going to hit. Miller's desk phone rings and he picks it up. I listen as I go about gathering my raid gear for the San Leandro warrant. It sounds like he's talking to Alberto.

Sergeant Roberts comes back in. "Change of plans fellas." He wipes the time off the grease board with his palm and writes in 3 p.m. "San Leandro moved it back a couple of hours."

"Good," says Miller, still holding the receiver. "The Big A has a buy ready to go right now." Miller goes back to the phone. "We'll meet you at the taco trailer in five minutes."

He hangs up the phone. "This is it, Soto! You buy from these guys, and you'll have done something that's never been done by a cop before." I know other cops have bought heroin in the past, so I'm guessing he means these dealers in particular.

Roberts claps his hands together. "Let's get you wired up."

It came up a little faster than I had anticipated. I mean, I know I already have one whole drug buy under my belt, but this one feels different. Marty English was a twit—a scrawny white kid with no brains and a heroin habit. The guys Alberto knows run the entire heroin trade in the Sonoma neighborhood. They're a tight knit group of Mexicans.

I'm standing with my arms raised as they tape the wire down. "These dudes are no joke," says Cad. *Thanks for stating the obvious.*

"This isn't a buy-bust," Miller reminds me. "It's a buy-walk. We're going to let the money go without making an arrest, and hopefully you'll be able to go back there another time and buy more, without Alberto."

"Who's the guy I'm buying from?" I ask, trying to appear calm and collected.

"It's Beto Salazar."

I recognize Salazar's name from my time on patrol, though thankfully I haven't had much contact with him. He shouldn't recognize me, and I sure hope nobody else down there does. Miller tells me that Salazar is one of several low-level dealers in the Sonoma Street area, and that most of them are selling for the Zamudio family.

"Doesn't matter who you buy from Soto," says Miller. "They all have prison records, so we'll be able to ID them later."

Miller and I jump in his car together, followed by Cad and Roberts in the van. Van Kirk apparently had something else to do. We test the wire and a squelching feedback of my own voice comes across the radio. Roberts flashes a thumbs-up out his window. They peel off and park the van in a spot next to a gas station. Miller and I continue another block to a gravel parking lot where a line of day workers wait outside a decrepit aluminum trailer for their lunch.

"Remember, we're not even going to charge this buy in court. Otherwise Alberto would be a material witness. Just let The Big A duke you in." Miller slaps forty bucks in my hand. "All you have to do is let

Salazar get a look at you so he'll remember your face when you come back."

I see Alberto milling around the side of the trailer. The brownness of his skin contrasts sharply with his clean white tee shirt and khaki pants—both of which are several sizes too large.

"You don't look like a cop," Albert says as we start on foot toward the neighborhood.

"That's good." I flash a tentative grin. "Better for you, right?"

"Better for you!" Alberto continues to evaluate my appearance as we walk. "Miller wanted me to bring that Van Kirk guy down here once but I said, 'fuck that shit.' Dude looks like a farmer or something."

We cut through an empty lot where I once responded to a gang shooting. I remember exactly where the kids were hanging out and drinking beer when the car rolled up and opened fire. A 16 year-old boy was hit in the chest. He reacted instinctively by turning and trying to run, but he dropped only a few yards away. I look down at the very spot where he died. I never imagined I'd be . . .

"Roll your sleeves down," Alberto barks, interrupting my thought. It occurs to me that my inner arms are too clean to be a heroin user.

I quickly stretch my shirtsleeves down as far as they'll go. "Will he try to check for tracks?"

"There's Beto," says Alberto without answering me. "The old dude standing on the porch."

I take a deep breath to calm myself and casually glance up, then away, as if I'm making sure there are no cops around.

"Need a twenty," Alberto says to the guy without any preamble.

Beto reaches into his pocket and produces a handful of rolled balloons. "Who's he?" Salazar asks with nothing more than mild interest.

"My homeboy," Alberto says. "Name is Soto."

The guy nods slightly and I nod back. I'm bolstered by the fact that my look hasn't seemed to raise any red flags. "I could use some too, if you got it." I say, pulling the two twenties from my sock.

Beto snatches the bills and slaps two of the balloons in their place. He looks around nervously, making me feel as if I had screwed up by flashing the bills in the open. As quick as it unfolded, the deal's over.

Had he seen enough of me to remember me? Would he sell to me when I come back alone? How bad did it look when I held out the money?

We step off the porch as two other guys approach—presumably Beto's next customers. One of them hobbles with a pronounced limp, swinging a crippled hand wildly with each step. He eyes me openly, and then twists himself around to watch us walk away.

Alberto pays no attention to him. Instead, he turns to me with an open palm. "Why don't you slip me one of those bags, Homes?"

"Miller will pay you. With money," I add with a laugh. Then I whisper toward the mic. "Headed back to the taco trailer now. Sold me two twenties."

Alberto looks surprised, as if he hadn't known I was wired.

Miller meets us there and flips Alberto forty bucks. "If Salazar sells to Soto when we go back I'll give you more."

Alberto heads off in the direction of Beto's house. As we drive back, Miller explains to me that withholding partial payment gives the CI incentive not to double cross us.

Back at the office I'm welcomed with high fives and backslaps. The deal went down as planned, and a presumptive chemical test verifies that what I bought from Beto Salazar was in fact heroin.

Miller logs the dope into evidence while I write a quick statement. Before my mind is able to stray too far into my first real narcotics success, we're rallied to the back parking lot. Sarge got another phone call from San Leandro narcs. They've been surveilling the home of their suspected dealer and he's just arrived. They've changed their timeline again and things are suddenly kicked into high gear. Van Kirk is on the phone and only partially paying attention. It sounds like he's talking to one of his CI's.

"I'll be right back," he says, grabbing his keys.

"Where you headed, Kirkie?" The sergeant's voice has a hint of frustration. Miller rolls his eyes and shakes his head.

"I just got to meet with Jimmy for a quick second." Van Kirk races out, leaving the office door ajar.

Roberts shrugs it off. "Saddle up, boys. Meet you in the back lot in two minutes."

Miller, Cad, and I are left to ourselves. "I guess Van Kirk is out of pocket," says Miller.

"Who's he meeting with?" I gather my gear.

Miller grabs a set of keys off his desk. "Some worthless informant of his we call Jimmy the Gimp."

We toss our gear into the van and strap on our ballistic vests, gunbelts, and raid jackets enroute. We roll up beside San Leandro's narc sergeant who's got two other plain clothes detectives with him. A third detective is a few blocks away watching the house and giving updates over their radio. We get a quick brief on their suspect, Jordan Fowler, a mid-level meth dealer with a record for weapons. According to their sergeant, Fowler lives alone in a duplex, and there's nothing to indicate he owns a dog. The weapons thing tweaks me a bit, but I've been on SWAT for a couple of years now, and I'm used to executing raids using the military tactics I've been taught.

Cad jumps into the car with a San Leandro detective so we'll be able to coordinate our arrival over both radio channels—theirs and ours. We circle the block and pull up on the side of the building where the suspect's view of our approach will be obscured by a carport. The detective who had been watching the house jumps out of his car and we all approach the door in an unwieldy, serpentine line. It seems to be tactically sound until this point. Their sergeant pounds on the door yelling, "Police! Search warrant!" Almost simultaneously, Cad and their detective rear back with the huge metal key. Apparently their other detective heard something inside that sounded like running, so he picks up a flowerpot and throws it through the window behind us. Glass rains down on the group at the back of the line. The noise scares the shit out of Sergeant Roberts, who had no idea the guy was going to break the window. Roberts dives off the porch aiming his gun at the window, probably thinking he was coming under fire. Luckily he doesn't shoot, but he ends up spraining his ankle. By now there's a thunderous noise as the key blows through the door's deadbolt, taking a six-foot section of doorjamb with it.

I charge into the house with my gun in front of me, thinking these fiascos are undoubtedly where cops get killed. Me and a San Leandro detective locate their suspect in a bedroom. He's lying on his bed, watching TV. He doesn't look all that surprised that we're there, only pissed off about the fact that we've broken his door and window, and dirtied his carpet with remnants of a flowerpot. "I would have let you in if you had given me half a second," he says.

The place is clean, both literally and figuratively. Other than the soil-stained carpet, it's a tidy unit with nothing disgusting that I have to dig through. The bad news for San Leandro is that there is no dope. Not even packaging, notes, paraphernalia, or any other indication that there ever was dope there. Their sergeant isn't convinced, and keeps us searching for what seems like hours. It's dark now, and we're all hungry. Their sergeant grills the guy, but he's got a look on his face that could be either innocence or a *got-over-on-you* smugness. They run a check on him and find a $130 traffic warrant. By traditional standards it's nothing, but it's enough to bring him to jail. A marked patrol unit pulls up and the illegal-parking desperado is walked out the back door in handcuffs.

I happen to be looking out the kitchen window when I see the San Leandro sergeant remove his raid jacket, gunbelt and vest, and stash them in the trunk of his car. I continue watching as he takes a detour on his way back in to the house. He steps across the small driveway toward the adjacent unit—which makes up the second half of the duplex. As the sergeant knocks on the door, I realize he doesn't want whoever lives there to know he's a cop. I quickly remove all my gear, tossing it on the kitchen table as I scurry out the back door. When I emerge from the side yard, I slow my stride to casual and relaxed. I join the sergeant on the porch just as a young woman, who looks like she's seen her share of barrooms, opens the door.

Acting on nothing more than a hunch, the sergeant says, "Jordan told me to come over here and get his stuff back."

She looks stares back and forth at us with a confused expression. Tentatively, she says, "I don't know what you're . . ."

But the San Leandro sergeant stays with it, cutting her off in the middle of the sentence. "You know what I'm talking about. C'mon, c'mon, we don't have much time. Jordan said the cops are coming to raid his place!"

Now she looks even more bewildered. She takes another second to study us, and then her eyes show a glimmer of reliance.

"He wants us to stash it somewhere else before the cops get here," I say. "I don't think he wants you to risk getting into any trouble."

The resistant look on her face melts into partnership. "Let me get it," she says. A minute later she comes back to the door carrying a metallic item wrapped in a towel, and a brown wooden container about the size of a small jewelry box. "This is all of it," she says, handing it to the sergeant.

He asks the girl if she's certain there isn't any more and she says she is. He unwraps the towel and finds a small gram scale, which he hands to me before opening the box. It contains wads of cash and two cylindrical sandwich baggies filled with meth.

The sergeant looks delighted as he hands it over to me. He pulls out his badge and tells the woman he's a cop. She's horrified that she's about to be arrested for felony drug possession when it wasn't even her stuff. She pleads with us not to take her in. The sergeant apparently had no intention of arresting her. He just wanted to get her to the point of panic, so she would readily give a written statement implicating Jordan. She does.

We get back to the jail and amend Jordan's charges to include the felony possession for sale. He won't know that his neighbor friend gave him up until later, when his attorney gets a hold of the report. Hopefully by then the woman will have moved out.

The office is crowded with narcs—both theirs and ours. Van Kirk arrives back from meeting with his CI and is laughing hysterically when he walks in.

"Jimmy the Gimp gave me some good information about a new drug dealer down on Sonoma! His name is Soto!"

Everybody laughs and I realize that the crippled guy I saw after my buy from Salazar must have been Van Kirk's informant, *Jimmy the Gimp*. What's even funnier is that he snitched me off to the cops. It does a lot to ease my fears about not looking enough like a drug addict. On top of that, San Leandro's sergeant tells everyone how well I played along with his ploy with Jordan's next-door neighbor.

* * *

I head to work the next day thinking I've got to get an informant of my own. The notion is driven home every time a phone call comes in for one of the other guys. I stop on the way and buy a pack of cigarettes to help with the effort.

Before things get too busy, I decide to go downstairs to the jail and check out the day's residents. I glance through the stack of booking sheets and find about two-dozen prisoners are being held. The jailers are preparing for the morning court run where most of the detainees will either be released on bail or taken to the county jail.

"Better hurry if you want to talk to someone," warns a petite girl in a jailer's uniform. "We're about to transport them out." She points to a booking sheet sitting apart from the others. "Except that one. She just came in and won't be going anyplace until tomorrow."

I check the sheet to find that 28-year-old Maria Cardenas had just been brought in on a shoplifting arrest. Normally a minor charge, but Maria is being held on a felony because of previous theft convictions. I recognize the profile as a common one for drug addicts. They'll often commit thefts and then fence the merchandise for drugs or drug money. I pull her name up on the jail's computer and find she has a string of previous arrests for prostitution as well. *She's perfect. With my extensive experience of two heroin buys and an almost prostitution case, we'll have plenty in common to talk about.*

I have one of the jailers bring Maria to a small interview room off the main booking area. It's a cramped cinderblock enclosure with a high ceiling, making the space feel more like an elevator shaft. I'm seated at a table when the jailer unlocks the door and leads her in. I nod and a second later the jailer is gone. Maria stands there with a curious look, studying me as I study her. The woman is the same age as I am, but her weathered face and flaccid body make her appear older. Still, Maria's not unattractive. Her full lips are set partly open, as if in the middle of an unfinished conversation, and her deep brown eyes – minus the teardrop tattoo in the corner – could otherwise be on a fashion magazine. Overall though, Maria's air is one that hints at a lifetime of struggle, and a keen sense of the street that makes me feel like a neophyte.

"Hi, Maria." I reach to slide the other chair out for her, then pull the pack of cigarettes out of my pocket. "Would you like a smoke?"

"Thanks." She flashes a brief smile before moving to the chair with a sultry draw that is both raw and unclean.

I start into my spiel. It is an invitation to help me nab drug dealers in return for my assistance in getting the charges against her dropped. She listens quietly, inhaling deeply then blowing double streams of smoke from her nose. My delivery is rough and clearly one that will need to be perfected over the next few years, but Maria doesn't seem to notice. I sit casually, talking slow and soft, and trying hard not to sound like I'm selling her a used car. Her intermittent smile puts me at ease, and my pitch finally becomes more natural.

Maria seems amenable. She asks if there is any way I could get her out today. She swears on her kids' lives that she will give me "solid information" within a few days.

I tell her the best I can do is to get the D.A. to release her in the morning on her own recognizance—essentially on her promise to appear in court later. "At that point, any information you give could get the case dropped altogether."

"I have four kids to take care of," she says. "I really need to get out today." I suspect that her urgency has more to do with her addiction.

I decide to ask her. "Are you going to be alright or will you be sick?"

There's a pause, and then Maria shrugs. "I won't feel good, but I'll be okay."

"How much do you use?"

"Not much," she says. "I'm not a junkie, I just chip a little."

The term *chip* means injecting the heroin under the skin rather than directly into the vein. I know the most common place to chip is into the back of the hand, but I don't see any fresh marks on Maria's.

Any further discussion about her drug use seems worthless. And since the topic of providing information has also petered out, I'm half figuring this was a waste of time. I pull out a business card and write my office number on it. I tell Maria I'll do my best to get her released tomorrow. She stubs out her cigarette and we both get up.

I can feel Maria looking at me from the side as I ring the buzzer for the jailer. "I promise I'll call when I get out," she says.

I hand her my card. "I hope so." I say it with a light smile so that she won't take it as a threat. It truly isn't meant as one. She's my first attempt to flip someone as an informant, and I feel as if we've made a connection.

The jailer opens the door for us and Maria turns back to me. "You know what? Out of all the times I been to jail, you're the only cop who ever tried to get me to snitch."

I watch as she's escorted back to her cell, and I'm wondering if there was a deeper meaning in her comment. Had she taken my offer as an insult or a compliment? I guess I'll find out when she's released.

I use the next few hours to finish my search warrant; all but the address verification.

In the later part of the afternoon, I head across the parking lot to the courthouse for a meeting with the district attorney regarding Maria's case. The deputies working there give me dirty looks, and if I didn't know better I'd think they all want to kick my ass. I get to the metal detector and discreetly show them my badge. Their disgusted expressions slowly transition to skeptical acknowledgment of our brotherhood, and they hesitantly gesture me through the machine.

I sit down across the desk from Gordon Bartell, a curly headed guy with a jovial face. I introduce myself and hand him one of my business cards, which he promptly tosses into a drawer filled with other cards. I embark on a long-winded explanation of my meeting with Maria, her promise to provide information, and her extensive criminal history.

Bartell interrupts me halfway through with a drum of his fingers on the desk. "Bottom line, you want me to drop the charges against this broad?"

"Well, not quite yet." I adjust myself in the chair. "I was hoping to get her released from court in the morning. Then, if she calls me with verifiable information, you could possibly drop the charges."

"What do you mean *if* she calls you?" His jovial face now replaced by that of a shrewd gamesman. "Is she going to call you or not?"

I suddenly feel like a grammar school kid who's been caught embellishing a story. *Had I overstated my advocacy for Maria?* Suddenly I hear my own voice. "Yes, she'll call."

Having backed me into a corner, Bartell now smiles. "And she'll give you some good information?"

I decide not to risk what little credibility I have on this. "I certainly hope so." I return the smile. "All I can promise you is that I'll do everything in my power to make this worth your time."

He signs the release form. "Hey, I get paid by the hour. It's the State of California's time."

I thank him and make a quick exit before he decides to start grilling me some more. I breeze across the lot on a cloud of satisfaction. I was finally able to accomplish something on my own.

The daylight is almost gone and a damp wind whips at my pant legs. I cling tightly to my papers as I jog the last few yards up the steps to the back door. I get to the office as everyone is leaving.

"We're all heading up to the PBA tonight, Soto," the sergeant calls out. "See you up there?"

I'm not usually one for long nights of drinking. In addition, Gale and the girls have been waiting all day to see me. "Maybe just one," I say. "I have a quick stop to make on the way up there."

I call Gale and let her know that I won't be home for dinner. I tell her that the guys are going up to the Police Benevolent Association's bar, not too far outside the city. She seems fine with it. After all, it's just this once. And what with being the new guy and all, it's probably the social thing to do.

On my way to the bar, I pull off Foothill into a hilly neighborhood east of the highway. I open my case file and glance at the address listed on the search warrant Miller gave me.

The blue and white, two-story house is at the corner. It looks like there's a basement level below it, on the backside where the hill drops away. The address matches the numbers on the front of the house, and I decide to get a better look at the layout. A corrugated plastic sheet blocks my view into the back yard. It's obviously been nailed tightly against the house along the fence line. It leaves me wondering what he's hiding back there.

I check the opposite side of the house, but there's a driveway with two cars under various stages of disrepair, and it's littered with car parts. I could try to climb over them, but getting to the fence would increase the chance of my getting caught. I decide instead to drive back down the hill and see if I can get to the yard from the block below. I'm in luck. A gas station borders the bottom of the property, separated from the yard only by an empty lot with a scraggly row of bushes and a more accessible fence.

I park my car near the air compressor. As I climb through the bushes, I notice a small homeless encampment with nobody around. I'm paranoid about being seen, so I use a knothole to discreetly look into the yard. All I can see is the dark outline of shrubs—rows and rows of them. I pop my head over the top of the fence and am struck with the wafting tang of growing marijuana. The yard is full of similar-sized sensimilla plants, cultivated and in neatly aligned rows. I duck back down and inch my way along the fence to another spot. *I've hit the mother lode!*

I want to get a quick, ballpark count for my warrant. I'm about to pop my head up again when I hear something rustling on the opposite side of the fence. I stop in my tracks, listening to an edgy stillness. It's interrupted occasionally by erratic breathing—which I hope is only mine. It's not.

I slowly raise my head above the fence and find myself peering into the angry end of a shotgun. I stumble backwards, throwing my hands into the air in submission. "Hey, hey, be cool, man."

"What the fuck are you doing here?" A man's voice blasts back; the gun still leveled right at my face.

"I stay here sometimes," I slowly back down the incline. "That's my stuff over there." I motion toward an old sleeping bag without breaking eye contact with him. "I don't want no trouble."

With the barrel still aimed at me, his enraged expression morphs into a grimaced smile. "I know what you want, you son-of-a-bitch!"

I've backed far enough away that I figure I now stand about a 50-50 chance of avoiding serious injury from the shotgun pellets, should he decide to shoot. I also assume that he would have already shot me if he wanted to. "I'm gone, okay?" I turn my back now and start toward the lights of the gas station. "I'm outta here, dude."

He offers a parting threat as I stumble through the bushes. "If I ever see you back here I'll kill you."

I reach the safety of the paved lot, imagining the possibilities of who'll do what to whom the next time he sees me. Strangely, the whole episode has left me exhilarated. The momentary fright, then the anger, and finally thoughts of vengeance, are all sentiments that take a backseat to the thrill of having fooled the guy. I could have pulled my badge and gun. I could have shot him. But I remained in character. What would have been a terrifying experience as a uniformed cop didn't affect me the same way now. It wasn't the cop he was aiming at; it was a fellow doper who he thought was coming to rip off his plants.

I bound into the PBA with a story to tell. The icy beers are lined up and the guys have started a boisterous game of liars dice. "Someone get Soto some bones!" yells the sergeant. Miller slides me a leather cup full of dice.

I take a long frothy swig of beer and start into my story. The game ceases as they follow along, rapt in my Hitchcockian narrative.

"That son-of-a-bitch!" hollers Van Kirk. "We're gonna shove that shotgun up his ass when we hit the place."

Sarge seems more concerned that I went off alone and could have been shot. Miller orders another round. I'm hungry with excitement, and ask what they have to eat.

"Chips," says Cad.

"Or pork rinds," Miller adds.

"Hotdogs," says the sarge with authority. As he slams his dice cup down, he calls out to the bartender. "Larry, get Soto a barker!"

4

The Big Secret

An old guy wearing a button up sweater greets me on my porch as I step out my front door. He introduces himself as "Ed" and points out his house across the street.

"Wife and I been here for thirty some-odd years."

"That's great," I say. Even though I'm eager to get to work, I linger there in order to make friends with my new neighbor. "We moved in over the Labor Day weekend."

Ed bobs his head as if he already knows that. "So what is it that you do?"

"What do I do? You mean for a living?"

"I see you coming in late at night sometimes."

I scratch my crude goatee. "Bartender." Then in an effort to shift the conversation elsewhere, I tell him that my family and I really like the neighborhood.

The old guy eyes from top to bottom. "Yeah, we haven't had any burglaries or anything like that." Then he looks me right in the eye. "I hope we don't start having them now."

Ouch! That was one hell of a welcome wagon. Glad I waited around. "Thanks for stopping by, Ed."

I get to work early and find a frenzy of activity outside my office. The investigators, most with rumpled clothes and bleary eyes, move purposely from desk to desk like ants on a picnic table. Cad whizzes past me into the office. As I follow him in, I ask what's going on.

"Homicide last night," he says as he pops open a filing cabinet and fingers through a bunch of mug photos. "The guy was found stabbed to death over on Havana Street."

I know the neighborhood well; it was my beat when I was in uniform. It's a rough area known for gang and drug violence, so the discovery of a dead body isn't exactly the shock of the century. Cad fills me in on the rest of the story and only then does the heightened activity make sense. The victim was neither a gang member nor a drug dealer. He was a 68-year-old retired airline pilot by the name of Arnold Bascomb. He had walked down the street to a local bar and was apparently heading back to his home when he was killed. "Looks like it was a street robbery," Cad says. "His watch and wallet were missing."

Cad tells me the homicide crew is already focusing on a couple of suspects who were seen in the area earlier, though he subtly neglects to mention the two by name. As Cad pulls a couple of photos from the drawer, he actually adjusts his body to shield my view. I follow him back out to where a clot of investigators are huddled, anxious to see the photos of their suspects. The fact that we happen to have them in our narcotics files will save a lot of time waiting for the county photo lab, and getting the witnesses to identify them. I nose over the shoulder of an investigator friend, so I can view the culprits. The photos are of two brothers, Art and Ernie Fausto—a couple of troublemakers who live in the South End. I've run into both of them in the past, but neither would have jumped out to me as cold-blooded killers. As far as I know, their histories are limited to drug use and maybe an occasional fight with the cops.

I head back into the office, leaving Cad to hang out and hobnob with the big boys a little longer. I guess he thinks that pulling a couple of photographs makes him an honorary homicide detective. *He's definitely got the top-secret thing mastered.*

Miller slipped into the office while we were with the investigators, and the sergeant and Van Kirk are right behind me as I come back in. Miller hangs up the phone and gives me a sheepish grin. "The Big A is ready to roll with another intro buy."

Roberts claps his hands together. "Let's get you wired up, Soto!"

Cad comes in and stands behind me, listening. Van Kirk picks up his phone and begins talking to someone—presumably an informant. Meanwhile, I'm standing in the middle of the office holding the lunch bag that I haven't even had time to put in the refrigerator yet.

"It's Mexican tar heroin," says Miller. "They're slinging it out of a motel in East Palo Alto."

"Name a motel in East Palo Alto that somebody *isn't* selling heroin out of." Cad steps around me to his desk. "What do we know about the suspects?"

Miller shrugs. "Not much, but Alberto can get Soto in the door."

"EPA is a dangerous place." Cad turns toward the sarge. "Do we know anything about the complex? The layout?"

Miller wrinkles his brow. I'm watching the exchange like a tennis match, only my life is the ball they're batting back and forth. The sergeant finally weighs in. "We'll check it out once we get over there. If it looks bad, we can call it off."

The so-called decision is clearly meant only to cool the friction between Miller and Cad, but it does little to alleviate the security concerns raised on my behalf.

We take the van, planning to meet Miller near the bridge approach after he picks up Alberto. Cad drives his own car—partly because he's annoyed that his point was ignored, and partly because he's too big to be crammed into the back of the van. Van Kirk is cracking jokes and sparing with Roberts in the front seat. As freeway traffic whizzes past, I'm sitting alone in the back of the van, wondering how concerned for my safety I should be. I'd really like to stash a gun somewhere on me during these buys, but I remember they told me not to.

Miller pulls behind Cad who's parked behind us, and I get out of the van. We switch places, so now Miller is riding in the van and I'm driving Alberto at the rear of the procession.

On the other side of the bridge we take the University Avenue exit. We follow it through a worsening collection of dilapidated apartments, liquor stores, and burned out cars. The streets are bustling with activity, yet completely devoid of children, old people, and white people. The place has clearly been abandoned by working folks, and surrendered over to street thugs.

We take a left, and the roadway wraps around to a weed and garbage-strewn lot, beyond which I can see the backside of a faded clapboard motel. The van pulls over with Cad behind them, and they signal for me to drive on in. *So much for checking the place out.*

I pull next to Cad and flip on the wire to test it. He nods with a sorrowful expression that tells me he's sympathetic to my concerns. As I continue past the van, I see Van Kirk engrossed in some animated horseplay. There's no telling if they're even monitoring me. I shake my head and continue toward the target with Alberto seated next to me.

"They're in room eight," he says, fidgeting in his seat like a guy about to go into withdrawals. "But don't worry, you can also buy from any of the other rooms. Everyone in the place is working for them." It occurs to me that we still don't even know who *them* is. If I get shot to shit, all they'll have to go on is an entire complex full of illegal Mexican immigrants.

As we're making the turn into the property, I notice two guys who appear to be hiding. They're hunkered down against a dumpster at the back of the building closest to us, inching their way through the weeds. I recognize them as guys I've run into in my own city on the other side of the bay. They're probably hiding from the local police, or maybe looking for a discreet place to shoot up. Whatever the case, I haven't the time or interest to figure it out now. I've got my own problems.

The rooms are laid out in a semi-circle around a dirt parking lot, allowing every resident to view arriving vehicles long before they even come to a stop. The place comes alive with whistles and signals, chirping like a National Geographic documentary. As I step out of the car, I wonder if my head is in the crosshairs of someone's riflescope. I follow Alberto to the open door of unit number eight. A young Latino woman sits on the bed watching a Mexican soap opera while she nurses an infant.

"How much you want?" calls a voice from the kitchenette.

"Two," I respond.

A thin, bare-chested guy emerges with a cupped hand. His look is deceivingly non-threatening, probably because his room is surrounded by people that would back him up in the event of any trouble. He gives me a tiny speck of brown putty, twisted tightly in plastic wrap about half the size of a kernel of corn. Had I not seen Mexican tar heroin before, I would be suspicious that I'd just been ripped off. It's supposed to be much more potent, since it hasn't been cut with anything yet.

"I give you one big one." The guy holds out his hand and I pass him the money. He doesn't even register Alberto, if in fact they've even met before. It's clear to me that I could have come over here and bought cold, without The Big A.

It goes down without a hitch, and for that I'm thankful. I'm still unclear about our investigative goal here though. It's unlikely we'll ever be back to buy more. Even if we do, I doubt the same guy will be here. Buying drugs out of this place, though potentially dangerous, does not leave me feeling as if I've accomplished any great feat.

The van pulls from the curb in front of me and Cad falls in behind me. We jump on the freeway and head back across the bridge. I'm relaxed now, and feeling pretty comfortable with Alberto. We talk a little about the heroin scene down on Sonoma Street, and I ask him if he knows where the dope is coming from.

"Zamudio," he answers without hesitation. "Victor and Rafael get it from a connection in Oakland."

I remember Miller telling me that the Zamudios were neighborhood kingpins. "Any chance we could buy from either of them?"

Alberto lets out a chuckle and shakes his head. "They sell weight, Homeboy." He flashes a row of nasty tracks on his inner arm. "They'd never let a dope fiend like me in the door."

Feeling the same relaxed kinship that I had been feeling, Alberto jumps on the opportunity to hit me up again for a piece of the tar. This time it's me who chuckles, and again I tell him that Miller will pay him when we get back to the station. He looks like shit by the time we pull into the lot, and I'm wondering how much of his habit we're financing.

I get back inside the police station and my drugs test positive. I log them into evidence downstairs and then return to my office to type the report. Miller has left to give Alberto a ride, and Cad has maneuvered himself into a detectives' meeting about last night's homicide. Van Kirk and the sarge ask if I want to go eat with them, but I decline. I chow on a piece of barbecue chicken brought from home while I work on my report. My typewriter, already on its last legs, finally quits and I have to use Miller's to finish it.

The phone rings and I see it's the general office line. The lady on the other end wants to complain about her neighbor who she believes is dealing drugs.

"What makes you think it's drugs?" I ask.

"Lots of people coming and going," she says. "Mostly on foot, and mostly young kids."

"How young?"

"Teenagers, almost all of them. After school lets out is when it's the worst. Sometimes they stay in there for a while, and then come out all hopped up on grass."

I smile at the term. Sounds like something my grandmother would have said. *Hopped up on grass.*

It's 2:33 p.m., almost time for school to get out. The woman won't give her name, but provides me with the address and description of the suspected drug house. It's only three blocks from the high school. The rest of my unit is still out, so I decide to investigate the complaint alone, hopeful that I can finally develop a case of my own.

I find the house situated on the corner, and I have a perfect view from the parking lot of an adjacent apartment building. A group of high school age kids stroll by, but show no interest as they continue on past the house. I sit for another half-hour without any activity, and my mind drifts to my interview with Maria Cardenas. It's been two days since we talked in the jail, and she should have been released from court yesterday. I really hoped she'd have called by now.

A small bronze colored Datsun buzzes around the corner with only one person visible in it. It parks right in front of me and a kid of about 17 or 18 gets out. He jogs across the street and up the front steps of the house I'm watching. I see there is some kind of security door at the front, which is opened by a woman. I use my binoculars to get a better view. She appears to be a white woman in her thirties, with long black hair and a slightly roundish figure. After a couple of minutes, the kid comes out and gets back into his car.

Normally, that's not enough evidence to take any action. I couldn't write a search warrant for the place, or even detain the woman based solely on what I just saw. Even if I stop the kid in the car, anything I find will be inadmissible in court and any arrest would be thrown out.

But I'm not looking to arrest the kid. All I want is an informant that can get me inside the house, legally. I follow the Datsun down the street until we're a good distance from the house, and then I pull him over. It's the first time I've used my unmarked car to make a stop, and plugging the strobe into the lighter port and finding the siren button takes me a couple of clumsy minutes.

The kid pulls over and I quickly turn off my lights and siren, so as not to draw attention to us. When I get to the driver's window, I see that the kid looks like he's ready to shit his pants. He shows me his license. I run a check and find out he's eighteen and never been in any trouble. His name is Peter and he lives with his parents in a nice neighborhood in the next town of Castro Valley.

"Can I ask why you stopped me?" he ekes out the question.

I decide to make the most of his nervousness and take the direct approach. "I wanted to talk to you about the weed you just bought from the woman in that house back there."

The poor kid's eyes pop out and he immediately begins to sweat. He swallows hard and starts to give me some lame story about just visiting a friend.

I ease my eyes closed and shake my head. "Don't . . ." I hold up a hand. "Let's not get started on the wrong foot."

His head drops to his chest and I can see his neck pulsing. I kneel down so my face is right even with his, only a couple of inches away, and I lower my voice to a soft whisper. "It's okay, pal." I put my hand on his trembling arm. "You're not the one I want. This is how it's going to work: you're going to give me the dope you bought, and tell me all about the lady who sold it to you. Then I let you go without any charges, and your name never gets used in any reports."

Almost before the last word leaves my lips, he reaches under his seat and pulls out a plastic baggie of marijuana. "That's all of it, honest. And it wasn't for me; it's for a friend. I've never used it or bought it before."

I ignore his rambling soliloquy of innocence. "Here's the catch," I say. "If you tip her off or tell her anything, I file charges against you and arrest you right out of Mom and Dad's house."

He gets it. The kid spills his guts about the woman. Her name is Darla, she lives alone, and has been dealing marijuana and hashish to kids from the middle school and high school for at least a year. She also takes in stolen property as barter for the drugs. While the kid is talking to me, I'm detecting a strange food odor emanating from inside the car. The more he talks, the hungrier I'm getting. Finally I have to stop him.

"What is that smell?" I stick my head in the window and sniff.

He lets out a nervous laugh. "Oh that? It's piroshki."

"What in the hell is piroshki?"

"It's like a Russian pizza sandwich." He reaches into the back seat to show me a whole bag of them. "I work in a piroshki factory. My shift just got over."

The smell is amazing. If I hadn't just taken the kid's drugs and conned him into ratting out his marijuana connection, I might have tried talking him out of one. But I've caused this kid enough grief. "Okay Peter Piroshki, you can go ahead and leave." Then, something pops into my mind and I hold up my hands. "Wait! I have one more question. Do you think Darla has any stolen typewriters?"

I drive back to the station eager to start work on a search warrant for Darla's house. I'm already planning on serving a warrant this week on the marijuana grower who pulled a shotgun on me, but now it looks like I have another one. A gust of wind blows my car and I notice the darkening sky. *Got a couple of heroin buys down, and by next week I'll have a couple of search warrants to my credit. Finally starting to roll like a real narc! I wonder whatever happened to Maria.*

I spend the afternoon at Cad's desk. He's still helping the homicide detectives find their suspects, and that means his typewriter is free. By mid afternoon the place is swarming with activity again. Apparently they've picked up the two brothers, Art and Ernie Fausto. Cad comes in and eyes me shadily. "Don't you have a desk of your own?"

I tell him my typewriter is on the fritz, and he frowns. There's an air of importance in Cad's movements though, and Miller, still steamed from Cad's earlier inquiries about the East Palo Alto case, decides to press him on it. "I hear you and your new partners made an arrest in the homicide case."

"Two arrests," Cad retorts. "As of right now they're being held on probation violations, but we'll find evidence on them soon enough."

"*We?*" Miller cries out in laughter.

Cad whirls around toward the door. He stops and turns back with a piercing glare at Miller, then shifts his gaze to me. "And don't forget to put the plastic cover over my typewriter when you're done!" Cad's exit is punctuated by a slammed door. Miller is still laughing as he picks up the ringing phone.

He covers the mouthpiece with his hand. "It's for you, Soto."

The other end is silent, and then in hushed tones I hear Maria's voice. "I told you I'd call."

"I never doubted you." I try to sound as sincere as possible. "Did you get released from court okay?"

"Uh-huh. Thanks."

I look at the clock and it's about time to head home. I'm hungry for a nice dinner, and it's now storming outside. "Did you want to meet?"

"I'm over at the welfare office with my baby. Can you pick me up?"

I toss my head back and roll my eyes. "Sure. I'll be there in five minutes." I drive the few blocks to the county offices, wondering if Maria can sense how green I am. *Maybe she's already manipulating me. A ride for she and her baby? C'mon!*

They're standing under the shelter of a bus stop, whipped by wind and splashed by passing cars. The baby looks to be less than a year, and I'm mindful that Maria has three more at home, or somewhere. I pull up and she climbs in. Her tiny son is halfway covered by a plastic bag, and watches me through huge, almond eyes.

"Thank you," Maria says.

I think about all of the rainstorms when there was no ride for Maria and her kids, and I'm suddenly disarmed. "You're welcome." I pull back into traffic. "Did you want to get something to eat?"

A smile creeps across her face and she unconsciously fluffs her hair. We end up at World's Fair, a cafeteria-style restaurant divided into six separate ethnic buffets and a donut shop. I hold the door for them, and Maria giggles with a schoolgirl candor that goes against my stereotype of her. It's as if I had taken her to a high-end restaurant for cocktails and a steak.

She picks out a plate of pork chow mein and a large Coke, and we take a seat at a corner booth. Maria pokes at the noodles and we talk casually for a few minutes about people we both know. To her they're friends and family, and to me they're people I've arrested; Little Tiger Lopez, Fat Girl, Crazy Lucy, Stabbin Steven Rodriguez, the entire Tofilau family, etc.

I check my watch and realize I've probably missed my own family dinner by now. I haven't gotten to this stage with an informant before, so I'm trying to think of a smooth way to steer the conversation toward the drug information I'm looking for. I don't push her, and instead I hold the baby while Maria takes a few bites of food. Suddenly she stops and sets her fork down.

"I didn't just call you because I needed a ride." Her expression takes a sudden turn to serious. "I have something to tell you."

I nod and set the baby on my knee so I can look directly at Maria. Her eyes are beginning to tear and she turns away so I won't see.

"It's okay," I say. "Whatever you want to tell me, it's okay." As soon as the words leave my mouth, I wonder why I made such an impulsive promise. What if it's *not* okay?

"It's a secret." Maria is now covering her face with her hands, and her voice is broken and quivering. "It's a big secret that involves a lot of other people. But I have to tell someone. I can't hold it in anymore."

The baby reaches for her mother, intuitively sensing something isn't right. She takes the little boy in her arms and now I can see Maria's eyes. Her cheeks are streaked with runny lines of mascara. She's weeping hard, trying to catch her breath. I realize that this is something more than the name of the guy she buys her drugs from.

"Arnie was such a nice man," Maria sobs. "He would never have hurt anybody."

My ears ring with the familiarity. *Is she talking about the guy who was killed? Arnold Bascomb?*

"Are you talking about the homicide?" A shot of excitement courses through me. "We arrested the suspects in that case," I tell her. "We think the Fausto brothers did it."

"Yeah, I heard." Maria shoos the air toward her wet cheeks. "Arthur and Ernie couldn't rip off a can of beer without screwing it up. You got the wrong guys." There is no uncertainty in her words.

I give her a minute to calm down, and then ask her to start over. "Tell me everything you know, from the beginning."

My heart is racing as she explains it to me. Aside from knowing that Bascomb was robbed of his wallet and watch, she knows several other details that haven't even hit the press yet. I can't believe I'm getting this information from my first informant ever. Well, my second informant counting the piroshki kid.

When Maria is finished with her story I excuse myself from the table. I go to the phone booth tucked around the corner from the restrooms and dial the detective bureau. Most of the squad has left, but the two main investigators on the case are still at their desks.

I get one of them on the phone and tell him I'm on my way in with an informant who's got information about his case. He's immediately hesitant, and tries to give me the brush. I get it; he's been up for nearly 24 hours, and they think they've got the scenario pretty well figured out. They've already made arrests.

"You know we already have the two guys in custody," he says.

"Yeah, the Fausto brothers." I take a breath before my next words. "You got the wrong guys."

A long, uncomfortable silence follows and I wonder if I sound too sure of myself. The last thing I want to do is piss off the investigators. I hear him cover the phone with his hand. There's a garbled exchange that I can't quite make out, and I assume it's between the two lead detectives. He comes back on the line with a pacifying tone that hints of condescension. "We'll stick around for a few more minutes until you get in."

Whatever! "We're on our way."

Their facial expressions when they see me walk in says it all. I'm in the company of a heroin-addicted prostitute, carrying her baby in my arms, and looking like a piece of shit myself. Who could blame them for smirking?

We all sit down in a tiny interview room, and Maria looks at me. "It's alright," I say. "Just tell them like you told me."

An odd look comes across her face, and for a minute I'm not sure what she's going to do. Finally she clears her throat and starts talking. "They released me from court the day before yesterday, but the paperwork took a long time and I didn't actually get out until late. I finally made it to my parents' house around four in the morning."

I already know that isn't true. She was released around 2 p.m. yesterday, and probably had to get her fix before going home. The minor point of fact doesn't really matter. The detectives are listening patiently.

"When I got there, everybody was up." Maria adjusts the baby in her lap. "My mom was crying and my little sister was freaking out. Everyone was yelling at my sister's boyfriend, Carlos."

"Why were they yelling at him?" asks one of the detectives.

"For what he did. Because of stabbing our neighbor, Arnie. Only at the time we didn't know it was Arnie he had stabbed."

The two detectives exchange looks. "What made your family think Carlos stabbed someone?"

Maria's face has a puzzled look, as if she can't believe they're questioning her veracity. "He did it, okay? He came running into the house covered with blood. He had the wallet and the watch that he took. He was all wild-eyed, and wanted them to help him get rid of the knife."

Now they both straighten up. They each slip their pens out and exchange glances with one another. This time it's more of an *Oh shit* look. Their investigation had just taken an unexpected turn, in a direction they hadn't put any work into. They have a lot of catching up to do. Both detectives pick up their note pads and start firing questions at Maria, lots of them. Only now she stays quiet. The next words out of her mouth establish her as the streetwise negotiator I had suspected she was.

"I'll answer the rest of your questions under two conditions," Maria says, as she toys playfully with her son's hair. "Nobody in my family goes to jail, and my name doesn't show up on any reports." She glances over at me as if I'm representing her in this exchange—which I guess in some ways I am.

Then, as calmly as she had brought it up, she drops it. "Is there a bathroom?" Maria picks up her son. "I need to change him."

I walk her across the floor and use my key to let her in the women's room. When I get back to the interview room, the two detectives sit glaring at me. They've apparently gotten over the surprise of having arrested two innocent men, and now they're onto a new focus: me.

"You two make a nice couple," one says. "The Soto Family."

The other detective raises his eyebrows. "Has anybody done a paternity test on that baby? He has your nose."

The barbs have an underlying significance that puts my mind at ease. It's a form of approval, and their way of thanking me for helping them out on a high profile case. I pretty much know it's the only recognition I'll get, but that's of little concern to me. Even if nobody else in the department knows, they do. I hope it will be a foundation block as I try to build a reputation as a good narc.

They record Maria's statement for the next two and a half hours. She comes out with even more information, including the fact that her family had hidden the suspect while the police were searching the neighborhood, and they helped him launder and ultimately burn his bloody clothes. The detectives had already agreed not to arrest any of Maria's family.

It's nearly 9 p.m. when they finish. I drive Maria and her baby into her neighborhood and drop her a few blocks from the family house. She thanks me and I thank her. Her information had identified a killer who may have otherwise gone free. Not to mention saving the two knuckleheads who were in jail for something they didn't do. My first experience with an informant couldn't have unfolded any better.

I don't see the road in front of me during my drive home. As if I hit a mental replay button, my mind is busy reliving the day's events.

The girls are asleep when I get home, and I give them both a kiss goodnight anyway. I spring back into the living room and fling myself onto the couch, eager to share my story. Gale heats up some leftover spaghetti for me and turns down the TV show she had been watching.

Between heaping mouthfuls, I enthusiastically recount my meeting with Maria. The details pour out of me in undercover parlance that

Gale only half understands, yet she nods earnestly. Her expression shows equal measures of thankfulness that I'm home safe, and delight that I enjoy my new assignment.

I ask Gale about her day and she starts to tell me. With the TV volume still down, I see that her show is over and the 10 o'clock news has come on. The vivid picture of their lead story sets my heart racing. I dive for the volume control and turn it up.

"Two local men were shot to death at an East Palo Alto apartment house today," the newscaster reports. "Police are calling it a drug rip-off gone bad."

"I was there!" I cry out, cutting Gale's story short. "I bought heroin at those apartments today, and I saw those two guys sneaking up from the back of the building. I missed being in the middle of that shootout by only a couple of minutes."

The exhilarating coincidence doesn't affect Gale the same as me, and she grows quiet. We watch the rest of the newscast together as I polish off the bowl of spaghetti, and then I take a quick shower before climbing into bed.

We both lie quietly in the dark, wrapped in our own thoughts. We both find it hard to fall asleep, but for two very different reasons.

5

BIRTHDAY DANCE

Between the undercover buys, helping my partners on their cases, and finding a typewriter that works, I've finally managed to squeeze a couple of days into writing my own search warrants. By the end of the day I've completed my marijuana cultivation warrant—the one where the guy stuck a shotgun in my face. And I'm nearly done typing the weed-dealing woman that the piroshki kid gave me.

I come in early to finish writing, and then I get both warrants signed by a judge. While I'm at the courthouse, I stop by D.A. Bartell's office. I remind him about the informant, Maria Cardenas, whom I went to bat for last week—the one he damn near made me swear on my life for.

"She gave us information that helped clear a homicide case," I say, trying not to sound boastful.

Bartell's face is set in business mode. "Yeah, I signed off on the arrest warrant charging Carlos Tellez yesterday afternoon." Finally, his demeanor softens and he nods. "So, our girl is the mystery informant behind the arrest?"

Oh, I see . . . now she's "our girl." I thank him for helping me get her out of jail, and I make like thanking him is my sole purpose for stopping by. Although that's part of it, I also want him to know that I'm not some bum, and that my word is good.

I pass a briefing in the conference room down the hall from my office, and listen at the back of the room as the op plan is laid out. It involves a stakeout of Maria's family home for Tellez. A map projected on the wall shows that Bascomb was found only a block from the home.

The detective sergeant suddenly stops talking and nods toward the back of the room. Everyone turns. "The narcotics unit gave us a hand in this case, and I should acknowledge their work," he says, almost grudgingly.

Cad is seated in the last row, and looks like he's about to stand up and take a bow.

The sergeant continues, "The narcs came up with a confidential informant who provided a useful piece of intelligence on the case."

Yeah, like the name of the person who did it.

By now, Cad realizes the sarge is talking about my help and not his. He folds his arms across his chest and slumps down in his seat. I'm guessing he'll no longer let me use his typewriter.

When I get back to the office, Miller is in a hurry for me to get back down to Sonoma without Alberto. "Let's see if Salazar will sell you another bag," he says.

I'm eager to make another buy, but I'm also wondering how long my luck will last. So far this whole drug-buying thing has been a breeze. Sooner or later someone is going to wonder who the hell I am, and confront me. I have no track marks to prove I'm a user, and no gun to protect myself if they figure out I'm a phony. Even if Van Kirk and Roberts are paying attention to my wire, a nagging voice inside keeps saying I should be ready to save my own ass in case they can't get to me in time.

They wire me up again and we head back down to the neighborhood. Van Kirk and Roberts are in the van a few blocks away, and Miller drops me at the end of El Dorado. I walk in from there.

I get to Beto's place, but he's not out on the porch like last time. I'm not sure if drug buyers knock or ring the bell, so I end up just sort of milling around in front of the guy's house. The door opens and out comes Jimmy the Gimp, stuffing a balloon in his pocket. Beto stands in the doorway looking me up and down, as if he doesn't remember me.

"Can I get another twenty from you?" I say to Beto, as Jimmy passes me on the porch.

"Where's Alberto?" Beto makes no move in or out.

I shrug. *At least he remembers me as the guy who was with Alberto last week.*

"I don't sell to nobody I don't know."

He's still standing in the doorway, and I'm not sure if I'm now supposed to argue the point. I'm also vaguely aware of The Gimp hovering behind me.

"He knows me," I suddenly blurt out, motioning toward Jimmy. The Gimp's head bobs back as his eyes register surprise. He looks like he's about to tell Beto that I'm a liar and he doesn't know me, when I step in close to him and toss my arm around his shoulder. I lean up to his ear and whisper, "I saw you going into the police station the other day. Unless you want me to tell Beto that you're a snitch, you better cosign for me so I can get my bag."

Jimmy sputters a few incoherent syllables before saying, "I know him. He's cool, Beto."

I get my bag of dope and then actually walk with The Gimp for a couple of blocks. He makes a pathetic attempt to explain why he was at the police department, denying of course, that he has ever snitched.

"Sorry for putting you on the spot, man." I sniff and rub my nose. "But I need to fix really bad."

Jimmy tells me that he knows some other guys in the neighborhood who have better dope than Beto. I pull out another twenty, and tell him I want to get another one. He hobbles up to another house and has me wait on the walkway in front. There's a brief conversation at the door, but I can't see who he's talking to through the screen. After a few seconds Jimmy motions me up.

Frankie Ortega is standing there eyeing me through the screen door. I know him from uniformed patrol, but not well enough for him to recognize me now. My beard has evolved to a motley Foo Manchu, my greasy hair is slicked back and my clothes look like hell.

"How much you need, Homes?"

"I only got enough money for one."

He nods, then reaches through the cracked door to snatch the bill out of my hand. He pushes it open a second later, glances around furtively, and then hands me a small, knotted balloon.

As we walk away from the house, Jimmy hits me up in his nasally voice. "Hey, you gonna cut me out a taste for helping you?"

I look at the balloon, wondering how much a *taste* is—not that I would give him some. "Sorry, this is for me and my old lady," I tell him. "I'll get you next time."

At the corner, he goes one way and I go the other. I meet Miller, Van Kirk, and the sarge down a few blocks, and then head back to the station. On the way back, I mention my search warrants to Sarge. He says we'll schedule them when we get to the office.

The cultivation paper is on the board for 2:30 p.m. today, and the weed lady is set for noon tomorrow. It'll be my first briefing, and I'm a little self-conscious about giving it. The guys from my unit will be there, and so will a couple of uniform cops from patrol. I spend the next hour writing up an op plan and copying photos and information to pass out.

"We know our suspect is likely to be armed," I begin the briefing. I pass around his mug photo and give them all the particulars. When I describe how the guy shoved a shotgun in my face, the uniformed cops visibly tense up. Having just come from Patrol, I know how they think and feel. You're an easily identifiable target in a uniform, and always defensive—always on high alert. On the other hand, I'm trying to project an image of a seasoned narc, immune from such pedestrian fears. I sit on the corner of the desk, the knee of my torn blue jeans casually draped over a chair, as if it's all pretty routine stuff in the world of undercover work.

I assign Miller and one of the uniforms to take positions in the rear, in case my suspect flees out the back of the house. Van Kirk and the sergeant will use the *key* to batter down the front door. I'll be at the front of the line to bang on the door first, and give the legally-mandated warning demanding that the suspect allow us entry before we force our way inside.

We pile into the van from the gas station at the bottom of the hill, leaving Miller and the uniform to make their way up the embankment to the fence. They'll be in the same spot I was when the shotgun incident happened, and they both appear pensive as they leave the van. I'm feeling the weight of responsibility for everyone's safety, but at the same time I'm getting an ego charge from the fact that all this tension surrounds my big case.

The uniform cop in the front catches my eye and gives me a silent thumbs-up. I nod with raised eyebrows as if to say, *We'll see.*

Miller's scratchy voice comes over the radio in a tone that's mostly somber, but with just a hint of glee. "Soto, the backyard is empty. There aren't any plants."

The van jerks to a stop and we stumble out in a headlong sprint for the door. I haven't had time to absorb Miller's radio transmission, other than knowing that I'm screwed. I fumble with my radio as I run toward the house. *What should I do now? Do I call a timeout?*

I see by the look on the sarge's face, it's too late now. I pound with the authority of Barney Fife, and in a deflated voice I say, "Police department, search warrant! Demand immediate entry! Open the door or we'll . . ."

The heavy battering ram swings forward and the door lurches awkwardly. It swings partially open, littering the carpet with the remnants of the strike plate and deadbolt housing. I'm standing stupidly, looking at my watch's second hand and wondering why we didn't wait the proscribed time for the occupant to let us in.

The team rushes past me and I hear yelling and swearing. I'm trying to gather myself, and at the same time I'm wondering if I could have been wrong about the marijuana plants I saw that night. I go straight for the window that overlooks the yard. There are no plants.

"What'd we do, Soto?" Sarge asks. "Hit the wrong house?"

Before I can tell him that it's the right house, Miller comes into the room dragging my guy by his cuffed hands. "Found your suspect hiding in a crawlspace in the bedroom closet."

Van Kirk laughs. "Suspect? What's he suspected of?"

Sarge searches the sofa for weapons first and then sits the suspect down where we can keep an eye on him. I have an overwhelming yearning to jump on top of my handcuffed prisoner and threaten his life if he doesn't admit to everybody that he *did* have a backyard full of marijuana plants just last week. I imagine myself slapping him in the face, first with an open hand and then with a backhand. *"Admit it, you son-of-a-bitch!"*

The suspect watches us while we search, but he says nothing. Finally, Van Kirk comes in from the garage wielding a Mossberg shotgun. "Hey Soto, is this the one he made you suck on?"

I roll my eyes, not wanting the suspect to put it together that I'm the same guy he threatened. "Leave it on the table and I'll log it into evidence," I say.

After an hour, everyone is tired of searching. I sit at the coffee table next to the suspect and begin filling out my evidence seizure paperwork. So far, I have one shotgun and some utility bills showing that my suspect, Derrick Clark, is in control of the residence.

I open what we call the raid kit, and pull out the receipt forms to start filling out. Dejected, I take off my raid jacket and bulletproof vest and hang them on the chair. Sergeant Roberts takes a seat next to me, gazing off like he's deep in thought. "Hey, Miller," he calls out over his shoulder. "Show me where Clark was hiding."

Miller shuts off the TV and saunters back into the dining room. "You mean, when he *came out of the closet?*" Pleased with his clever double meaning, he leads the sarge and me up a short stairway to a bedroom and then pulls back the closet door. "He was hunkered down in here."

Boxes are stacked in one corner and all the hung clothes have been shoved to the opposite side. We glance up at the ceiling and see an attic opening covered loosely by a piece of sheetrock. Sarge looks at me with a knowing grin. I steady the boxes while Miller uses them as a ladder. Sarge holds a flashlight on the opening with one hand, and aims his handgun toward it with the other.

Miller slides the sheetrock covering out of the way and slowly pokes his head into the attic. He rotates all the way around with his flashlight held out in front of him, and then a sheepish smile crosses his face. "He's got your dope up here, drying."

Miller climbs all the way inside and I follow. The heat in the attic is stifling, and the weighty scent of marijuana hangs in the air. Dozens and dozens of withered marijuana plants are strung upside down on ropes running the length of the attic.

It takes two more hours to photograph, disassemble, and cart all one hundred seventy-eight plants through the house and out to the street. During that time Miller explains to me that the buds at the ends of the plants' branches are the most valuable part of the crop. By hanging them upside down, the euphoric THC contained in the leaves drains into the tips during the drying process, making the end product more potent—thus more valuable.

A crime scene tech is summoned with a property truck, and he transports the harvest back to the station for us. I get a few swats on the back for *my* successful search warrant, but I'm more than aware that it was a sympathy case donated to me by Miller, the bounty of which wouldn't even have been detected if not for the sarge.

There is a fair amount of work involved in processing the evidence and writing the report, and both Miller and Van Kirk help me get it done. When Clark's finished being booked, I pull him into the interview room. He eyes me with curiosity as I read him his rights, and he stops me midway through. "I'll tell you what you want to know, off the record."

I agree, even though technically there is no *off the record* once I've advised him his rights. He admits growing and harvesting the plants, but says he was only part of a four-person partnership in the operation. He won't give me the names of the others involved, however.

"You look kind of familiar," he says.

"I get that a lot."

"Anyway," he continues. "We decided to pull up the plants earlier than we wanted to."

"Why's that?"

"We were about to get ripped off."

I glance down at my notepad and bite my lip. Trying not to laugh, I ask, "What made you think you were going to get ripped off?" I gather my things and press the buzzer for the jailers to come open the door.

"Caught some dude climbing the fence into my yard." He follows me out and back down the hall.

"Can't trust anyone these days." I shake my head in disbelief as I open his cell door. "Did the guy ever come back to take your plants?"

"No way. I scared him off pretty good," he says with a satisfied nod. "I doubt that guy will ever come back."

I walk out of the jail and up to my office, chuckling at my own cleverness. On my way out for the night, I notice I'm on the board for another search warrant tomorrow. It will be the first order of business after our noon starting time.

Headlights sweep across my face on the way home, and I see my reflection in the rearview mirror. I look grubbier than my suspect, Derrick Clark. My hands are sticky with marijuana sap and I smell like I just came from Woodstock. I'm eager to get home, but even more eager to do my second search warrant tomorrow—one that I know I worked up from scratch, completely on my own.

* * *

My search warrant has been bumped to 3 p.m. because of the Carlos Tellez surveillance. Sarge says there's a better chance we'll catch my marijuana gal selling to the kids after school lets out, anyway. He's got a good point.

I mention during the briefing, that the woman's house has a wrought iron security door over the entry, but that it didn't appear to be locked when I watched my informant go in. "My plan is to simply go up and knock," I tell the skeptical group seated around the office. "It's about the time when her customers usually start showing up, so I'm hoping she's left it unlocked again." We decide to have Cad and Miller carry the *key* with them, just in case.

We do a quick drive-by in the van, but there's no visible activity at the house. Sarge parks us all down the street and we watch for a while. After about ten minutes, the back of the van is like a sauna and everyone is uncomfortable. To spare my comrades further aggravation, I decide to go ahead and hit the place without waiting any longer.

I jump from the van wearing my raid jacket with the big POLICE lettering on it, and I slip my dark sunglasses into place. I'm wearing my bulletproof vest over a cotton tee shirt, and my pistol and a pair of handcuffs are tucked into my Levis. I jog up the steps and see that the security door is not only closed, but it's locked. It's too late to change course now, so I give the door a good rap.

"Who is it?" a pleasant voice calls from inside.

"It's Phil."

The dark-haired woman suddenly appears on the other side of the screen. She's wearing a red kimono cinched at the waste with a tie. A huge smile materializes across her face as she unlocks the security door for me.

"Come in, Phil," she calls out over her shoulder as she prances away.

"Hold it," I say, fumbling to get my badge unclipped from my belt. I thrust it out in front of me. "Police officer! I've got a warrant to search this premises!"

The woman laughs jauntily as she plops down, cross-legged on the sofa. "Go ahead, Officer Phil, do your thing."

She seems too giddy to be a drug dealer about to be arrested. Though I've still got my badge out, I have the feeling she doesn't believe I'm a cop. I turn to show her the handgun tucked into my pants and she claps her hands excitedly.

"I'm a police officer," I say, pulling out my handcuffs.

"Oooh," she cries out in delight. "You're going to go all the way and handcuff me? This is great!"

Her response is so far from anything I expected that I'm caught in momentary paralysis. I'm still standing in front of her, all my gear in my hands as proof I'm the real thing, and then she starts chanting.

"Take it off, take it off!" She does a wolf whistle. "Take it all off, Officer Phil!"

There's a sudden rumble up the stairs behind me, and in come my partners with their guns drawn. "Police officers! Search warrant!" they scream out as they funnel inside.

The woman's jubilation peters out and her face goes slack. The sound of one last pathetic clap hangs in the air. "You mean you're a *real* cop?"

I flip my sunglass off and frown at the impertinence. "Uh, yeah. That's what I've been trying to tell you. Who did you think I was?" My partners have now put their guns away and are standing there waiting for her answer.

"I thought you were a male stripper." Her face is flushed with embarrassment. "Today is my birthday . . . and well, when I saw you at my door in that sexy getup . . ."

I can't hear anything else she says because the guys are laughing so loudly. The sergeant starts going with it, twirling his raid jacket above his head and throwing it seductively to the floor. Then, he unbuckles his gunbelt and tosses that aside as well.

"Hold on," the woman says, the reality of her situation finally sinking in. "You guys are really here to search my place for drugs?"

I assure her that we are.

"Oh hell, I'll just save us all time and tell you where they're at." She points to a coffee table across the room. "All my weed is in that drawer."

Cad slides it open and pulls out a large zip-lock baggie with about a half-ounce of loose marijuana. It's a paltry amount, hardly worthy of all the work that went into seizing it. In fact, I might have recovered much more on any given night of uniformed patrol.

"What about the stolen property?" I ask.

She rolls her eyes and points to a coat closet. "In there."

I open the door and am greeted by a jumble of bags, clothes, phones, and a clot of stereo and television cables. I dig through the pile, finally finding what I'm really after: an electric typewriter. There's also a fairly nice coffee maker amongst the mess. I snatch that as well and slap evidence tags on both items. Though they're technically property of the police evidence room, they'll be temporarily stored in the narcotics office where I can make good use of the typewriter, and the guys will make use of the coffee pot.

In the jail she gives me a statement admitting that she routinely sells to kids from the local high school. Not that they couldn't find another source, but the fact that I've put her out of business gives me some solace. I convince myself that even given the insignificant amount of pot recovered, it was all worth it.

When I leave the jail, Van Kirk and Sergeant Roberts help me carry the raid kit and bags of evidence upstairs. The sarge hands me his bag and goes straight into his office when he sees that the investigations lieutenant is waiting for him there. They close the door and I have the strangest feeling they're talking about me. Van Kirk slows at the window and I'm guessing he thinks they're talking about him.

The investigations secretary, Eiko Sasaki, rounds the corner waving her hands in the air. "A young man is waiting to see you, Officer Van Kirk."

"Where is he?" We both ask at the same time.

Her eyes dart to the door right next to me, and as if in slow motion it begins to open. I hear Mrs. Sasaki start to apologize, but I've already turned away and am diving for my office door. It's too late. Jimmy the Gimp stumbles out of the interview room and stares at me with a baffled expression.

"You!" He eyes me up and down. Then turns to Van Kirk and in his nasally voice says, "That's the Soto dude I been telling you about!"

I realize my heroin cover has just been blown out of the water. By tomorrow morning, every dealer in the Sonoma area will know I'm an undercover cop.

Jimmy scratches his head, then his mouth gapes open and his eyes register some semblance of acuity–like a kid who suddenly figured out there's no Santa Clause. *And just when I thought the Gimp's light had finally come on, it goes dim again.* He turns to Van Kirk. "Wait just a minute . . . this guy's snitching for you, too?"

I try my hardest to look insulted, but I can barely conceal my laughter. "Hell no, I'm not a snitch!" I hold up the evidence bags in my hands. "The cops found some stuff of mine that got ripped off."

Van Kirk clears his throat. "Yeah, we're just returning his stolen property." He pushes me toward the elevator. "There's the way out, Mr. Soto."

Mrs. Sasaki watches the whole exchange from her desk. She raises an eyebrow as I hustle past her into the elevator. In the background I hear Van Kirk laying into The Gimp. "Stop trying to play detective, Jimmy. And get your gimpy ass back inside the interview room."

A few minutes later I pass Mrs. Sasaki again, sneaking my way back into the office. She's as confused as Jimmy.

I'm fifteen minutes from finishing up for the night, when Van Kirk comes in like he's got a Jalapeño pepper in his shorts. I surmise that he's gotten rid of the gimp, and now at the end of the night, wants to roll with something else. "Wanna buy some PCP, Soto?"

Miller wheels around in his chair and does an exaggerated check of his wristwatch.

I haven't bought PCP before, and I'm instantly engulfed in the fear that I might be expected by the dealer to try it out. I've heard that the stuff is so potent it can actually be absorbed through the skin.

"Yea, I'm game." I hear myself agreeing to it before I finish the thought. "Who am I buying it from?"

"Black Al."

Now Miller perks up. "You got a snitch into Black Al?"

While the two of them go back and forth about what a big deal it will be to put a case on this dealer, I replace the batteries in the body wire. "Do we know his real name?" I take off my shirt and work the sling over my head.

Miller shakes his head. "We've heard about this guy for over a year. As far as PCP goes, everyone on the street knows Black Al's the man with the fat sack in the South End."

"Haven't had a CI who could buy from him," says Van Kirk. "Much less intro a cop to him."

I feel the cold wire being taped to my skin. "Who's the CI? Please don't tell me it's Jimmy."

They both laugh. "Just about as bad," says Van Kirk. "His name is Ray Rodriguez. We call him RR."

Van Kirk and I move to the interview room next door while Miller makes copies of the cash I'll use to buy the drugs. I find the informant sitting on the corner of the table. He's a dark complected guy who could pass for Filipino, Indonesian, or any Hispanic ethnicity. He's wearing some sort of striped hat and his nose is noticeably large and purple.

"This is RR," Van Kirk barely gets the words out before he stares up at the guy's cap and breaks into laughter. "What the hell kind of hat is that?" he says. "You look like a goddamn railroad conductor. That must be what RR stands for. I'm gonna start calling you the RR Express!"

The guy is quiet and seems self-conscious. He walks a few paces behind us and I use the distance to quietly ask Van Kirk, "What's with his nose?"

Van Kirk shrugs. "I don't know . . . it's purple." Then he turns to RR. "Hey, what in the hell's wrong with your nose, anyway?"

The guy looks humiliated. "Doctor says it's a blood clot."

Van Kirk turns back to me. "Blood clot."

Thanks for clearing that up.

RR and I get into my car, and Miller and Van Kirk follow us in the van. We turn onto Dixon Street and the van peels off down Valle Vista.

"It's back there," RR says, pointing to a narrow dirt driveway between two apartment buildings. We pull all the way to a dark dead-end. I see it's one of three old cottages, crammed onto a small lot backing up to a set of train tracks. I take a second to rehearse the street terminology for PCP: crystal, KJ, angel dust, super joints. Since I haven't bought it before, I figure to just follow along with RR. Like buying from the heroin dealers on Sonoma, I want to be able to return for more without RR.

As soon as we step onto the landing, the door opens my heart skips a beat or two. The woman holding it open for us is Eva Flores, a notorious PCP user. I'm pretty sure I've arrested her before, and I know I've stopped her a half-dozen times. She's also the daughter of State Assemblyman, Glen Flores. She's not a bad looking girl, and I've always wondered how she got mixed up in the PCP scene. Right now I'm just wondering what I should do.

I hesitate a second as RR goes inside, and I weigh out the things that could happen if I follow him in. There's a real possibility she'll recognize me immediately. Not knowing who else is inside, it could turn into a real mess real quick. I make my decision, and step past her into the shadowy cottage. I feel Eva eyeing me as I go by, but I work hard to keep focused elsewhere. I'm afraid if we lock eyes, mine will betray me. On the other hand, if I avoid her too much it will look like I've got something to hide. I hear the front door being locked behind me.

I steady my breathing and turn toward her with buoyant coolness. "How ya doin?"

Eva studies me for a couple of beats and then nods. "I'll go get Al."

RR stands with his hands in his pockets, seemingly unconcerned. Presumably he knows how things normally go down, and I'm hoping he would sense if there was a problem. Eva returns to the room in less than a minute. Again I feel as if she's studying me, but I can't tell if it's beyond the normal checking out of a new customer. Finally she and RR start talking. I'm listening hard to detect if there's any tension. They obviously know one another, and the interaction seems light and laid back.

I discreetly take in a deep steadying breath and mask it by running my fingers back through my hair. As I let it out, I finally begin to gain control of my nerves. I force a yawn and scratch my goatee in an effort to look unruffled. I hear a bedroom door opening off to my left, where I suppose Al has been. An indistinct figure emerges in my periphery, but other than a black man, I'm unable to make out any features. I have to work at not letting my eyes dart around the room like a cop, and again, I try to appear indifferent to my surroundings.

RR turns to greet the dealer. "What's up, Al?"

I turn at the same time. My mouth goes dry and I suddenly feel as if I've been lit on fire. What I had thought was a worst-case scenario of running into Eva Flores, pales as the light of the window illuminates Black Al. He's Aldean Harris, a guy I went to high school with. In fact, we were in the same homeroom class for two years. I recognized him the second I saw him, and there's no possible way he won't recognize me—even after six years. And I'm pretty sure the fact that I became a cop is well known throughout my class.

"This is Phil Soto," says RR. "He's a partner of mine and he's looking to score some KJ.

I want to put my hand over RR's mouth before he goes too far out on a limb for me. Once they figure it out, RR's a walking dead man. And I wish he hadn't used my first name. Aldean will put it all together for sure.

Eva stands at his side, watching closely but saying nothing. Aldean glares at me with brown eyes that flicker in the room's dim light. His white teeth slowly reveal themselves and his dark face morphs into a smile. I'm certain he knows who I am.

"How much you need, Phil?"

Could this really be happening? I fumble forty dollars from my pocket and my hoarse voice barely answers him. Eva starts chatting again with RR while me and Aldean complete the deal.

Easy as that, I walk out of there with four PCP joints. On the porch I turn back with a newly fortified backbone. "If it's good I'll come by in a few days for more."

"Don't worry, you'll like it." Eva follows Al back into the cottage and closes the door.

We meet up with the van in a parking lot a few blocks away. Miller asks if the woman was Eva Flores, and I tell him it was.

"I thought I recognized her voice. We've busted her before." Miller turns to Van Kirk. "Except, since she didn't make the deal we really don't have anything on her this time."

"And we still don't have an ID on Black Al." Van Kirk tosses his notepad onto the dash.

I leave RR alone in the car and walk around to Van Kirk's open window. In a low voice, out of RR's earshot, I tell Van Kirk Al's full name and how I know him. Van Kirk is nearly peeing in his pants he's laughing so hard. Miller seems more amazed than humored, and reaches over to slap hands with me.

We get back to the station and I weigh and test the dope before logging it into evidence. It's the real thing.

The office is empty except for me. I flick the light off on my way out and nod goodnight to the sarge. He's in his office next door, talking with the investigations lieutenant. They wave me in, and I cautiously enter. *I knew they were talking about me.*

I open the door and they exchange looks as if trying to figure out which one is going to tell me. "We got a lead on where our homicide suspect is staying," the LT says. "They figure on making an arrest sometime tomorrow." He usually comes across as having an overblown impression of his own importance, and this time is no different.

"The SWAT team is going to be on standby starting in the morning," says Sergeant Roberts.

I'm thinking this is their way of telling me to double back early, since I'm on the SWAT team. I'm about to ask what time they want me in when it becomes apparent that they've got other plans.

"We've already talked with the SWAT commander, and you're not going to be part of tomorrow's operation." The lieutenant glances at a notepad balanced on his crossed legs. "We're going to need you here."

"Here?" My mind quickly runs through a short list of possible uses for me. "What do you need me to . . .?"

"You're going to be in jail with the suspect." The LT answers over the top of my question, then leans back in his chair. "We need you undercover and wired for sound."

I almost chuckle at the *wired for sound* comment. Nobody says that except TV cops. They tell me they hope to get a warrant signed and hit the place around 10 a.m., and they want me here by then.

I get home way too late to see the girls. Gale tried to wait up, but fell asleep on the couch while watching *Falcon Crest*. She's left a plate of leftover dinner for me on the kitchen counter. I devour it while giving Gale the play-by-play of the day's cases. She smiles at all the right places and seems genuinely excited for me. When I'm finished she picks up my plate and goes to the sink. She's quiet for a minute and then turns toward me.

"Does it make you feel bad?"

I wrinkle my brow in confusion.

"About your friend, Aldean. Does it make you feel bad that you're eventually going to have to arrest him?"

I wave the question off like I'm swatting a fly. "It's his own choice to sell drugs, not mine."

Gale asks me if I'm ready for bed and I tell her I have a few things I need to do first. I've had a couple of close calls already: being seen by Van Kirk's gimpy informant, and now doing business with a guy from high school. Considering all the heroin they have me buying, I want to keep the odds in my favor as much as I can. Gale goes into the bedroom and I wait until she's in bed before starting my little project.

I take a book of matches out of the kitchen drawer—the one where we keep the birthday candles. I get some rubbing alcohol and a sewing needle out of the medicine cabinet, and find a graphite pencil in a drawer. I go into the bathroom and quietly lock the door. In order to make my tracks look real I'll need to create three stages of injection sites. The first are recent punctures—raised and red and oozing. I sterilize the sewing needle with alcohol then pull the skin away from the vein on my inner arm. I poke several holes through the loose flesh, pushing the needle through the skin until it comes out about a quarter inch below. I'm careful to follow the vein line without going deep enough to hit it. I hold the lit match to the end of the needle until it is black with soot. With that I make a few more holes, this time leaving a slightly darkened residue in the skin. I imagine it's the same principle as getting a tattoo. In any case, it gives me the desired stage of old tracks that have turned to scar tissue. The bruised color is deepened when I run the pencil along the vein. The middle stage of scabbed injections will come naturally as these all begin to heal.

I hold my handiwork up to the light in admiration. It's not the arm of a lifelong addict, but I'll definitely pass for a guy with a decent habit. As long as they have me buying heroin, I'll have to remember to update my tracks occasionally with more pencil applications.

In the dark of our bedroom I can't tell if Gale is awake or not. In my exuberance I forgot to tell her about my upcoming role as a jail cellmate to a murderer. I climb in next to her and lay staring up at the dark ceiling. In my mind is a picture of Aldean back in high school, clean and innocent. He's smiling the same way he did when he sold me drugs. I keep replaying Gale's question about taking him to jail. As remorse starts to seep in, I quickly push it out of my mind.

6

Cellmates

I have some time, so I swing by my daughter's preschool on the way in to work. She's playing with a few other kids in the fenced yard, and I watch from the adjacent parking lot. The weather is cool and the sky is overcast, but my daughter has on only a light sweater. *Why do they have these kids outside?*

A blond boy uses a plastic bat like a sword, and I have the urge to jump the fence and snatch it from the kid before he hurts my little girl. One of the teacher's aids steps in and curtails his swashbuckling, which allows me to remain incognito for the time being. The aid starts rounding up the kids to get them in, out of the cold.

A woman going to the library next door, blatantly scrutinizes me as she steps from her car. Her sizzling scowl is a reminder of how out of place I must look—a grimy pervert alone in his car, watching all the little kiddies at play. I decide to leave before she calls the cops.

I get to work well before my curtain call. The SWAT commander is conferencing with the investigations lieutenant, and as I glance through the window I see they both have the same pissed off look.

One of the lead investigators is at the copy machine and I ask how the stakeout for Tellez is going.

"Not so good," he says. "It doesn't look like he's hiding out where we thought he was, so we're back to square one."

Word of the cancelled surveillance operation has apparently spread to the rest of the narcs, and they've already put me down on the board for another heroin buy on Sonoma. It doesn't sound like they have any particular target in mind, just hang around and try to score a bag from one of the neighborhood dealers.

I glance out the window. The wind is really starting to blow and now it's begun to sprinkle. I go down to the parking lot and pull a long, olive-colored trench coat from the trunk of my car. I picked it up for eleven dollars at a thrift store over the weekend, thinking it would really bring my look to that next level. I'm eager to take it on a test run today.

Back in the office, I take off my shirt so they can wire me up. Van Kirk gets a load of my new tracks and bursts out laughing. Miller inspects them curiously and then gives me a hardy slap on the back before joining in the laughter.

Smitty walks in sucking on his pipe, and stops abruptly to give my arm the once over. "Look at this piece of shit," he says. "Somebody get a piss test from him so we can see if he's loaded."

"Go back to your illegal Bingo cases." I turn to put my shirt back on, content with my spontaneous comeback.

"No, no. I wouldn't want to miss this," he says. Then, as he looks out the window, "Who do you think is going to be out there slinging dope in this rain?"

I shrug it off and head for the back lot. A clerk who used to be friendly with me passes me in the hall without a word. I realize that the combination of my stringy hair, goatee, earring, and now the trench coat, has got everybody in the building thinking I've turned into someone else. I know the contrast with my clean-cut patrol look is staggering, and most of them probably wonder if I've lost my mind. I can almost feel my posture slouching and my feet shuffling more and more with each disgusted look I get. I find myself thriving on the negative attention.

Smitty takes his unmarked vice car, and Miller and Van Kirk let me out of the van a couple of blocks from the neighborhood. Smitty was right; the streets are empty. I wander past Beto Salazar's house, and up and down a couple of side streets. I'm determined not to go back empty handed.

The rain has turned the tail of my hair into tiny rings that funnel the droplets down the back of my neck. My eleven-dollar coat is soaked and I'm shivering like the wet dog I probably smell like. I whisper into the wire, "I'm going to stay out here a little longer."

I can almost hear their collective groans from wherever they are parked. I schlep around the corner onto Yolo, and hunker down beneath the overpass where A Street crosses the train tracks. It gives me a little break from the chilling wind. I wipe my nose and stare out at the corner house—a single-story dump with chipped white paint and faded blue trim. A broken down camper sits behind a high wooden fence in the back, and a "BEWARE OF DOG" sign hangs from a cyclone gate in the front. It's the Zamudio house—the alleged source of the local heroin trade. I remember hearing about the family from the time I started as a rookie on patrol.

I'm squatted down in the shadows, the concrete girders trembling as trucks rumble overhead, and I'm thinking about how great it would be to put a case on one of the Zamudio brothers. I make a mental note to ask my informant, Maria, if she knows them.

I straighten my frozen legs and I head back past Beto's place. I try knocking on the door, but there's no answer. I loiter there for a few minutes and then take a slow pass around the block. I come out on the backside of the Zamudio house, and I figure, *what the hell.* I shuffle around to the front and stand under the meager shelter of a withered tree. A cloud breaks and I'm momentarily pelted with a torrent of hail. I lift my coat to shield my head and hunch against the tree trunk. I can see the foggy exhale of each quivering breath. I'm a half-second from giving up when I hear a door creak open and a voice calling unenthusiastically through the rain.

"Hey . . . hey Homeboy, what you need?"

I wipe my nose and sniff hard, just like an addict about to go into withdrawals. "Me?" I cautiously step toward the warning sign on the gate.

"Yeah you." A heavy guy with a shaved head and neatly trimmed beard motions to me from the doorway. "I knew you was a straight up dope fiend when I seen you out the window. Who else is stupid enough to stand out in the rain for two hours?"

I come face-to-face with him in the doorway and I see that it's Rafael Zamudio, himself. He clamps his arm around the back of the door and blocks me with his body. "Who you know down here?"

I wipe my nose again and aim my boogered sleeve down the street. "Beto knows me."

"Why don't you go buy from him then?" Zamudio's eyes are serious and cold.

"Not home," I shiver out my answer.

"Who else you know?"

I try to suck my cheeks in a little as I talk. "A lot of dudes, but I don't ask their names." *Sounds like a reasonable answer to me. These are street drug deals for Christ sake, not Chamber of Commerce Mixers.*

Zamudio eases the door open and eyes me carefully as I step inside. He leads me into the kitchen where his whole operation is spread out on a small table. I'm being watched closely as I survey the gram scale, plastic wrap, matches, and the golf ball-size blob of brownish tar heroin. *Must be about a quarter ounce.* I think about giving the bust signal and having my backups burst in to seize it all. But that would blow all my other buy cases, and since he has yet to sell me anything, it would only leave us with a possession charge. I quickly decide to stay the course and put my best effort toward getting a chargeable sales count against him.

Just then he reaches under his shirt and pulls a handgun out of his pants. It looks like a small, .38-caliber revolver. He holds it for a second, not pointing it at me, but not pointing it away from me either. It seems more like a not-so-subtle warning not to rip him off, snitch him off, or otherwise double-cross him. He slowly sets the gun on the table next to his drugs. Zamudio takes his seat at the head of the table and I tentatively lower myself into a chair across from him. I hand him forty dollars and he eyes me carefully the entire time he's bagging up my dope. He twists the plastic-wrapped ends tightly, and then singes them with a flame before handing them to me.

I put the score in my pocket, and at this point I just want to get out of the house. But before I can, there's a rumbling sound behind me and several voices emerge up from the basement stairway. Zamudio's brother, Victor, is leading the way and three other guys are with him. They are all high, and I'm certain they've been downstairs shooting up. They all look familiar to me, but besides his brother, Victor, I can only think of one guy's name off the top. They are the who's who of heroin sellers and users in the north end of the city. I've stopped worrying about getting recognized as a cop, but right now I have a lot of anxiety about passing myself off as a heroin addict. I realize I may have oversold how many people I know down here, since not one of these guys will recognize me as a buyer.

They all stop to look at me, and it's clear from their impassive expressions that they're unconcerned. I'm guessing they assume that since Rafael is selling to me, I must be okay. Rafael catches their placid looks and seems equally at ease. Since none of them have reacted to me, he's obviously under the mistaken impression that they recognize me as a fellow addict. I glance back at the table and the gun is no longer sitting there.

We all make our way through the back door and out onto a pitted dirt area behind the house. It's a gloomy place cast in the shadows of the overpass. I casually glance around the yard. With the exception of a rusted weight bench, a beat up motorcycle, and a few various car parts, the place is barren. Thankfully there are no dogs. But I notice there are no cars on the street and no other people—which would also mean there are no witnesses. I take notice that the gate out to the street is open a few inches, and decide that is where I'm heading if things start to go bad. I also know that Van Kirk, Miller, and Smitty are listening to everything over my wire. All I have to do is give the bust signal and they come save me.

One of the guys makes some noise about wanting me to go with them into the basement so we can all shoot up, and the others grunt their endorsement of the idea. It heartens me that they seem to accept me as one of them, however I'm not sure how long it will be before they figure out that nobody knows who the hell I am. Besides, the last thing I want to do is get stuck in the basement where I might be forced to inject myself with heroin. Although, from their demeanor I suspect they're more likely interested in getting out of the rain or using some of my drugs for themselves than they are in trying to test me.

"This shit isn't all for me," I tell them. "I got someone waiting on me for half of the fix." Victor slides onto the old motorcycle and starts it up, apparently giving up on the idea of talking me into the basement.

A couple of the other guys press the issue more forcefully though, as Rafael stands behind me in silence. He crosses his thick, tattooed arms, and the more I resist the more concerned he looks. Adding to my dread is the gnawing fact that he's got that gun tucked under his shirt.

It seems reasonable to me that an addict wouldn't want to share his stuff with a bunch of guys he doesn't know, but at some point very soon my excuses are going to start looking weird. I realize I'm going to have to find a credible way to exit, and I'll have to do it soon. Seeing Victor on the motorcycle suddenly gives me an idea.

I tell them that my "old lady" is sick with withdrawals at home, and I need to get a bag to her. "Otherwise this stuff would already be in my arm," I add. I jump on the seat behind Victor. "Give me a ride to the bus stop, Homes. I'll cut you out a pinch."

A second later we're out the gate and heading up the incline of the overpass, my wet trench coat flapping wildly in the wind. The position in which I've put myself dawns on me with chagrined exhilaration. I'm a passenger on a ratty motorcycle, being driven in the rain, by a guy who's loaded on heroin, and I'm not wearing a helmet. It also occurs to me that I just got a chargeable, felony drug-sales case against a major dealer that no one's ever been able to get close to.

Victor pulls off about a half-mile up the road and I squeeze a speck of the tar onto his fingernail. He makes a pitch for more, and I stay in character as a stingy addict.

Victor's motorcycle is barely out of sight when I hear Smitty's cantankerous voice. "You trying to get yourself killed, dumbshit?"

I climb in with him and we're followed back to the station by the other two in the van. Turns out that the wire's transmission was spotty, and they didn't initially know I had taken a ride with Victor. Smitty just happened to take a listening post at the bottom of the A Street overpass, and saw us cruise past on the bike.

When we get in the office I can see they're all concerned that it could have turned out badly, and I might have been hurt or killed. I explain that I needed to come up with a convincing reason as to why I wouldn't shoot up right there. "I had to convince them I was in a real hurry," I say. "It was the only thing I could think of at the time."

They've done undercover buys before, and they seem to get it. And when it finally sinks in that I actually bought from Rafael, they're no longer upset. They call the sarge in from his office next door and tell him the whole story. He can hardly believe that I bought directly from the main guy without ever getting intro'd by a CI.

Miller pulls out a file marked *Sonoma Street – Heroin*. As he scans over it, a huge smile crosses his face. "Hey, Rafael is also on state parole. Having possession of the handgun is another felony violation against him."

"Where the hell you been, Soto?" Cad storms in, oblivious to the buy I just made. "That CI of yours, Maria, has been calling." He flops into his chair. "She said she'd call back at two o'clock."

I type up my buy report on Rafael Zamudio while I'm waiting for Maria's call, and I give it to Miller. He tells me that his plan is to keep sending me into the neighborhood to buy from as many of the dealers as I can. After a few months, he'll get arrest warrants for all of them and then organize a big sweep to round them all up. Miller seems determined, but I feel he's overly optimistic. It's been three weeks and I've only bought from a few guys.

"Sarge agrees with me," Miller says. "We want to get you back into Zamudio within the next couple of days."

I act as if I'm excited to do it, but a voice inside is telling me the Zamudio brothers will have figured it out by then. It's inevitable; sooner or later they'll all talk and compare notes, and they'll realize that I'm virtually an unknown. My only other buys on Sonoma were from Beto Salazar and Frankie Ortega, and I doubt either of them would cosign for me, even if Zamudio bothers to ask them. I'm also troubled by the fact that Rafael is armed and I'm not. The whole gun thing has got me feeling pretty naked.

My line rings and it's Maria. She's talking in a hushed tone, but sounds anxious about something. "Meet me by the pond at Weekes Park in ten minutes."

I grab my keys and a hundred dollars from my informant funds, and head out to my car. It's no longer raining, but the hard wind is gusting out of deep gray skies. I find Maria wrapped in a heavy, hooded coat, and sitting on a bench near the pond. I pull to the curb and she climbs inside. As her hood drops, I'm bombarded the smells of sweet perfume, hairspray, and cigarettes. She's clearly gone to some trouble to look attractive, yet she keeps focused on the business at hand.

"Carlos knows the cops are looking for him," she says. "Some detectives were snooping around the motel he was staying at and he split before they got him."

I ask if she knows where he is now, and she says she doesn't. "But at night he sleeps in a friend's car in the parking garage under the Holiday Bowl."

Maria doesn't have many particulars, but she describes it as a primer gray, panel van with a flat tire. She says that only a couple of people know he stays there, and asks that we try to "play it off" somehow so she doesn't get burned.

I don't want to offend Maria, but I go ahead and offer her the money. "I know you didn't tell me about Carlos because you want money." I fold the bills and slide them into her jacket pocket. "But you have gone out on a limb for me, and I really want you to have this." I feel a little cheesy since it's the city's money and not mine, but the sentiment behind the gesture is sincere. Besides, I know she can use it. She flushes, but takes it just the same.

I find a phone booth and call the lead detective in the Bascomb homicide. I fill him in about Carlos Tellez and the van parked beneath the bowling alley. He says they'll set up surveillance on it right away.

Maria has shed the jacket by the time I get back into the car, and I see she's got on a yellow halter-top. She's done her best to display some cleavage, but her four kids and her harsh lifestyle has flattened them like mudcakes. "When this is over with, I got another guy you should investigate." She smiles eagerly. "They call him Cliff, and he lives down off of Miami Avenue. He's a connection for lots of raw heroin."

She says she knows the house, so we take a swing by. Maria points out a brown stucco, single-story place in a working class neighborhood. She hasn't bought directly from him, but she's waited outside in the car for other people who have. I jot down the address and a couple of license plates before dropping Maria off back at her house. I thank her again for everything she's done.

Cad nearly knocks me over as I open the office door. "Don't go anywhere, Soto. We've got a new lead on Carlos Tellez's whereabouts." He rushes past me with a printout in his hand. "The detectives are setting up right now, on a van where he's purported to be laying his head at night."

Imagine that. "How fortunate for them," I say with a roll of my eyes. Cad continues on his way and I start checking the files for this big dealer, Cliff, who lives on Miami. I find the Cliff's name on notations made from other informant interviews, but nothing to indicate we've ever opened an investigation on him. I run the license numbers that I copied from the cars in front of the house, and they both come back registered to that address, under the name Clifford Foster. I write his name and address on a file folder and slip in into the holder on my desk.

By now it's dark out, and I'm getting pretty hungry. I thought I'd be home in time for dinner tonight, but the potential arrest of Tellez is going to keep me here in limbo. I give Gale a call and let her know what's going on. She puts each of the girls on the phone to say good-night to me. I'm looking at their pictures on my desk while we're talking, and the contrast between their innocent lives and what mine has become brings a lump to my throat. I tell them all how much I love them and I assure Gale I'm being careful.

There's a palpable change in activity on the floor outside my office, and rather than easing toward quitting time, the detective bureau is suddenly infused with energy. The majority of the SWAT team has been sent home, but a few who are still on duty are called in for an urgent briefing. Minutes later there's an exodus of unmarked cars from the back lot, probably heading for the Holiday Bowl parking garage.

While I wait, I run a records check on the possible dealer, Clifford Foster. He's only got one violation—an arrest for drunken driving. I pull a mug photo of him to show Maria, and put it in my new case file. Basically I'm just milling around the second floor, making myself visible to the investigations lieutenant in case they arrest Tellez.

It's about 7 p.m. when Sergeant Roberts comes in with the news: Tellez is in custody. He helps me get into the wire while one of the detectives runs down the gist of their investigative needs. We quickly rehearse my role as a fellow prisoner, and then they handcuff me. Sarge says it'll look better for the other prisoners to see me brought in that way. While Tellez is still being transported in from the scene of his arrest, they walk me into the jail and go through a mock booking and fingerprinting process. As I'm washing the ink off my hands, I catch my reflection in the metal jail mirror. With my dark hair slicked back and gnarly features, I figure to blend perfectly with the evening's jail crowd. My white *"beater"* shirt and khaki pants definitely add to the look.

It seems to be a relatively slow night, and at the last minute the detectives opt to move a bunch of prisoners out of a dormitory-type cell I was supposed to be put into. Instead, they want me in there alone when Tellez is brought in. The reason they give is to eliminate background noise over the wire for recording purposes. It makes sense, though my ego hopes it isn't just being done for my safety.

The door closes behind me and I have a few minutes alone in the cell to collect my thoughts and get into my role. After recalling the eighteen months I spent working in the jail before becoming a police officer, I decide the most realistic thing to do is stretch out on a bed and go to sleep.

I'm lying on one of the flat plastic mattresses when I hear the cell door rumble open. I stay put with my eyes closed, as if I've been in there for hours and couldn't give two shits about anyone else. My face is pressed against the mattress, swathed in its musty odor, and I momentarily imagine the chaffed particles of disease and fungus that have been deposited here. The door slams closed and I hear my new cellmate yell out to the jailers. "Hey, when do I get my phone call?"

I wait another few seconds before starting my performance. I take in a deep breath of air that smells curiously reminiscent of feet and ass, and then I stretch lazily as I roll over. Squinting through one eye, I give Tellez a look of slight annoyance. He's younger looking than I expected, and I realize he's probably never been in an adult jail before. He's got to be scared shitless. I replay Maria's comment that Tellez killed Bascomb to impress her older brothers, and it helps me decide how to play him.

"Relax, Homeboy." I slowly swing my feet to the floor. "They never let you use the phone right away."

"How do you know?" The kid gives the door a weak punch before taking a seat on the bed across from me.

I let out a demeaning huff without answering, and then lay back down with my eyes closed.

"You been in here awhile?" Tellez asks.

I slowly open one eye. "A few hours."

"You get your phone call yet?"

"Who I'm gonna call?" I close my eyes again.

A few seconds pass and I hear him get up and walk to the door. "Hey, I need a blanket!" His plea is to nobody in particular.

I roll over slowly to a sitting position. "Listen up, youngster. This ain't the Embassy Suites. You keep that shit up and them cops are gonna come in here and stuff a blanket up your ass."

He comes away from the door and this time takes a seat on the bed next to me. "You been in here before?"

I answer in a bored tone. "Yeah . . . I been here before."

He glances down at my arm and I see his eyes focus on my track marks. "What'd you do?"

"They say I jacked someone's car. Also got a parole violation slapped on me." That last part lets him know that I've done time in prison. "What'd you do?" I ask with a slight chuckle. "Throw a rock through someone's window?"

He shakes his head.

I smirk. "I know, you stole a candy bar."

He shakes his head again and slides over until he's right next to me. "Killed somebody." *Not bad—he admits it to me in less than ten minutes.* His words were just a little louder than a whisper, but since the wire is taped to my chest just beneath my shirt, I'm certain his comment was picked up.

"You?" I look him up and down. "What happened, you run over someone during your driver's test?"

Tellez stands up and motions me over to the center of the cell. I get up and follow along. He leans close, almost on top of the wire. "They might have microphones up there," he points to the air vent above us. "Don't want to say it too loud."

We shuffle over to the far corner of the cell, out of view from the door and away from the vents. I give it my best to look uninterested as he glances around the empty cell.

He steps in tight again. "I killed an old man."

I look at him, leaving a skeptical silence between us.

"Stabbed him with a knife." Then he demonstrates it to me as if gripping a knife in his hand. He uses a fluid thrusting motion with his right fist, followed with an arching overhand blow into the air.

Though I don't know the autopsy results, I'm going to guess they'll come back with two stab wounds, the locations of which will match perfectly with Tellez's gratuitous reenactment. *Thanks for that.*

I quickly look around, raising a hand in brotherly warning. "Be careful, they could have cameras in those vents, too."

The kid walks back to his bunk, cautiously eyeing the vents. I lie back down on my mattress and close my eyes contentedly. A few minutes later the door rumbles open and a jailer calls out, "Soto?"

I nod to him. "That's me."

"C'mon out. We're moving you to another cell."

The PBA is hopping tonight. There are sheriff's deputies, local cops, nurses, and even one of the judges is drinking at the bar. By the time I walk in, Roberts, Van Kirk and Miller have told them all about my feat in the jail cell. Music is playing and I'm wildly exhilarated by my new persona. I hang my trench coat on a hook and I see one of the nurses watching me. I'm pretty sure it's because she's never seen a cop look so much like a street thug. She whispers to her girlfriend and they both giggle. A seven-and-seven is waiting for me when I take my place next to Roberts, and he hands me a cup of dice.

"I ordered us something to eat," he says.

A couple of narcs from the South County Task Force come in and they congratulate me for successfully buying from Zamudio. They pull up to the bar with us. We talk about case strategies and our plan to go back and buy from him again. I'm mentally sidetracked by images of the .38 in Rafael Zamudio's waistband though, and the dread that he and his boys will confront me more vigorously the next time.

Larry steps up from behind the bar and I'm aware of his presence just standing there watching us. I look up and he's holding my hotdog in his outstretched hands, waiting for me to finish my conversation. "Your barker, sir."

A few rolls of the dice later and my consternation over Zamudio has dissolved like the ice cubes in my drink. We close the place down.

I amble in the front door at home, just before the sun comes up.

7

New Tracks

I've managed to stay busy for the past week, secretly hoping Miller and the sarge have forgotten about sending me back to Sonoma. I was lucky to have gotten through my last buy down there in one piece, and I'd rather not tempt fate. It's winding down toward the end of the day and I can see headlights from the commute traffic outside the window as they pass our building. I'm about to take a bite of my salami sandwich when Miller comes into the office.

"The Big A needs some money," he says, "and that means we gotta get you back down to buy from Zamudio."

An image suddenly appears in my head: I'm dead, killed by the Zamudios, and The Big A shows up at my funeral in a new car and wearing an expensive suit—all paid for with informant funds.

Miller leaves the office to get new batteries for the wire and I turn to Van Kirk. "I got The Big A's money right here." I grab a handful of my crotch to illustrate the point.

A few minutes later I've got sixty bucks in my pocket, a fresh wire taped to my chest, and we're ready to roll. As I finish my sandwich on the way to our cars, I mention again my concern about Zamudio. "By now they'll have figured out that I'm pretty much unknown in the neighborhood and that it was a mistake for Rafael to sell to me."

"The worst that happens is he shuts you down this time," Miller says.

Again, I'm imagining a much more ominous scenario. "What do you think about me carrying a gun, just in case?"

Miller shakes his head. "Too risky. They know what police-issued guns look like. If they spot it on you, your cover is blown."

And poor Alberto won't get his money. I say nothing, but my insides are churning with doubt. I always promise Gale that I'll be safe, and this time I know I'm walking into a situation that goes against my better judgment. It's pitch black on the streets. *Why couldn't we have done this earlier, when at least I had the advantage of some light?*

They drop me on the far side of the overpass and I climb through a dilapidated cyclone fence. I make my way over the train tracks, past broken glass and gang graffiti. Two dark figures approach from further down the tracks, but they're too far away for me to make them out. In my greasy pants and old coat I doubt they view me as someone worth robbing. However, they could mistake me for a rival gang member and kill me just for the hell of it. I suddenly hunch forward with my hands on my knees and gag loudly, faking the act of spitting out the remnants of my curdled, drug-addicted stomach.

Whoever they are, they seem to have lost interest in me. By the time I get to the street, they've disappeared into the night. I consider mentioning that I'm okay for the benefit of Van Kirk and Miller, whom I'm certain heard my act over the wire. But I'm too close to Zamudio's place now and I'd hate to be overheard by one of them.

I get to the door and the house is dark. A good part of me hopes nobody is home and we can just call it a night. I take a breath before knocking, and hold it in as I listen. The lights remain off, but there's a tapping sound at the front window to my right. "What do you want?" A voice asks, sounding like an irritated Rafael Zamudio.

"What's up, Homes?" I take a step back so he can see me. "Got a couple of twenties for me?"

I can see him squinting at me through the darkness, and then a flicker of recognition in his look. He lets the curtain go and suddenly the door creaks open. Rafael eyes me for a minute before asking me who I am.

Is it a game? I know he remembers. "Phil Soto. You helped me out with a couple of bags a while back."

He stands there behind the door, eyeing me without a word. "I ain't got it on me," he says, leaving the sentence hanging as if there's more. I give a slight shiver and stare back. "Go around back and wait under the overpass," he says.

I nod and step off the porch. *Why does he want me back there by the train tracks, in the dark?* I consider the very slim possibility that he really doesn't have any on him, but out of the kindness of his heart he's going to go get a couple of bags and bring them to me.

I skirt the short block without seeing a soul. The streetlight is gone, either burned out or shot out long ago. It's way too dark underneath the overpass, so I stand in the street where the dim light from a warehouse a block away might help me discern approaching trouble. I keep glancing behind me though, to make sure someone doesn't surprise me from the train tracks. Besides trying to keep up 360-degree awareness, I occasionally peer over toward the rear of the Zamudio house. It's still dark.

After about ten minutes I hear low voices approaching from that direction. I can make out the shapes of three men as they round Zamudio's back gate and head toward me. I shove my hand into my empty coat pocket, thinking how much better this would be if I felt a gun there.

"Three," I whisper into my coat, hoping that my partners will hear it. A motorcycle engine starts up and I see a single headlamp come on behind the fence at the back of the house. By now, all three guys have nearly reached me. Two of them were at the house when I bought last time, and I don't recognize the third. I unconsciously glance back toward the hole in the fence near the tracks, and realize the window for me to take off running is quickly closing. The three guys split apart and form a semi-circle around me, effectively sealing the window. Out comes the motorcycle with Rafael's brother, Victor, driving it our way. Rafael is still nowhere to be seen.

This sure looks like a whippin' out in the woodshed for me!

"Where's Rafael?" I say with a pathetic gesture toward the house—a useless demonstration of familiarity.

They don't answer, with the exception of one guy who mumbles something unintelligible.

Victor stops directly in front of me, straddling the idling bike. At first the headlamp shines directly in my eyes, and after I exaggerate a painful squint he aims the handlebars away. It is not lost on me that they are all in a position to make a hasty exit if they were to kill me.

The three on foot could easily head down the railroad tracks and pop out blocks away, and Victor could ride off in a hurry by simply letting go of the clutch. Mine wouldn't be the first dead body found in a heap on this desolate stretch of road.

"What's up?" I say to Victor, with a nod toward my captors.

"My brother says he don't know you."

I shrug. "We did some business a couple of weeks ago." I look around at the other guys. "You saw me."

Victor ignores the point. "You a dope fiend?" he asks, his eyes sunken and bloodshot.

"I only chip once in a while," I say, mimicking every drug addict I've ever arrested.

He seems unmoved by the answer, and suddenly Rafael appears at the back gate. They all watch him in silence as he comes our way. The two brothers confer just out of my hearing range.

"Check his arms." Rafael motions to the guys to either side of me.

One guy casually flips open a gravity blade and twirls it in his hand. Another one reaches over and pulls the sleeve of my coat back. They all strain to see. Victor takes aim with the bike's headlamp, directing it at my arm.

I feebly pull my arm away from the guy, as if to say I'll do it myself. I yank my sleeve all the way up and thrust my arm forward into the beam. I sure wish I had touched up my tracks before coming down here. Some of the pencil lead has worn off, and the raised *injection sites* are no longer swollen. But tiny scabs have formed, and one in particular has what looks like a permanent discoloration beneath the skin.

They look at one another and then back at my arm. "Those tracks ain't shit," says Rafael with an air of disgust. I know he's right, but I also know there is enough to convince them I'm a legitimate heroin user.

Rafael seems mildly placated, and Victor has now turned the headlamp away. The dude with the knife flips it closed and slides it into his pocket.

I sense the momentum turning and decide to capitalize on it. "Now how about fixing me up with some shit before I'm too sick to make it outta here?"

Rafael nods to his brother on the bike, having apparently given him the drugs to hold during my interrogation. Victor pulls two balloons out of his sock and I hand him forty bucks. They turn and hurriedly go their separate ways, as I slip beneath the overpass and make my way across the tracks. As I crawl through the hole in the fence I'm wondering where the hell my backup was. Miller and Van Kirk must have heard what was going on. Didn't they realize I was an inch away from getting my ass sliced off?

By the time I reach the van, I'm over being pissed off and I'm euphoric about now having a chargeable buy against Victor. Miller and Van Kirk seem startled when I throw the side door open and dive in.

"Did you do it, Soto?" Miller turns in his seat.

"What the hell do you mean, did I do it? Weren't you listening?"

"The wire took a dump and we couldn't hear anything."

Van Kirk chimes in. "I was so concerned that I was just about to do a drive-by to check on you." He waits a beat—long enough for me to bite the hook. "But Miller was sleeping so soundly I didn't want to wake him up."

We exchange a couple of *fuck you's* and *eat me's* before heading back to the station. When I tell them how the deal went down, they're as stoked as I am. Miller thinks we'll also be able to throw another sales charge on Rafael for facilitating the deal.

Having now been sold to twice and thoroughly vetted by the main guy, this buy case is really starting to have legs. We all agree that I now have the credentials to pretty much buy heroin from any of the dealers in the Sonoma neighborhood. Still, I've made a decision about the gun thing.

After logging the dope into evidence and typing up my supplement report, I head downstairs to the property and evidence room. The unit supervisor takes me into the labyrinth of storage lockers, finally stopping in front of a huge bin with a half-dozen rollout drawers—each one full of handguns tagged for destruction. I pick through them until I find a particularly grungy little revolver with a broken grip. I dry-fire it a few times to make sure it'll shoot. Its serial number has been filed off of the frame, and it looks like anything but a cop's gun. Just to be sure, I get some gray duct tape and wind it several times around the busted grip. I pick up some round-nose practice bullets from the SWAT armory and load her up. The little five-shot isn't the best protection, but definitely better than what I've had until now.

* * *

A few days later, I make my third buy from my old high school classmate, Aldean. He still hasn't recognized me, and he's still got the fat sack of PCP. Not that I have a heart for the dude, but I'm starting to feel like a chump for running up the score on him. Two chargeable sales counts are enough, and I tell Van Kirk it's time to close the case out and get an arrest warrant. He looks at me like I'm nuts, but he doesn't argue.

I'm at my desk typing when Smitty comes in with a young female patrol officer. She's fairly new to the department, and Smitty has her dressed in regular clothes. He motions for Roberts to join us, so now we're all crammed into our office waiting for Smitty to tell us what the interruption is all about. He closes the door behind Sarge finally fills us in.

"A few days ago I sent Laura into Hog Heaven to do a little sniffing around," he says. "Turns out they're selling more than motorcycles out of their showroom. One of the salesmen took a real interest in her, and offered to sell her some coke."

Roberts raises an eyebrow. I know that he and Smitty have a real hard-on for the motorcycle dealership because of rumored links to organized crime. But as far as I know, nobody's ever been able to put together any kind of case against the owner.

"Laura told them she doesn't do drugs," Smitty says with a sarcastic chuckle. "But she did tell the guy about her brother."

Now I raise one eyebrow.

"The salesman wants to get in Laura's pants so bad, that he agreed to sell her brother some coke, sight unseen." Smitty points to me. "And you'll be playing the part of the brother. You're meeting the guy tonight in Walnut Creek."

"Walnut Creek?" I look down at my torn Levis. "You sure I'm not too throw-down for the Walnut Creek cocaine crowd?"

Roberts and Smitty exchange shrugs. "You're right. The guy might think you're there to rob him," says Smitty. "We'll probably have to clean you up a little."

In my locker I find a pair of dark slacks I used to keep there for court, and I borrow a knit shirt from Van Kirk. The clothes clash a little, but not as much as they clash with my grizzled appearance. I'm told to take Cad's big car, which jumbles the image even more: A Latino addict, dressed like an altar boy, driving a pimp's car.

The guy must be eager to bed my sister, because he doesn't even flinch when I pull up to meet him. He motions me over to his black BMW, and I get in. We're in the parking lot of a shopping mall, but he pulls around back to a dark spot near a loading dock.

"Here ya go," he says, handing me a paper bindle. "A solid eighth O-Z."

I carefully unfold it, as if I can tell anything in the dark. It could be talcum powder for all I know.

"Aren't ya gonna try it out?" The guy smiles, and I get the hint he wants to party with it.

"Yeah, just keep an eye out." I use the fold to funnel a line on the flat part of my hand behind the thumb. Just before I lean into it, I glance out the window on his side of the car. When he turns to see what I'm looking at, I dump the line into my lap. By the time he glances back my way I'm snorting the empty backside of my hand.

"Pretty good stuff, huh?"

Fueled by the cleverness of my illusion, I funnel a line onto his hand and he sucks it in like a vacuum cleaner. He's so into the head-rush that I'm able to dump yet another batch, pretending to have snorted it. *I'd better stop my ingenious little performance before there's none left.*

I pay him for the dope and he drives around to the front of the store to drop me at my car. I open the door to get out and the interior light comes on. At the exact same moment, we both look down at my dark slacks. They glisten brightly as if covered by a blanket of new fallen snow. We look at each other and we both start laughing.

"Do you believe this shit?" I try to appear disgusted with my clumsiness. "I spilled it all over myself."

"You probably got a half-gram you can snort off your pants when you get home."

I tell him thanks, and he tells me to have Laura give him a call. *Laura? Oh yeah, my sister.*

* * *

Several days have passed since the last Zamudio buy. I've gone down to the neighborhood a couple of times, once on foot and a couple of times on a bicycle, and I've had no trouble scoring heroin from any of the numerous other sellers there. I guess I've been seen in the area so much by now that nobody even questions me. We're up to ten buys, with charges against seven different people. Additionally, Miller has had Alberto intro me to a couple of new dealers outside of the city—one in unincorporated Alameda County and another in Oakland. Both were heroin buys that went down with no problems.

My desk phone rings and it's Maria. Her gravelly voice is low and tranquil, almost seductive. I can't tell if she's trying to sound that way or if she just woke up. It's 11:30 in the morning, and I have no idea how late heroin addicts or prostitutes sleep on weekdays. Or on weekends, for that matter.

She wants to meet me at a coffee shop near a freeway onramp at the far north end of the city, which surprises me since she lives on the opposite end. There are a number of gritty motels near our meeting place, which makes me wonder if she's been working out of one of them. The pretext for our meeting however, is that she has more information about Clifford Foster, the heroin connection she told me about who lives on Miami Avenue. I grab some money and the case file with Foster's mug photo, before heading to meet her.

I buy Maria some pancakes and watch as she smothers them in syrup. I get myself a cup of coffee and we talk while she eats. The topic of where she's been staying or why she's up this way doesn't come up. I get the feeling that she's avoiding the subject, though I think she knows I know.

Maria tells me that Cliff is a bigger dealer than she originally thought. "He doesn't do any business at his house anymore," she says. "He has kids, and doesn't want anything coming down on his family."

I ask how he does his deals, and she tells me that it's all by phone and meetings on the street.

"Do you know where he goes to make his calls?" I motion to the server for more coffee.

"The phone booth at the gas station on Calaroga and Tennyson. He makes most of his deals there."

She takes a look at his mug photo and confirms we're talking about the same guy. I pay the bill and slip her sixty bucks for her trouble. She smiles coyly, as if the gesture was totally unexpected. I ask if she needs a ride anywhere, and she gives me the same smile.

"No, that's okay." She hangs back as I leave, presumably so I won't see her walk to the motel next door.

I'm driving back to the station after meeting Maria, and I cut over to Mission Blvd. I pass an older woman standing in the sun on a corner, just steps away from an adult bookstore. I make eye contact with her and she maintains it until I've passed. I glance in the side mirror and see the woman's following gaze.

I hit the corner, loop around the block, and come back past her a little slower. I get a better look this time, noting that the woman is bone thin, with sucked-in cheeks and wicked acne pits on her face. Though she's probably in her 50's, she's wearing tight-fitting jeans and a skimpy blouse. I pull to the curb about twenty-feet ahead of her, and she glances around before walking up to the open passenger window.

"Whatcha looking for?" her snaggletooth grin taking up my entire field of view.

"You, mama!"

"I'm Linda." She tosses open the door and jumps in. "You got money, honey?"

I give her a wink as I pull back into traffic. We continue on Mission, all the while she's sex-talking it up. "I'm gonna get you all sticky and gooey," she says, exposing more of her poor dental work.

"Can't wait!"

She rubs her hand on my thigh and I tell her she's about to make me crash the car. She laughs.

"What's it gonna cost me for some Linda?" I ask.

"Twenty for head." She smiles eagerly.

She could kill someone with those teeth! "Sure, okay. I know a good place we can park."

We pass the library and she cranes her neck to view the who's who of downtown drunks gathered on the benches outside.

"Anybody you know?" I ask. I've already got enough to arrest her, but now I'm just playing around until I find a good time to make the pinch.

"It's just Ernie selling weed to some of his friends."

Hmmm, weed you say? "Let's go get us some," I say with delight.

I stop the car at the curb, and Linda and I walk over to join the group. I realize that my look has now become bottom-of-the-barrel bad. I'm so into the part that I no longer give a thought to being recognized.

I toss an arm around Linda as we swagger up. "Ernie! How about hooking us up, Homeboy?" I come off like I'm just part of the downtown bum crowd.

He sells me a few joints as if we are all longtime friends. I'm just about skipping with glee on my way back to the car. Linda and I get in and she reaches her clawing fingers toward me like a kid eager for a treat. "Gimme, gimme!"

I take Linda's hand and hold it in mine, as if I'm about to put something into it. She beams back at me. Then I snap one cuff around her wrist and the other to the steering wheel. Linda's eyes study it curiously, and I can almost see her trying to figure out if it's some kinky play I have in mind or if I'm a psycho about to sexually assault her. Finally, the confusion clears as she grasps a reality worse than the first two. "You're a cop?"

I nod. "I'm a cop." I reach beneath my seat to a police radio hidden there, and I pick up the mic. "Nora forty-six, is there a walking beat unit downtown?"

The dispatcher asks for his location and he advises that he's only a block away from the library. It's Thurmond Morris, the guy they call

Morris Code. He's a walrus-looking cop who took the foot patrol assignment to lose weight. It didn't work.

"Have Morris respond to the east side benches and take Ernie Diaz into custody for me, and send me a transport unit to D and Mission."

I return to station after my meeting with Maria, with arrests for both prostitution and marijuana sales. I know that taking Linda into custody without backup is not within policy, but nobody usually scrutinizes undercover operations too much. Our unconventional methods are pretty much a widely accepted fact.

The sarge also overlooks the poor tactics, and seems elated about the prostitute. Apparently he had tried to flip Linda as an informant after a previous arrest and she never got back in touch with him.

During the booking process, I notice the hooker's address is on a street in an upscale neighborhood in Fremont, near where my captain lives. I use the opportunity to let the big boss know about his nefarious neighbor. The captain is an ex-narc himself, and loves to talk about dope cases. Though I've hardly ever said two words to any of the second floor brass, Captain Evancheck and me really seem to hit it off. I end up spending about fifteen minutes with him, telling him about my arrests downtown. I have him in hysterics by the time I leave his office.

The next few hours are spent logging the marijuana into evidence, taking statements from my two arrestees, and typing up both reports. Ernie doesn't have anything to say, but Linda wants to work her case off. Probably the same song and dance she gave Sergeant Roberts last time she was arrested, but I listen to her just the same. She claims to know a big methamphetamine dealer, Reggie Cuthbertson, who lives on Southgate. I know the area, and used to work the neighborhood when I was on patrol. Though the name sounds mildly familiar to me, I can't place it.

"You know this guy well enough to buy from him?" I scribble notes onto my pad.

"I'd probably have to blow him first," Linda says. "He's a trick. He pays me with meth sometimes, and when he does he's got a lot of it."

"Do you think you could intro me?"

She shrugs. "He gets a little paranoid, but we could try. He'd never make you for a cop in a million years. You arrested me and I still can't believe it."

Sometimes lately, I have trouble believing it myself.

Having given Linda instructions to set up a meth buy once she gets out, I return to my office. I'm eager to start doing some research on her speed-dealing John. It's late in the day and I expect the place to be quieting down. When I open the door I'm greeted by loud laughter and a room full of narcs.

"Soto," my sergeant cries out. "T-NET needs your services tonight." I immediately recognize the four visiting narcs as guys from the Tri-Cities Narcotics Enforcement Team.

"We've got a new CI who can intro a cop into a heroin dealer." Their sergeant says it like it's a once-in-a-lifetime opportunity, too unbelievable to pass up. I also sense where they're heading with it, since other than me there are few if any undercover cops in the county who buy heroin.

"They need you to be their buyer," Roberts says. "Chop-chop, we gotta get rolling."

There's a knock at the office door and DJ Thompson from the probation department steps in. He's a crew cut, no-nonsense, hard ass who's garnered the nickname, Bullet Head. The guy loves to ride along with the cops whenever they're dealing with one of his probationers. Apparently the guy I'll be buying from is one of his.

The briefing is slam-bam and on the fly, because apparently the informant has to make the buy during his lunch break at work. *A dope informant with a job; now there's something you don't see every day.*

We drive to a restaurant called Masala Bombay at the north end of Fremont, where we meet the informant, Sundip. I'm already having doubts, and I haven't even met the seller yet. Sundip is a smooth-faced 20 year-old, dressed in a collared shirt, fitted jeans, and white high-top tennis shoes. He may pass for a heroin user in South County, but in my world he'd be lucky to score a weed joint.

We're dropped off near the dealer's house, a mediocre flattop in a working class neighborhood. It's dark outside, and I follow Sundip up the cracked walkway to the front door. Three backup cars are deployed nearby; the van containing Van Kirk and Roberts; Miller and the probation guy, Thompson, in Miller's little Toyota; and the four T-NET guys in their sedan.

We're standing at the front door and suddenly the oddness of our contrasting looks strikes me. How could anyone believe Sundip and me are drug-buying pals? This dealer, whoever he is, must be watching us through the window right now. My mind races with doubts about whether or not Sundip can pull it off, and whether or not this dealer will even fall for it. I'm feeling a sudden surge of anxiety as Sundip knocks for the second time. I can hear someone moving around on the other side of the door, and I'm mollified by the fact that my duct-taped revolver is tucked under my shirt.

The crack of a gunshot rings out of the dark, startling the hell out of both of us. I instinctively drop and dive away from the door. Sundip stumbles backwards, and for a minute I think he may have been shot.

"Are you okay?" I whisper.

He nods nervously. "What was that?"

I shrug back, but I know we're both thinking that his dealer friend may not be so friendly. My hand is on the butt of my gun as I survey the windows facing out to the porch. I see a withered face peering out from behind a curtain. He seems as concerned as me, and his eyes are darting back and forth as frantically as mine. The guy cracks open the door and regards us both without saying anything.

"Mike, it's me." Sundip eases himself back to the doorway.

"Did one of you guys shoot a gun?" the dealer asks.

We both tell him that it wasn't us. "I thought it was you," Sundip says.

Mike shakes his head, looks us over again, and quickly waves us in. The interior of the house is dark and there doesn't appear to be anyone else inside. There's no weapon visible and this guy, Mike, seems mild mannered. Still, I'm eager to get this over with and get the hell out. Sundip tells Mike that I am a friend of his, and that he brought me there to score a bag. Mike appears to be a low-level user who probably supports his habit by selling powder heroin diluted with Similac or whatever. He produces an oversized balloon, which confirms my suspicions. Nobody sells that much product unless it's crap. Doesn't really matter to me though; a sale is a sale—so long as there's some heroin in it.

We get out of there right away and meet up with the other units around the corner. Everyone is strangely quiet, and I'm sensing something's going on that nobody wants to talk about. I figure we'll drop Sundip off and then I'll find out what it is.

The T-NET cops pay their informant a few bucks and leave him at the restaurant. We all meet up at an empty lot around the corner. I lean back against the car and study the faces of the group. "Is anybody going to tell me what the hell happened?"

The probation guy, Thompson, is white as a ghost. Miller thrusts his hands into his pockets and stares at the ground. Roberts rolls his eyes and Van Kirk bursts out laughing.

"I had an accidental discharge," Miller says. "I was showing Thompson my new gun and it went off."

"Inside your car?" I glance at Thompson as he runs a nervous hand over his flattop. All I can think of is his Bullet Head nickname.

Miller nods. "It ricocheted around the Toyota and whistled right over DJ's head. Luckily neither of us was hit."

"No shit." I'm laughing as I hand the T-NET sergeant the heroin balloon. "And I thought making the buy was the dangerous part."

Back at the office I settle in at my desk to type the buy report for the T-NET guys. They're long gone, but I've agreed to fax it to them by morning. Roberts and Van Kirk drop their things in the office and leave for the night. Miller sits at his desk, pensive and quiet. I suppose he's replaying the blunder in the Toyota and imagining how much worse it could have been. He finally gets up and slogs out in silence.

When I finish my report, I walk out to the fax machine in the investigations secretary's area. The entire second floor is empty and most of the overhead lights have been turned off. I fire up the fax and sit waiting for it to calibrate. In the meantime, I type the name, Reggie Cuthbertson, into the computer. I'm anxious to find out why Linda's meth-dealing customer is familiar to me.

"Working late?" A voice bellows from across the room.

"Oh, hello, Chief." I hold up my report, as if the gesture explains what I'm doing sitting alone in the dark. The police chief heads directly through the maze of desks and stands over me. He's a towering beast, and I have to twist clumsily in my seat in order to look up at him. I don't know if he expects me to continue what I'm doing or stay poised to answer him.

The chief casually strolls around me in a half-circle, examining me head to toe. "You really pierced your ear?"

I pause, trying to think of a response besides yes. "Uh, yeah," I finally say, pointing up to my left ear.

"So tell me," the chief says with an air of belittlement. "What does it mean when a man has an earring in his left ear?"

"What does it mean?" I touch my earlobe reflexively.

"Yeah," the chief nods. "I heard it means he likes other men to piss in his beard."

I blink several times trying to process his bizarre words, and I find myself unconsciously rubbing my beard.

This is the same guy that hired me as a cop, made me a field-training officer, and put me on the SWAT team after only two years.

The chief walks back toward his office, laughing at his own joke. I fax my report to T-NET, still a little stunned at my boss's remark. I glance at the computer next to the fax machine and see the results for my name search. Thirty-five-year-old Reggie Cuthbertson shows an address on Southgate and an arrest record for domestic violence, drug possession, and a host of less serious traffic offenses. Still can't draw him out of my memory.

I lock up the office and head to the parking lot. I sit silently in the dark of my idling car, waiting for the heat to work its way out of the vents. I find myself wondering how the police chief's opinion of me went from being a good police officer to a piss-craving man-lover. Or did it? Maybe it's just his way of warning me not to go too far astray. *Piss in my beard. Fuck him!*

I'm pulling into my driveway at home when I suddenly realize who Reginald Cuthbertson is.

8

PREGNANT PATTY

Testifying in court takes up all of my Monday morning, and I finally get into the office at 11 a.m. Cad passes me in the doorway carrying a bunch of things from his desk.

"You can have my typewriter." He tucks a lamp cord under his arm. "It's better than that piece of shit you seized in a search warrant."

"Where the hell are you going?"

"Transferred out to the floor," he says. "Going to be working fraud cases."

One thing you can depend on at the police department is that changes happen fast, and often without much warning. I don't know what to say to the guy except, good luck. He was a little overbearing at times, but he helped to break me in and he always watched out for my safety. I guess having his nose pressed up to the glass during the Arnold Bascomb homicide finally paid off for him.

I find Miller and Van Kirk at their desks. "Who are we getting in place of Cad?" I ask, sliding my file back into the drawer.

"The Salami." Miller shakes his head. "Can't picture him as a narc."

Van Kirk turns in his chair. "He'd have to be an improvement over Cad. The guy never bought so much as an aspirin."

I sit down, smiling to myself. The guy nicknamed Salami is an older cop who I've known since I was in high school. Ed Mooney used to come to the campus in uniform to watch his nephews' sporting events. I remember back to my first night on patrol when I was riding with my training officer. We were called to a near-riot, and somehow I had managed to lose the face shield off my riot helmet. Mooney pushed me out of line in front of all the other cops and cracked a joke about my helmet being on backwards.

Over time though, I've grown to appreciate his humor. I was never sure how he got the nickname Salami, but if you ask him it's because he's so well endowed. I'd be more inclined to believe it's because he's got a nose like an old Italian. Nevertheless, Mooney is one of the guys I've always looked up to—which now feels like a strange twist of fate. I'll be senior to him in the unit. As much as I'd like to take Cad's typewriter and leave my piece of shit for the new guy, I can't do it to Mooney.

A message on my desk says Linda called for me while I was in court. I see that the sergeant took the call, which makes me a little uncomfortable since she never called him back after her last arrest. I dial the number and get the desk clerk at the Red Carpet Motel on Mission. I ask for Linda and he connects me to her room before I even say her last name. Must know her pretty well, I think to myself. She probably trades sex with the dude for a free room.

Linda tells me she'll intro me to Reggie, and she's ready to bring me over to his house whenever I can do it. "He has a quarter ounce of meth right now," Linda says.

I figure two o'clock gives us enough time to rally everyone and put together a decent briefing. I write the 2 p.m. UC buy on the board, and I start making copies of photos and rap sheets to pass out.

The sergeant comes in and nods at the board. "Whatdaya got, Soto?" I tell him about Linda's intro and he pauses a second or two before telling me he's good with it. Van Kirk and Miller say they'll also be free to help out on the surveillance.

I stare at Reginald Cuthbertson's mug photograph, happy to have finally remembered who he is. He lives in a different area of the city now, which is part of what threw me. I remember a few years ago when I was working the night shift in uniform, and I had developed a street informant named Isabel Cota. She was always telling me about some white biker who dealt meth from his cottage near her place. I had found Cuthbertson's name back then by running the motorcycle's license number. I spent long hours each shift parked in the dark, watching his place from the other side of Mission Boulevard. I even followed a guy one night out of Cuthbertson's driveway, and ended up arresting the guy with meth and a loaded gun. I suspected he had just scored the dope from Cuthbertson, however I was never able to catch Cuthbertson dirty. I eventually moved to another beat and lost interest.

I'm stapling my packets together when someone knocks at the office door. We all quiet down, and I'm momentarily reminded of the hush that descended on the office whenever I, as a young uniformed officer, would come to the door. Miller opens it and we see it's the investigations lieutenant.

Lieutenant Preston, a tall lanky guy with thick glasses, stands there awkwardly. It's as if his body is too big for him and he doesn't know which leg to rest his weight on or which hand to tuck into his pocket. "You guys look like you've been snorting some of your own heroin evidence," he finally says. It's his lame attempt at transferring his discomfiture to us.

Van Kirk and I don't react at all. But Miller forces a small chuckle, mercifully saving the stiff from himself. *You don't snort heroin anyway, dumbass!*

"I need you and you," he says, pointing to Van Kirk and me—clearly unconcerned as to whether we were in the middle of something.

We glance at each other and then slowly get up and follow Preston to his office. Before we can sit down, he hands us a sticky note with a handwritten address and the names of Rolf and Anise Gordon. "These folks are members of our Neighborhood Alert Program," he says, placing a hand on the door. It's a clear signal he's got no intention of entertaining us any longer than he has to. "I'd like both of you to go down there and make contact with them. They've got some urgent drug information to pass on, and I told them I'd send representatives from our narcotics unit." He purses his lips as he looks us up and down, as if disgusted that we're the best the department could come up with.

Van Kirk looks like he wants to kick the lieutenant in the balls. It would be of no use to tell the guy that we have a buy set up in twenty minutes. I put a hand on Van Kirk's shoulder before he says something he'll regret, and we both leave the office. The whole ride down to the Gordon's is a flurry of curses, threats, and things we'd like to do to the ass-kissing, promotion-pandering lieutenant. Van Kirk is convinced he picked us for the mission because we didn't laugh at his stupid joke.

We knock at the Gordons' door, and they immediately come off as an uppity couple who appear as if we've somehow inconvenienced them by showing up on their doorstep. They want us to hold our badges up to the window, so they can see if we're indeed who we say we are. And then they leave us standing on the porch, conversing with us through the kitchen window rather than inviting us in. Van Kirk doesn't help matters when he intentionally mispronounces Anise's name as *Anus*. It goes downhill from there.

"We specifically asked for a sergeant or higher rank to respond to our complaint," says Mr. Gordon. "You know, we're very good friends of Commander Stravinski."

"We have no rank of commander," I tell them.

Van Kirk curls his lip. "And Stravinski retired over five years ago." He turns toward me. "They must have been *really* close with the old man."

It turns out that the Gordon's hot narcotics information is nothing more than someone smoking pot in the park down the street. The Gordons claim to smell it when they walk their Pomeranians each evening.

I go back to the car for a pen and take my time, just to screw with Van Kirk. As if I'm the only one who really gives a shit about their complaint, I return with a hustle in my step and start scribbling illegible rubbish onto my notepad. Van Kirk can see what I'm doing, but thankfully the couple believes I'm hanging on their every word.

We jump back in the car and take off like we're following up on their big lead. "Fuck the Gordons," Van Kirk yells out. "And fuck that fatass, Preston!"

We get back to the department nearly a half-hour past our planned briefing time. As we pass the lieutenant's office, I hold up the notebook to show him we've taken care of his precious constituents. Van Kirk won't even look at him.

The sarge isn't in his office, and now nobody can find him. We check Smitty's office and we're told that Smitty and the sarge are on the street, working hookers. I let out an exasperated sigh.

I return to my office and change the status board to show my UC buy at 3:30 p.m., hoping everybody will be back by then and Linda will still be able to do it. Miller tells Van Kirk one of his informants, the RR Express, called with some info. Van Kirk gets in touch with RR just as Sergeant Roberts slips back into his office. When Van Kirk gets off the phone, he tells us that a pregnant woman is dealing PCP out of the Phoenix Lodge on A Street. They all turn in unison to look at me.

"So much for *my* buy case." I take off my shirt and start taping the wire down. It isn't until we get to the motel that I learn I'm not even going to be intro'd. They want me to show up at her room alone, and try talking my way inside, cold. All we know about her is that her name is Patty, she's in room 10, and she's pregnant.

I find the room on the second floor near the front of the building. I knock, but hear nothing at first. Several seconds go by before I detect muffled movement, as if someone is sliding furniture around. I'm thinking through things I might say to bamboozle my way in and get her to sell to me. I'm wondering if it would be best to throw out a made-up name of someone who sent me, or try to convince her that we already know each other. The latch flips and the door eases open, and I realize I don't have to worry about either scenario.

A young woman with colorless skin and huge brown eyes stares back at me—her mouth hanging open as if she forgot to close it. The look in her eyes is a million miles away as she licks her cracked lips with a dry, pasty tongue. Behind her, a swirl of acrid smoke slowly settles to the floor. I peer past the mother-of-the-year to make sure nobody else is in there.

I nod and walk inside without a word. She's slow to react, and I'm already sitting on the bed by the time she does a robot-like, turn to face me. I can see she's trying to formulate a few words, but she's too high. Now that I'm inside, I get a full view of Patty. Her dark hair is long and stringy, and she's more than a little pregnant. The woman's belly is so big that I'd bet she's about to give birth any minute. With all her senses deadened by the PCP, I wonder if she'd even know she was in labor.

Patty closes the door and lights up a PCP joint. I'm concerned about my own exposure to the drug through normal breathing, but I find myself really angered about the baby's exposure.

She sucks in a long drag before finally speaking. "Who are you?"

"Phil." I step around the bed and open the window. "You told me to come over and you'd sell me a couple of joints."

"I did?" She rummages through her purse.

I'm trying to breathe the fresh air without being too obvious, but I realize it doesn't matter. She isn't picking up on any of it.

"Here." Patty hands me a couple of joints in return for a wad of folded bills. "Wanna party with me?" She extends the lit joint and I take it.

I hold it down at my side while she stares blankly at the money I just handed her. She's not counting it; she's just staring at it in her hand. I don't even have to pretend to take a hit. Instead, I just stub the joint out and toss it in the sink.

"Wanna party with me?" she asks again, still transfixed on the money.

"Yeah, sure." I walk out with a knot in the pit of my stomach. "We need to call CPS," I say into the wire. "This chick is going to have a baby any second, and she's a goddamn zombie."

We briefly discuss the options once I'm back in the van. We could go back in and arrest her right now, which is what I'm pushing for. Sarge wants to write up the report and send it to the district attorney's office for an arrest warrant. He's not fond of bringing a woman to our jail in her condition.

"We don't even know her last name," I say. "How are we going to get an arrest warrant without a full name?"

There's some talk about going back to the motel later to do more follow-up, but our course of action is never really made clear. I get the feeling the consensus is that it's too late in the day to do a whole lot with it. *I feel like dogshit.*

Back at the station I find out one of the whores that Smitty arrested wants to talk with me. Her name is Becky, and I've arrested her a couple of times in the past: once on patrol for under the influence, and again about a month ago for prostitution. I go downstairs and buzz myself into the jail. I wait near the door so none of the prisoners can see me, and I have one of the jailers bring Becky out to me. I walk her upstairs and into the interview room next door to our office.

Plain and simple, she wants me to help her out of this case. She's pretty up-front that she won't give me any heroin connections, because that would cut off her supply. But she knows a lot of meth dealers, and has no problem giving them up.

"I can snitch off financiers all day," she says.

I'm thinking, there was a time I'd take whatever she gave me and I'd be happy for it. Things have changed though. Now I've got bigger cases, better informants, and I'm buying drugs just about everywhere in the East Bay. To waste a bunch of time on users or small time dealers would be about as satisfying as my big PCP buy from Pregnant Patty. "What about labs?"

"Crank labs?" Becky shakes her head as she lights a cigarette. "You talk labs, you're talking about the Hell's Angels. Nobody messes with them."

I take down the names of a few dealers she knows, but they all sell insignificant quantities. Somehow the conversation gets around to her brother, Kenny. She wants to know if the information she gives me could also be applied toward helping her brother out of a heroin possession case.

"Kind of like paying off a credit card?" I ask. "But you want to throw a little towards Kenny's bill?"

She laughs at the analogy. "He's got a worse habit than me."

"How'd that happen?" I put down my notepad and lean back in my chair. "You and your brother both wind up with heroin habits."

The smile fades from Becky's face. "My mom is a dope fiend."

"Your mom got you and Kenny into it?"

"Well, I wouldn't say she actually got us into it." Becky blows a smoke ring into the air above her. "It's just something that's been around us forever. She was always telling us, like, 'don't do it,' and shit like that. But when we started using it, what the hell could she say?"

I squint toward a spot high on the wall, trying to imagine a life like that. "What does she say now? I mean, do you slam it in front of her?"

Now Becky really laughs. "Fuck yes we get high together. She even bought some shit for Kenny on his birthday. It was her present to him."

I slump forward in my chair with my mouth agape. "Heroin for his birthday . . ." A few seconds pass as another question occurs to me. "How does your mom support her habit?"

Becky grins in anticipation of my reaction. "She's a whore, too!"

"Your mom."

Becky nods. "In fact, I was out there working the street with her tonight. We had just split up when Smitty got me."

The interview is concluded on that note, and I call for a jailer to take Becky back to her cell. I prepare a misdemeanor citation like I promised her I would, so she can get out tonight and avoid becoming sick. In return, she assures me she will work on turning up a meth manufacturing lab for me.

I head back upstairs feeling less like a streetwise operative than I did before talking with Becky. The whole family whoring together and shooting heroin together is a little more togetherness than I can stomach. My mind flashes forward twenty years to Patty the PCP dealer and her daughter, both of them slinging dope together out of the Phoenix Lodge.

It's dark by the time I get back in the office, and Miller is the only one there. I slowly erase my UC buy off the board, exaggerating it for the added guilt effect.

"Sorry, Soto. I got to roll out of here and pay Big A for some info. I'm going home after that."

I nod toward Van Kirk's desk. "What about him?"

"His kid had a game tonight. He was going to try to get by his school to see some of it."

"And the sarge?"

Miller shakes his head bleakly. "I think he headed up to the PBA for a soda." He gathers his things and leaves. I'm about to follow him out the door when my phone rings.

"Phil, it's Linda . . ."

I apologize for leaving her hanging about the buy today. I tell her something big came up and I couldn't get to a phone. I feel kind of crummy about it, especially since she was pretty good about getting right back to me. I suddenly wonder if she needs money. You wouldn't think a face like hers would get much business.

I agree to meet her, and I grab a couple of hundred bucks from my desk on the way out the door. She's at a bus stop downtown, and jumps into the car quickly when I pull up. For some reason the outfit she's wearing reminds me of a sailor. Her pants are denim bell-bottoms with some kind of zippered sides, and her blouse has blue and white horizontal stripes. *Maybe it's Fleet Week.*

I figure on kicking her down a little, maybe forty bucks, and then getting on my way. Because of whatever miscommunication however, she thinks we're going to do the Cuthbertson buy tonight. I know I've been playing it pretty loose with the whores, making arrests alone and whatnot, but it would be just plain stupid to try an undercover meth buy from a paranoid biker, alone.

We drive by Cuthbertson's house on Southgate, and Linda points it out. I recognize his motorcycle out front as the same one he had when he lived over off of Mission.

My buy case was blown off earlier for what? That pregnant chick? Then Sarge goes out with Smitty to do whores. I start the justification process in my mind. *And that idiot lieutenant sends us down to chase our tails over some pot smokers. I could have had this buy wrapped up by three o'clock this afternoon.*

"Does he have guns?" I angle the rearview mirror to better view myself. *The full beard is good. A better look for buying meth.*

"I never saw any guns."

"Is there anyone else there?"

"How should I know?" Linda fidgets in her seat. "Every other time I go there he's alone."

"Are you sure there's no guns?"

A little slobber escapes Linda's toothless laugh. "Now you sound like the paranoid one."

"Okay, in and out. Got that, Linda? You introduce me, we buy a gram, and we're outta there."

Next thing I know we're at the front door. Cuthbertson lets us in, but he's eyeing the shit out of me. He looks like the kind of guy who's been around the block. He probably knows that hookers are all snitches, and anyone a chick like Linda brings over is automatically under suspicion.

Linda tells Cuthbertson that I'm her friend, Phil. She's got her arm around my waist and she starts nuzzling against me. Her humid breath on my neck makes me want to gag. I slunk back onto his big, U-shaped sofa, and Linda reclines with me. She's half talking to him and half talking to me, hyper and giddy as if she's already snorted a few lines.

"You're not a cop, are you?" Cuthbertson says, out of nowhere.

I frown for a second, as if trying to process the sheer absurdity of the question. "Me? A cop?" I laugh. "Not in a million years."

"Phil's cool," says Linda, draping a leg across mine. "I've known him forever."

Now she's nervously rubbing my chest and trying to unbutton my shirt. I get that she wants to play this thing off, but really? Who comes over to buy dope and starts undressing her friend right there? I slide my arm from her shoulder, down to the narrow part of her waist and give it a firm squeeze. She yelps loudly, but seems to get the message to ratchet it down a couple of notches.

I sense that Cuthbertson isn't going to do business with me, which doesn't really matter since this is only an uncharged intro buy. He motions Linda to go with him, and I slip her sixty bucks. They're gone a while, and I'm sitting alone in the living room the whole time.

They come back into the room and the side zipper of Linda's pants is down. She nervously hands me a gram bag that looks a little on the light side. They're both a little hyper, which I suspect is because they snorted some of what was supposed to go to me. Not to mention that she probably blew him for the dope and hid my money up her ass. Whatever, the deal was made, he got a good look at me, and with any luck I'll be able to buy from him down the road without Linda. And without the pleasure of her full body massage.

It's nearly nine o'clock by the time I get my dope tested, weighed, and put into evidence. Like I thought, it's about a quarter-gram shy.

I race home and Gale is still up. She's kept some dinner warm for me, and has bought some of my favorite Ben and Jerry's ice cream. I jump in the shower first, trying to scrub off the day's nastiness. I look in on my sleeping girls, and then sit with Gale and eat my dinner.

9

Weird Science

I ask Gale to wake me when she gets up. Five o'clock in the morning is an ungodly hour that I should never have to experience, yet I struggle out of bed motivated by the fact that she does it every day.

I have SWAT training this morning, and though I'd rather work on my drug cases, it's an orientation of our new rifles. Missing it is not an option. Besides, I'd hate for the unit commander to think I'm more into my narcotics assignment than I am the SWAT team. Even though in truth, I am. We'll probably waste the whole second half of the day shooting.

We're up at the range by 8 o'clock. There's nowhere to sit because the night's dew has settled on everything, so we huddle like a bunch of green camouflage penguins against the cold. The commander doesn't want to risk the new rifles getting wet, so he's laid them out on the ground atop their cases, like presents on Christmas morning. To purchase ten high-quality rifles and scopes must have been a major coup on his part, especially given this year's tight budget.

He rounds us all up and walks us over to the spot near the parking lot where the guns are displayed. All twenty-four team members stand ogling over the rifles as the commander runs down their proper handling and maintenance. "These are really expensive pieces of equipment," he says, as if we're back in the second grade. "If we treat them right, they'll give us many, many years of efficient use."

The whole time my mind is on the Clifford Foster case. I think about Maria's information, that Foster does all his business from a phone booth on Calaroga. I can't help thinking I should be surveilling that spot right now.

I'm rousted from my thoughts as the group moves downrange. We stop near an earthen berm at the foot of the shooting lanes. The commander then goes into a dissertation about the metal targets we'll be firing at. After about an hour of instruction, everyone is getting antsy. The commander senses that he's losing his audience, and he summons one of his favorite guys to the front.

"Go get us all some coffee and a box of donuts," the commander says. He pulls some cash from his wallet and gives it to the errand boy. We're all a little shocked at the boss's uncharacteristic generosity, and figure his glee is due to our newly purchased arms.

The teacher's pet, eager to further ingratiate himself with the boss, jumps in the nearest patrol car and backs up, lickety-split. There's a sudden crunching sound, distinctive even though I've never heard it before. I can feel the laughter bubbling up from my belly even before I turn. But the idiot doesn't stop after the first rifle. Thinking he simply hit a rough patch of dirt, he gives it more gas. Now everyone is running toward the guy, waving their arms and yelling for him to stop. I'm at the rear of the group, doubled over my knees. When I see the patrol car lurching and bounding as it backs over rifle after rifle, I fall into uncontrolled hysterics.

By the time he's finished his destruction derby, a swath of shattered scopes, crushed stocks, and twisted barrels lay like corpses before us. The commander drops to his knees, cradling the remnants of a rifle as if it were a wartime comrade breathing his last breath. The rest of the team stands silent, afraid to say a word. I have to duck behind the equipment shed until I can gain composure.

I finally emerge, zipping up my pants as if I had gone to take a leak. Errand Boy is now out of the car, surveying the carnage. Horrified and bewildered, he steps tentatively up behind the commander. "Did you still want me to pick up some donuts?"

I've completely lost it now, and so have a few of the other guys. We have to take a long break in the parking lot to catch our breath. Besides a good laugh, the upside of the tragedy is that the afternoon shooting range is canceled. I'm now free to work on my cases.

Everybody heads back to the station after the range fiasco. Instead, I drive directly down to the gas station at Calaroga and Tennyson. After about a half-hour, I get bored and drive by Foster's house. There's a tan Toyota pickup in the driveway, but the drapes of the house are closed and I can't tell if anybody's home. I make a U-turn a few blocks up, and I see Clifford coming out the front door as I make my second pass. I continue on, keeping my head facing straight ahead. I pull into an empty driveway a block further, and wait.

It's tough to conduct a one-man surveillance. As I wait for Foster's pickup to drive by, I'm wondering if he saw me and went back inside, or if he's driving a different car—perhaps one that had been parked inside the garage. I want to turn my head and look, but he may drive by at that very moment and see me. Not that he would recognize me, but he's undoubtedly cautious and hyper-aware of anybody who doesn't fit. I'm also hoping this homeowner doesn't come out and kick me out of his driveway.

The tan truck finally passes and I can see Foster's willowy figure and long mustache in my mirror. I back out and loosely tail him onto Calaroga. I'm expecting him to continue to the intersection with Tennyson, and pull into the gas station. Instead, he takes a left turn and then a right, stopping in a Quick Stop parking lot near the high school. He immediately goes to the phone booth there.

I've now pulled into the campus lot across the street, where my car will blend better and I'll have a good view of the market. I make a notation of the time on my notepad as I watch Foster dialing the phone.

He's on the phone for three minutes, and hangs up at 12:18 p.m. I note that time as well. Foster glances up and down the street before going back to his truck. He sits in the lot for several minutes, and I'm beginning to think I've been burned. He must have seen me, and now he's waiting to see what I do. I sink as low in my seat as I can, and I wait. Nothing happens, and I wait some more.

At 1:46 p.m., a white, full-size SUV pulls into the Quick Stop lot and parks next to Foster. The windows are tinted and all I can tell about the driver is that he's male, and he's wearing sunglasses. Foster steps out of his car and leans into the passenger window. There appears to be some kind of exchange, and then Foster comes away with a folded newspaper tucked under his arm. I'm certain that there are drugs wrapped inside the paper, though it'll take some creative writing to articulate it in a warrant. I need to get the license plate of the SUV, but to use my binoculars might draw attention. I'm ready to follow one of them when they leave, but which one? To get a search warrant for Foster's house, I'll need to see him go directly back there, with the package. But I'll have to follow the SUV, at least for a few blocks, in order to see the license plate. I decide to drive by while they're both still in the lot.

I drive out of the school, and turn slowly onto the street. The SUV has started up, and begins to pull out in front of me. I slow and turn on my signal, as if I'm going into the Quick Stop lot as he's coming out of. He pulls out in front of me, and I covertly write the license plate number on my hand. Now I'm committed into the lot, so I continue past Foster and park. I exit the car without looking in his direction, and go into the market. I wait until Foster has pulled out, and then I jump back in my car and follow him the four blocks back to his house.

Before heading back to the station, I drive by the Quick Stop again and get the phone number from inside the booth he used to make his call. When I get to the office, I call Pacific Bell Security and ask if they can give me information about the call. The man is polite enough, but his message is disappointing just the same: "Not without a court order or a search warrant." He also tells me their main office is in San Francisco, and all requests would have to be served there.

I've never heard of a phone call warrant, but I sit down at the typewriter and start working on it. I'm hoping that the burden of proof is less for phone records than for someone's home. The extent of my justification is an informant's information, a phone call made from a public phone booth, and a meeting followed by a suspicious exchange of a newspaper.

I run the SUV's license number with the hope that it's registered to a known drug dealer, but my luck doesn't hold out. The plate comes back as reported lost or stolen. I assume the dealer in the SUV puts on the bogus license plates when transacting business, just in case someone like me is paying attention. Though it won't help me identify him, it adds more credibility toward my notion that it was indeed a drug deal I witnessed.

Not much else is going on, and I'm able to finish typing it by the end of the day. I plan to get in early in the morning and hopefully bring the warrant to Angus Daniels—the drunkard who barely reads them.

Sarge comes into the office and I give him the rundown on the case. He had heard about the fiasco at the range, and wanted to know if I was the knucklehead who ran over all the guns. I'm pretty sure he knows it wasn't me, and probably just wants to mess with me.

On his way out for the night, he pops his head in again. "Don't forget, Soto, we have the big California narco luncheon on Friday." He rubs his hands together. "It's all the way down in Santa Cruz, but it's one hell of a barbecue!"

* * *

I'm up early again, though not as early as yesterday. I remind Gale that I have the narcotics association luncheon tomorrow, and she reminds me that we volunteered to run a booth at the church festival on Saturday. I spend a little time playing with the girls before heading in to work.

I do a quick proofread of my warrant affidavit, and then walk across the lot to the courthouse. Unfortunately, Judge Daniels is in the middle of a trial and I end up with a newer judge by the name of Peters. He seems to like the idea of doing the phone records warrant first, rather than go right for the house. He signs it, and ten minutes later I'm on my way to San Francisco.

I serve the warrant at Pacific Bell's security office. They tell me it'll take a few days to get the records of the calls made, but they'll phone me with the results as soon as they get them. I'm overly thankful, considering the possibility that I may need their help again down the road.

It's after lunch by the time I get back. Everybody is in the office, including the new guy. Somebody evidently came up with information about a PCP dealer in San Jose, and they've given Salami the case to get him started. I suppose Miller or Van Kirk will walk him through it. It turns out to be a UC buy, and I'm going to be the buyer.

I get the wire on and we all pile into the van. According to Salami, the informant set up the deal over the phone, and he won't even be there. I'm supposed to meet a guy named Ruben at Capitol Park off of Story Road—wherever that is.

Salami directs us via a dated Thomas Brothers map, and after a few wrong turns we managed to locate the place. It's a sunny afternoon and we're all happy to get out of the sweltering van. I find my connection slumped on a picnic table near the bathrooms, a half-empty Tequila bottle embraced between his legs. He gives me a sly grin as I approach. "Homeboy said you might be late. Don't know your way around San Ho?"

I shake my head. "Don't get down this way much."

We talk a bit, and then he struggles to his feet. A bead of sweat drips down his sunken cheeks as he swigs from the bottle. "Let's do the deal down here."

Right away I'm thinking it's a rip-off. Dude probably has a partner waiting in the bushes for me with a knife or something.

Ruben shields his eyes from the glaring sun. "It's shadier under the trees."

Now I feel stupid. The guy's just trying to avoid getting skin cancer.

Beneath a drooping willow, Ruben hands me a sandwich baggie of parsley and salt-like crystals that I'm hoping is PCP. I hand him the money and he slips in into his jeans without counting it.

"It's good shit." He grins and I can see his tongue thrashing around, poking through gaps in his rotted teeth.

We start back down the paved trail and he sucks back another slug. Tobacco-colored liquid washes back into the bottle as he pulls it from his lips. "I like you, man." Ruben stops to examine the small amount remaining in the bottle. Another wide smile as he thrusts the Tequila backwash toward me. "Kill it, Homes!"

I accept the bottle, clenching my teeth so hard I'm afraid they'll crack. I close my eyes in silent prayer that whatever alcohol remains in the syrupy fluid, is enough to kill the germs I'm about to ingest. I grimace as I swallow the last of it.

Some cops receive medals of valor for risking their lives in such a manner.

We return to the station and I stay downstairs in the evidence room, weighing and testing the drugs. The presumptive results are positive for PCP, but the bag will have to go to the lab for a definite determination.

Miller and Van Kirk are huddled at Miller's desk looking at a map of Oakland when I get back upstairs. Miller turns to me. "Soto! Your CI, Becky, has been calling. She says she has a meth lab for you!"

I throw my paperwork on the chair and join them at the map. "Did she say where?"

"Yea, me and Kirkie are looking up the address now. She said it's on East 10th Street, near Fruitvale. She doesn't have the address, but she'll point it out."

Van Kirk swivels his chair around. "She'll be at the bus station downtown in a half-hour."

We decide that I'll meet with her in my car, and Van Kirk, Miller, and Salami will follow us in the van. I realize that if this is the real thing, we may have to pull an all-nighter.

My head is buzzing with excitement. I have to keep reminding myself that informants are notoriously flakey, and this whole thing could turn out to be nothing. Still, I'm nearly breathless as I cross the lot to my car. *A meth lab . . . how great would that be?*

Becky's already at the bus station when I pull up. She jumps in and we hit the freeway, northbound. I learn that she was actually inside the place the night before. A friend had taken her along during a buy that she estimated to be about a half-pound.

"A half-pound?" I repeat, a little more excitedly than I mean to. Now my mouth is dry and I'm breathing like I've just run a race. "You're sure?"

"Yeah, I'm sure. He cooks for the HA."

A Hell's Angels meth cook is a huge deal, and I'm starting to fear that I'm in over my head. I wonder if the whole case should be turned over to the feds.

"How much do you guys pay snitches for giving up a meth lab?"

I sit there for a few seconds. "I don't know. I'm not sure we've ever had one before." I check the mirror to make sure the van is keeping up with us. "But it'll probably be worth a lot."

Becky smiles. "Mind if I smoke?"

I shake my head, oblivious to everything around me. I'm suddenly seeing myself doing major cases. No more pint-sized marijuana grows. No more street-level dealers. No more . . . I have to stop and get a hold of myself. *This thing could be a big nothing!*

We take the off-ramp and Becky directs me around to a quasi-industrial area near several sets of train tracks. Across from them sits a row of old cottages, no bigger than about 20-feet square. They look like buildings that once housed workers from the train yards. I ask Becky again if she's sure this is the place. She says she is.

She points out one in the middle of the row. The light over the door is on, even though it's only dusk, and aluminum foil covers both the front windows. I jot down the address and description.

"It's the one in the middle," I relay over the radio to the guys in the van. "The one with foil over the windows."

I drop Becky downtown, and we all return to the station. Roberts is waiting there for us, and we run everything down to him. Van Kirk and Miller seem as eager as I am to run with it, but I'm sensing that the sarge isn't as enthused. Maybe he's got plans tonight, or maybe he just thinks Becky's info is a waste of time. After all, meth labs aren't usually that easy to come by, and Becky is unremarkable as far as informants go. In fact, she's only got a couple of validated tip-offs to her credit. The more we discuss it the more I get the feeling that the sarge's reluctance has to do with the luncheon in Santa Cruz tomorrow. He's probably afraid we'll end up working late and we'll be too tired to go.

We ultimately talk Roberts into it, and I get busy typing the search warrant. Miller helps me out by phoning the on-call judge and letting him know that we'll be dropping by his house tonight. Normally, getting it signed during business hours the following day would suffice, but this is different. I pump up the exigency angle in the affidavit by including the fact that labs, by nature, are transient, and the large amount of drugs seen by the unnamed informant are likely to be sold if we delay serving the warrant. That means we'll have to hit the place tonight.

I finish typing the warrant around 8:30 p.m., having only stopped once to grab a cup of coffee from the machine downstairs and to let Gale know what's going on. The rest of the crew took a dinner break, but I was too keyed up and I wanted to get the warrant written as soon as possible.

Van Kirk accompanies me to the Castro Valley hills home of the new judge, Gary Peters. He raises an eyebrow when he recognizes me from his chambers this morning. I raise an eyebrow back when I see his plaid bathrobe and padded slippers. It's like the first time you see your grammar school teacher in casual clothes at the grocery store. *You're a real person, with a real life?*

"You've been busy today," the judge says as he takes a seat under a desk lamp—search warrant and pen in hand. He smiles warmly, but when he puts on his reading glasses I know he means business. It seems like he's studying every word, tracing the pen over certain sections and rereading them. I can feel a bubble in my throat each time he furrows his eyebrows. He presses the pen to his lips as he flips to the last page. When he gets to the end, he thumbs back through it to the beginning. "You say here on page two, that your informant, referred to as "X", identified the location of the lab."

"Yes sir," I lean forward.

"Did he or she simply provide you with the address, or did the informant actually point out the house to you?"

"She pointed it out to me from across the street, your honor."

He smiles at my clumsy slipup, identifying the gender of the informant. Van Kirk nudges me and I roll my eyes at my stupidity. Not that I don't trust the judge, but I've obviously gone to great lengths to hide her identity. Most judges would rather not know anyway, for fear they might accidentally slip in court the same way I did here.

The judge has me pen the clarification, detailing the informant's means of identifying the target house. I print the change in the margin, and initial it. Other than that, Judge Peters has no other concerns. He endorses it for night service, which allows us to hit the place after 10 p.m., and then he signs it and wishes me good luck.

Oakland's narcotics people have all gone home, and I end up speaking to the desk sergeant on the phone. I try to give him a sense of what we're doing, without offering too many specifics. I get the feeling he never worked narcotics, because he seems less than thrilled about getting us some backup. Maybe I pissed him off with my evasiveness, or maybe they're just really busy tonight.

We gather in the Fruitvale transit station parking lot, a few blocks away from the target house. Standing around nervously, we wait there for an Oakland marked unit to show up. It's nearly 11 p.m. and the Thursday night sky is filled with sirens, barking dogs, car alarms, and occasionally the far-off sound of a gunshot. Two OPD units arrive, and it's clear they simply responded to another dispatched backup call, with no idea of what it's about. Under the parking lot's halogen lights, we spend about twenty minutes briefing the cops on our case.

"If anything goes wrong during entry, you guys will radio directly into your dispatch center," the sarge tells them.

I catch a look between the two patrolmen. "Miller and Van Kirk will be on the key." I turn to the Oakland cops. "And we'd like the two uniforms up front with us when we go in. I want to make sure these people know we're cops." Another look passes between them. Salami seems overwhelmed by the whole thing. He's probably wondering if every night is like this.

We roll up in the van, and the two marked patrol cars pull up from the opposite direction. The door is only feet from the sidewalk and the key swings into it as soon as I step onto the tiny landing. "Police! Search warrant!"

The key makes solid contact with the lock, but also catches the lip of the jamb. The door jerks partially open, and the top half of the jamb heaves from the sheetrock, momentarily blocking our path. A second powerful swing of the key wrenches it completely from the wall, causing an ear-splitting crack.

Already amped to the limit, we all instinctively duck at the sound, thinking it may be a gunshot. Suddenly a choking stench hits us. It's the unmistakable validation of a meth lab. The added fuel ignites a torrent of yelling as we charge into the cramped quarters. Pistols swing wildly amidst the shouts and threats. In the dim light of the room I see an image straight out of an old horror film. A man hunches eerily over a laboratory bench that spans the entire wall. Beneath him is an array of beakers, flasks, pipettes and cylinders—all bubbling and sputtering a thick, amber fluid. The madman slowly turns to view the intruders, his eyes wide and his pupils as large as a horse's. He raises his gloved hands in submission, but the shocked expression seems frozen forever on his face.

One of the uniformed cops yanks Boris Karloff out in handcuffs as the rest of us advance. A small kitchenette sits off to the side, and a curtain separates it from another room beyond. Miller and I jerk the fabric from the doorway and step into the room with our guns and flashlights extended ahead of us. A mattress on the floor goes from wall to wall, and we nearly trip on it. A haggard-looking woman and two emaciated children lie curled against one another on a heap of dirty clothes. Their eyes all bear deep circles, and their weary expressions convey an existence of isolation and misery.

We take the children into protective custody, and the next hour is spent arranging for their placement and transportation. The mother, though probably part victim and part moron, is arrested for child neglect. She gives a written statement admitting that she allowed her children to live 24-hours a day inside a one-bedroom home where their father manufactured methamphetamine. The chemical odor alone is enough to permanently kill off half the brain cells of those poor kids.

Sergeant Roberts surveys the whole setup and determines it's way beyond our capabilities. We'll need better-trained help to dismantle the lab, obtain test samples for the crime lab, and figure out a way to dispose of the chemicals. We call the Department of Justice, and they send out their expert. Narco agents throughout the state know him as *Mr. Meth.* He shows up around 2 a.m. with a beautiful blond woman on his arm. He gets out of the car, accompanied by an entourage of underling agents. My cohorts converge on him with the fervor of an Elvis sighting, and I quickly realize this is the big time.

He asks me a few questions about the case and congratulates me for coming up with a "working lab." Apparently as rare as labs are, those in full operation are even more so. Mr. Meth makes several phone calls from the scene, lining up state assistance for us, and arranging for a certified and contracted chemical company to come take the toxic mess away. On his way out he motions me to follow him to his car. He pops the trunk open and pulls out five sets of paper-like body suits and matching booties.

"We should all be wearing these." He hands them to me. "This shit is full of deadly carcinogens."

"It's my first lab," I say. "I didn't know how strong the chemicals were."

"I've been in lots of them." He leans close to me, out of earshot of his girl and his minions. "My doctor told me I can't have kids."

"Are you serious?"

He nods sorrowfully. "The stuff got absorbed by my balls, and now they don't work."

With that, he jumps in his car and he's gone. I stand there in the dark for a few minutes allowing the buzzing in my head to clear. I wonder if the guy was putting me on, or if the story of his impotence is true. I quickly put on my jumpsuit, just in case.

The sun is just coming up when we get the last of the evidence packed into the van. A crime scene tech has taken all the samples they'll need, and the chemical company has already come and gone. I glance at the lone remaining Oakland cop, a guy who probably would have rather been doing anything else than being assigned to stay with us. His patrol car is blocking part of the street and his overhead lights are on, but he's slumped over asleep behind the wheel. I tap on the window and let him know he's free to go. I thank him and he mumbles a response before taking off.

I, on the other hand, am still flouncing about like a hyper lapdog. It dawns on me that I may be feeling the effects from the chemicals I've been breathing in all night. We open all the van's windows and try to breathe in the fresh air as we barrel along the freeway.

We offload all the evidence at the station just as the day shift is hitting the back lot to go in-service. Several of them remark about all the boxes marked, *glassware*. By the time we've carried everything to the evidence lockers, the first floor is abuzz with talk about our big bust.

I flop down at my desk, feeling besieged by the lengthy report that lies ahead. I'm trying to decide if I should start on it now or head home for some food and some sleep.

Just then, Miller comes in laughing. "You won't believe it. Roberts still wants to go to the luncheon in Santa Cruz. I haven't eaten or slept in over twenty-four hours, but this barbecue is supposed to be the event of the year. Van Kirk is up for it, and so is Miller. Salami looks like he's ready to put in his transfer papers.

"I'm in," I say with forced enthusiasm. I take a sniff of my clothes. "I sure wish we had time to shower; I smell like those nasty chemicals."

"We all do, Soto." Van Kirk takes some aftershave from his desk drawer and splashes in on himself.

"Give me some of that." We all take turns dousing ourselves before we leave.

We stop by the probation building down the street, and pick up the guy known as Bullet Head and a female probation officer who calls herself the Queen of Hearts. We're packed into the back of the stuffy van for what seems like hours, and finally roll into Santa Cruz around 11 a.m. The barbecue is in full swing, taking place both inside and outside at a park and recreation facility. Over two hundred gnarly-looking narcs are there from all around the state. So is the legendary, Mr. Meth.

He's holding court near one of the bars, surrounded by eager lackeys. He calls out to me by name, and introduces me around the group. He tells them all of my previous night's case, and then he wants to buy me a drink. I stand there with my seven & seven, bathing in my own grandeur. I feel larger than life.

I finish my drink and another is plunked down in front of me. I'm smothered in congratulatory slaps on the back—many from narcs I've never met. They all seem to know about my case. Somebody is selling raffle tickets and I see Miller buy a shitload of them. I suddenly realize that I've abandoned my partners—left them alone so I can hang with the elite crowd. I feel a little like Cad; hob-knobbing with the homicide boys and thinking he's too good for the likes of his own unit. Somebody slides another drink in front of me and I lose my train of thought.

Damn it's hot! The top of my head seems to have absorbed all of the sun's heat. I see my hands outstretched for another rib, but they feel heavy and numb. I'm aware of my beard full of barbecue sauce, and I clumsily rake my arm and shirtsleeve over it. I take my drink and stumble into the auditorium. They're calling some numbers from the front of the room. *Is it a Bingo game?* I see Miller sitting with his back to me. He's checking the number on his six-foot strand of tickets. *Look at all those fugging tickets.* I'm on the floor, crawling between peoples' feet. "Scuse me . . . scuse me." *This is gonna be funny.* I inch up to the back of Miller's chair, where his raffle tickets dangle playfully in front of my blurry eyes. *This is gonna be funnier than shit.* I fumble a book of matches from my pocket and after several attempts, strike a flame. I light the end of his tickets on fire, then I slide backwards a few rows to watch the show. Smoke fingers up from beside Miller, but he's too engrossed in the next number to notice. I'm vaguely aware of laughter above and around me. Somebody finally taps Miller on the shoulder and tells him that his raffle tickets are on fire. The blaze is nearly up to his waist now. Miller lets out a high-pitched yell as he jumps up to stomp out the blaze. Somebody tells me I'm crazy as I struggle to lift myself off the floor. The room spins wildly and I stumble back outside to get away from it.

"Congratulations on your case," an unknown voice says. I feel the cool wetness of a beer being placed into my hand, and then everything fades into an unpleasant, catatonic blur.

10

Held Hostage

A harsh light pierces through my eyelids, and it feels as if someone is jackhammering inside my head. Gale stands at the raised blinds with an odd expression that I can't place. My head hurts too much to try.

"Get up, Serpico." Gale's voice sounds neither angry nor pleased, just stern. "You're working a booth at the church festival today."

"What happened?" I shield my eyes from the sun.

"You tell me." She moves to the closet and tosses me a pair of sweats. "Your friends dumped you off in front of the house last night and you passed out in the bathtub."

It doesn't ring a bell. "Did the girls see me?"

"The whole neighborhood probably saw you. You could barely walk." She sits at the foot of the bed. "You stumbled in while we were eating dinner, then went into the garage and took off all your clothes."

"I did?" Not that Gale would make up something like that. It's just that I don't remember it.

"You were mumbling something about dangerous chemicals."

"Oh."

"And then you paraded naked through the living room, down the hall and into the bath. Luckily the girls were watching TV and missed it."

"How did I get from the bathtub to the bedroom?" I sit up and the pounding increases tenfold.

"I had to pick the lock on the bathroom door and drag you into bed."

"I hope the girls didn't see . . ."

"No, thank God." Gale heads for the door. "Now get your hungover ass out of bed. We're leaving in twenty minutes."

* * *

We stopped by the station to pick up my car over the weekend. I got in and out of the lot quickly, avoiding anyone who may have heard about my antics at the luncheon. When I get in on Monday, the office is quiet. Miller's duffle bag is on his desk, so I know he's working. I check with the division secretary and find out that Van Kirk is on vacation, Roberts is in a meeting, and Salami is away at a school this week.

I sit down and begin the arduous task of typing up the meth lab report. Miller comes in and pauses just inside the doorway when he sees me. He shakes his head shamefully and then lets out a little chuckle. "Soto, Soto, Soto. Thought he was a hero and ended up a zero."

I guess I had that coming. "How bad was it?"

Miller wrinkles his nose and shrugs. "We've all been there."

I tell him what the secretary told me about Van Kirk and Salami being gone. Then I ask, "And what meeting is Roberts in?"

Miller sits down at his desk. "Chief, captains, lieutenants—all the stars and bars in the building. I guess the police department is going through some kind of audit, and they want all the honchos there."

"As long as it's not about me." I go back to my typing. I've been at it awhile when I notice a post-it note stuck to my phone. It says that Pacific Bell security called with my warrant information. I phone them back and speak to the investigator handling my case.

"A three-minute call was placed from that phone booth at 12:15 p.m. to 1553 Mangels Avenue in San Francisco."

I thank him, and I immediately dial San Francisco's narcotics unit. I tell the guy who answers that I'm working a case on a local heroin dealer, and that he had made a call to the Mangels address in his city. The detective doesn't seem to recognize the location, but checks some files while I'm on the phone.

"We've had a couple of domestic calls at that address, but nothing dope related. The utility information comes back to a Luke Talbott. Does that name ring any bells?"

I tell him it doesn't mean anything to me. I'm about to hang up when the detective comes up with something else. "You might be in luck," the guy says. "It looks like Talbott's got an arrest from three years ago for heroin possession. He just got off probation."

That fact will definitely help me get into Foster's house on Miami. I thank the SF detective, and let him know I'll give him a call with any additional information we find involving the house in their city.

"What's your name again?" I tell him my name, and I hear him laugh. "You were at the barbecue last week, right?"

I cringe. "Ah, yeah. I was there."

"You're the dude who lit his partner's tickets on fire."

Miller's pacing around me like he's got something important. It gives me the excuse I need to end my conversation with the San Francisco cop.

I think about apologizing to Miller for sending his potential raffle winnings up in flames, but decide instead to just let it die.

"Remember Smitty telling us about Frank Bellotti? Miller rifles through his files looking for the notes. "Bellotti. The guy dealing weight from his house in the Castro Valley hills."

I nod, even though I don't remember it.

"One of my CI's just called and said Bellotti's holding a shitload right now. She thinks the guy would sell to you without an intro, as long as you dropped the right name."

"And she gave you the name I'm supposed to use?" I feel the weight of doubt descending on me like a wave of quicksand. "This guy's a big dealer, and he's going to do business with a dude he's never met?"

Miller shrugs. "Davey."

"Huh?"

"Just tell him that Davey sent you."

I exhale a long, deep breath. For the first time, I feel like telling Miller to forget it, I'm not doing it. This whole thing sounds ridiculous to me. It's either a setup or just a stupid idea that'll never work. As I watch Miller change out the batteries in the wire, I start thinking about how he let me off the hook for my actions at the barbecue. He could have been pissed off, but he wasn't. He could have made a big deal of it, but he didn't. "Yeah, I'll give Bellotti a try."

I walk up the terraced walkway admiring the view. It's a nicely landscaped home with a set of double doors under a wide portico. *Just tell him Davey sent you. What a joke. Sounds like something out of a Jimmy Cagney movie.*

I ring the bell and Bellotti answers the door. I recognize him from the photo in Miller's file. The guy strikes me right away as part of the nightclub crowd. He's a good-looking guy—beefy like a football player, and his dark hair is slicked back.

"Hey, you Frank?"

"Yeah, who are you?"

"Phil Soto. I'm a friend of Davey's."

Bellotti regards me for a second before stepping back to let me in. "You know Davey?" he says from behind me.

"Yeah. He told me you could help me out with an eight-ball."

I see two other guys sitting at a table and my whole body tenses at the thought that one of them may actually be Davey. Bellotti tells me to wait here, and he disappears into another room. The two guys talk in low voices to one another, but say nothing to me. Bellotti comes out after a few minutes, and hands me a small zip-lock baggie. It looks about the right size, and its content is flakey and sparkles like coke. I examine it and hold it up to the light, then hand Bellotti the money.

The phone rings and one of the other guys picks it up. He mumbles an acknowledgement before hanging up. He then turns to Bellotti and shakes his head.

Bellotti slowly walks to the front door and slides the latch closed. "You're not going anywhere."

I glance from him to the two other guys, then back. "What's the problem?"

"Davey says he doesn't know you." Bellotti's eyes narrow. "I left a message for him when I was in the other room, and that was him calling back. He doesn't know anyone named Soto."

Dammit! I knew this Davey idea wouldn't work. Now I've painted myself into a corner. I suddenly imagine my own image playing on a black and white television. I'm trapped like a rat—entangled in a web of lies, panicking, wild eyes telegraphing my next move, bolting for the door like a clumsy crook on a Dragnet episode.

I suppose I could give the bust signal and wait for Miller and Smitty to come barreling in. Instead, I convince myself to stay calm.

"Davey." I shake my head, forcing an inept laugh. "He knows who I am."

Bellotti doesn't seem to see the humor of the situation. "Good. Because he's on his way over here right now."

I shrug as if I haven't a care in the world. I take a seat on one of the chairs while Bellotti and the guy who answered the phone remain standing. My mind races to come up with a game plan. I have an idea, but it will require easing them down from their hyper, hostage-guarding mindset. I only wish I knew a little more about Davey, like where he's coming from. I have no idea how much time I have to work with. The guy could live next door for all I know.

I'm aware of every tick of the clock, every passing car, and every look that passes between these three guys. I yawn, stretch my arms, and lean back in my chair. A couple of minutes pass and I casually glance at my watch. I want to let enough time elapse in order to appear legitimately annoyed, without waiting so long that the son-of-a-bitch actually shows up. I check my watch again after another minute, and let out a sigh. Several more minutes pass, and I think the time is right.

"Got a pen?" I ask, pulling my wallet out.

They look at one another, then Bellotti hands me a pen. I pull out an old receipt and tear a piece of it off. I scribble down the name Soto, and the undercover phone line number beneath it. *I've got to move fast, before they can react.*

"Enough of this bullshit." I stand up and slap the piece of paper onto the table. "I got things to do. Whenever that dumbfuck, Davey, decides to show up, have him give me a call." I toss the pen back to Bellotti and quickly head for the door. Having been lulled into a state of complacency, the group is now caught in a moment of confusion. In the few seconds it takes them to recover, I unlatch the door and make a hasty exit.

A car pulls to the curb in front of the house, and I'm relieved to see that it's Smitty and Miller in the Toyota. I climb into the backseat and we take off.

It turns out that Smitty and Miller had heard everything, and were debating how far to let it go before kicking the door. They had slipped in close, and would have made their move when Davey showed up. Though my heart is still racing, it feels good that they trusted me enough to let me talk my way out of it.

In any case, the sale went down and I got an eight-ball to prove it.

We get back to the office and Mrs. Sasaki, the division secretary, motions us over. "A young man is waiting to speak with an undercover officer." She bows her head slightly toward a small sofa. "This time I asked him to wait out here."

It's not the gimp, but a crazy guy I've seen come in a few times. He's a thin white guy, about 30-years old, with a prematurely bald head. Everyone in the unit just calls him Cone Head. Miller rolls his eyes and whispers to me under his breath. "I'll get this nutcase outta here quick."

Cone Head jumps up when he sees Miller. "Detective Miller, I need to talk to you about something. It's real important."

"C'mon back for a sec," says Miller with a wave of his hand. "This is Soto."

"Are you a policeman, too?" Cone Head quicksteps along between us.

I tell him that I am.

"What's your important information?" Miller asks, cutting right to the point.

Cone Head glances around furtively and then whispers, "The guy that built Pinocchio is buried in my backyard."

"Geppetto?" I ask.

Miller flips a quick U-turn, ushering Cone Head around with him. "Okay, thanks for the tip."

"So, you guys will look into it?

"Yep. We'll take it from here."

I finish typing the Bellotti buy report, and by the end of the day I realize that the undercover line hasn't rung. Bellotti and his friends are probably cleaning the place out in anticipation of a raid. I'm thankful that Miller doesn't want me to try going back. Instead, he's working on a search warrant for Bellotti's house. *What a waste of time.*

The sarge comes in just before we leave for the day. He asks what we've been up to, but as Miller runs it down it's obvious the sarge's mind is on something else.

"We're gonna have to clean up our act around here," Sarge says.

Miller and I look at each other.

"This accreditation audit thing is a big deal to the chief." Roberts runs a hand over his head. "They got some blue ribbon committee coming to check out everything this department does."

I lock up my desk drawer. "*We* don't have anything to worry about, do we, Sarge?"

The boss glances around the office and then shrugs. "I don't know. Maybe I'm just paranoid. We just gotta be real careful, that's all."

By the end of the week I've got my heroin search warrant signed for Clifford Foster's place on Miami. I went back to Judge Peters, partly because he's the one who signed the phone warrant on the case and knows the background, and partly because he seems to think highly of me. I heard he used to be a deputy district attorney, and maybe that's why he seems to like the way I investigate my cases. Can't hurt to have a judge in my corner.

When I get in to work the following Monday, I notice a flurry of activity in Lieutenant Preston's office. He's got five men in suits stuffed into the tiny room, and I can only imagine they're the *blue ribbon committee* that Roberts referred to.

Van Kirk slides up to the side of me and we both peer across the detectives' floor into Preston's window. His ungainly body, combined with his overly animated movements, makes him look like a convulsing spastic.

"Could the guy be any more obvious?" Van Kirk says. "He might as well get down on his knees and blow each of them."

We find Miller and Salami already at their desks, and Roberts is doing paperwork in his office. He sees us and joins the group behind closed doors. Roberts holds a loose meeting to find out what everyone is working on, and which things need to be scheduled on the board.

"The Amir Habibi case is going to trial," Miller says. "I've been subpoenaed for later this week."

"We'll have to get the drugs out of the safe deposit box," Sarge says. He turns to Salami and me. "It's a kilo of pure Persian heroin from a case Skip worked before he left the unit."

"And the dope is in a bank?" Salami asks the question I'm thinking.

"We decided that the chain of custody was tighter having the drugs locked up there, rather than in our evidence locker." Sarge moves to the board and writes down that he and Miller need to go to the bank regarding the Habibi case.

"I came in this weekend to meet with a new informant," says Van Kirk. "She's supposedly into a really big PCP dealer out of San Leandro. A guy by the name of Tony Fisk."

Miller looks over at me with a smirk. The look tells me Miller thinks there's more to Van Kirk's weekend meeting with his new informant.

"I want to set up a CI buy, and try to make the house where the dope is." Van Kirk is already counting out money. "Hopefully as soon as possible."

I get another smirk from Miller as the sarge writes it on the board.

"I've got a search warrant for Clifford Foster's place on Miami," I say. "Like to hit it this afternoon if possible."

Sarge puts mine on the board after Van Kirk's. Then he goes back to the top of the board and writes: *Call girl – Vagabond Motel.*

We all look at each other, wondering where the hell that came from. Roberts senses that the room has grown silent, and makes a defensive pitch for his case. "We need to stay up on these prostitution complaints. Otherwise the commanders are going to eliminate the vice unit completely." Roberts motions toward the vice office. "Smitty can't do it alone."

"*We* do more vice cases than Smitty does," Miller says.

"That's because he's heavily involved in tracking organized crime, and he just doesn't have the time." Roberts turns toward Miller. "I think we're saying the same thing."

Miller raises his eyebrows. It was a bafflingly clever way for the sarge to kill the discussion. *I think we're both saying the same thing. I'm going to remember that one.*

We find out that the sarge has already set up the call-girl operation. He phoned a local number he saw in an underground Berkeley newspaper, and told the hooker to meet him at his motel room at noon. The girl is evidently from the Sonoma neighborhood where I've been buying heroin.

I turn to Miller, the case agent of the Sonoma investigation. "I probably shouldn't go then."

Miller nods his agreement, but the sarge overrules him. "You can still go, Philly. We'll just put a bag over your head."

We all laugh, but Roberts isn't joking. He takes a brown shopping bag from the evidence kit and cuts two eyeholes in it. "Try it on for size."

Next thing I know, we're setting up the motel room for a sting. Roberts tapes the wire to the wall behind the headboard and then ushers us into the adjoining room to test it. Our handheld radios monitor every sound the sarge makes. He closes the door between the rooms and we wait.

There's a knock and we hear Roberts answer the door.

A woman's voice is barely audible. "Are you Bruce?"

"Yes. Yes I am, but my friends call me Boner." Roberts is playing it up like he's some kind of nerd. "And you must be Sophia. Gee, you're pretty."

The discussion about money goes quickly, and we're ready for him to give the bust signal.

"Ohhh, your titties look nice." Roberts takes in a gasp, as if he's never seen a girl. "They're quite round aren't they?"

"I guess." The chick is all business now. "I'll only do straight if you wear a rubber."

"A rubber?"

We're leaning against the door, laughing.

"Oh, you mean a prophylactic?"

Miller shakes his head. "The sarge is hamming it up too much."

"Do you shave your pubic hairs in that shape?" Sarge asks. "Or do they grow that way naturally?"

Sophia gives a short answer I can't hear.

Finally, Roberts gives the bust signal. “I wish I had a *beer* right now.”

I slip the shopping bag over my head, and Van Kirk throws open the door. “Police, you’re under arrest!”

I hear the girl scream, but I can’t see anything through these damn cutouts. I hear Roberts scream too, and I maneuver the bag so I get a view of what’s going on. Roberts has been handcuffed and he’s seated on a chair next to the bed. He’s wearing those ridiculous-looking reading glasses and his fishing hat.

The girl has completely stripped, and Van Kirk is taking a Polaroid photo of her. I don’t know if it’s evidence in the prostitution case or for the Beauty Queen of the Month board.

“I’m not a prostitute,” screams Sophia. “That guy is my boyfriend.”

Roberts uses his shoulder to push his eyeglasses back up his nose. “Prostitute? Did someone say prostitute? I had no idea she was one of those.”

Sophia stares at him with pleading eyes. “I’m your girlfriend, right? Tell them!”

“Fiddlesticks,” Roberts says in a huff. “And all this time I thought I was finally getting lucky with a girl. Wait until I get home and tell Mother.”

Sophia shakes her head in frustration. “No, no. Tell them I’m your girlfriend. There was no money, right?”

We all look at Roberts. “I’ll tell you everything you want to know, officers. This woman was going to do sexual intercourse and other nasty things to me, in exchange for cash money!”

Sophia rears up on the bed like a snarling attack dog, naked and handcuffed. “You lying son-of-a-bitch! I’m going to kill you when I get out! You hear me, Mother Fucker? I’m gonna kill you!” Van Kirk snaps another photo.

“Oh my,” says Roberts as Salami and I escort him out of the room. “Can you get me into a witness protection program?” After a few steps outside I take off the idiotic bag and we remove the sarge’s handcuffs. I ride back with he and Salami while Van Kirk and Miller grab the wire, check out of the room and transport Sophia to the jail.

After grabbing some lunch, Roberts and Miller go by the bank to pick up the kilo of heroin for the Habibi trial. I'm in the office when they get back, and I can smell the vinegar-like acidity right through the pillowcase they have it in.

They set it down on top of the file cabinets while Roberts heads downstairs to find a something to wrap it in before locking it into the cabinet. Van Kirk goes to the corkboard and pins up the photo of Sophia, the new Beauty Queen of the Month. It's one where she's about to take Roberts' head off. In the background you can see Roberts on the chair and me standing over him with the bag on my head.

There's a knock at the door and we all assume that Roberts forgot his key again. "Unless you have a key, stay the hell out!" Miller yells.

An awkward silence is followed by a guttural clearing of the throat. "It's Lieutenant Preston." The laughter in our office quickly dwindles. "And I've got the accreditation committee with me." Now the room falls deadly silent.

Our eyes dart back and forth at each other, all thinking the same thought: *we're screwed*. We can't leave them standing at the door while we run around straightening up the place. Instead, we each throw something into our typewriters and pretend to be working. I'm closest to the door, so I open it.

Preston stares down his nose at me through his Ward Cleaver glasses. "I trust you boys won't mind if the committee takes a quick look around the office?" He pushes past me without waiting for an answer.

"Not at all." I sit back down at my desk. "We just got back from an operation. Sergeant Roberts is down in the jail, and should be back any minute."

By now all five suits have barged in behind Preston. The room is cramped as it is, and now there's nowhere for them to move. Typical of Preston, he turns toward the nearest guy. "Why don't you explain to the committee how your unit operates." He's focused on Van Kirk. I stare down at my typewriter, knowing that Preston can't explain it himself, because he has no idea what we do.

There's a knock on the door, mercifully interrupting Van Kirk's pop quiz. I try to get to it quickly, but I can't reach it fast enough.

"It's me, Sergeant Boner. I forgot my key again."

The door swings open and I can see the dread on Roberts' face. He launches into a mad cacophony of facts and figures, scattered with a slipshod summary of our current cases. It sounds terrible.

I notice one of the suits sniffing toward the pillowcase, and I close my eyes. A hundred thousand dollars worth of pure heroin sitting out on a file cabinet; there's no way to explain that one. Another guy nudges a third and motions toward the corkboard. There's Sophia, naked as a jaybird, with Roberts on the chair in handcuffs and me under a bag. There's no way to explain that one either.

Preston starts talking about our evidence handling policies, and I see Roberts' eyes dart to the pillowcase. Beads of sweat are forming on his brow, and I can almost hear my partners' dry throats trying to swallow. Roberts' eyes flash across the room to the Beauty Queen and he makes a crippled lunge at it. He clutches Sophia's photo in his hand and yanks it off the wall. The move isn't discreet, and he's gotten the attention of everyone in the room. He slides the wrinkled photo into his pocket, and now everyone is staring at the spot Sophia formerly held on the wall. In his haste, Van Kirk had neglected to remove the picture of the prior Beauty Queen. I look up to see the Zucchini Girl, displayed for the committee in all her glory.

Lieutenant Preston frowns and shakes his head, as if he'd just been witness to unspeakable atrocities. Never mind that he was one of the commanders in the staff room for the zucchini film's private showing.

"Come along, gentlemen." Preston quickly guides the men out, though leaving himself just enough time to turn and throw us all a condescending look.

We pony up in the back lot for Van Kirk's big PCP surveillance, but the sarge's heart isn't into it. Poor guy probably sees his whole career going down the toilet. We tell him that we can handle the case without him, but he decides to go along.

Sarge, Smitty and Salami ride together in the van, and Miller, Van Kirk and I each take our own cars. Van Kirk peels off to pick up his CI, and then we all meet up at an Arco gas station a few blocks from the suspect's house. It's a throw-down area of unincorporated Alameda County, neglected by residents and disregarded by redevelopment efforts. As a result, cars with no wheels sit up on blocks in front of shoddily converted garages. The streets are narrow and rutted, and the whole place looks more like a collection of sheds than a neighborhood.

I can only see the back of Van Kirk's CI in the car, and I'm sure he intentionally parked facing away from us. It only makes us more curious. Miller and I give each other a wink, and then we both claim we suddenly have to take a leak. We pass the car without looking, and then wait a minute or two inside the gas station restroom. On our way out we both get a good glimpse of her. She's an exotic-looking gal with brown skin and a striking smile. Her hair is silky and black, and she looks to be in her mid-twenties. Nothing like the informants Miller and I have.

Van Kirk walks over and ushers us away from his car before we have a chance to talk to her. We huddle around him next to the van, and the other guys join us there.

"This guy is a pretty big PCP dealer." Van Kirk hands each of us a sheet with Tony Fisk's photo, address, and vehicle descriptions. "He usually keeps a good quantity at the house, so this should go down quickly. 'In and out,' is what I told the CI."

"Do we know who Fisk's connection is?" Miller and I are thinking the same thing. If this guy, Fisk, is that big, then his dealer must be huge. Unfortunately, Van Kirk's informant doesn't know anything about Fisk's supplier.

Van Kirk lets the CI out of his car and we track her up to Fisk's front door. The radio abruptly goes live with the CI's voice. Miller immediately comes on the car-to-car channel, laughing. "Did you know she was wearing a wire?"

"Nope." I let out a chuckle. "But I'm sure Van Kirk was gentlemanly enough to help her put it on."

"I bet that was cozy."

Van Kirk comes over the air. "Just so you guys know, Smitty's the one who helped get her set up."

We make a couple of cracks about Smitty being a dirty old man, and he finally comes on the radio and tells us all to shut up and pay attention.

I'm slumped in my car, parked under a nice shade tree about a block away. I assume the other guys are doing the same. I bolt upright when I hear Fisk tell the CI that he doesn't have enough on-hand.

"Did you guys hear that?" Van Kirk barks over the air. "Sounds like he might have to trip for it."

"I hope it's not too far," Roberts says flatly. "You gotta stay put and watch her, and that only leaves Soto and Miller to follow him and make the connection's house."

Without having said it, we all know that the van is nearly useless in rolling surveillances. It's big, awkward, and it's painted a ridiculous blue color that's hard to miss. Plus, we do most of our raids out of it. Had we known there was a potential for a vehicle surveillance, we would have probably parked Salami in it down the street and each had our own cars.

I hear Fisk in the background, involved in a one-sided conversation as if talking on the phone. I'm straining to listen, but the CI is moving around too much and it sounds like the wire is in a cement mixer. She finally settles down and I pick up the tail end of Fisk's conversation. It sounds like the connection has the drugs wherever he is. And then, in a final salutation, Fisk calls him by name: "I'll be there in ten minutes, Doug."

Fisk tells Van Kirk's informant to hang out there while he takes a drive to get it.

I start the car and pick up the mic. "You guys hear that?"

"Setting up for a trip," Van Kirk relays the information, just in case somebody missed it. He's on a fixed post across the street from the house, and I imagine his position is not a subtle one. Since we didn't expect Fisk to come outside, Van Kirk is most likely slunk down on the floorboard, trying not to be seen. He'll probably have no time to alert us when Fisk actually leaves.

A few seconds of tense silence passes and then Van Kirk abruptly comes on the air. "Fisk's out of the house and rolling northbound. Looks like he's driving the silver Jeep listed on the briefing sheet."

The guy comes flying out of his shantytown neighborhood, and I hear Miller pick him up. "He's on Foothill, number one lane, and he's moving along pretty good."

I roll up behind Miller and see he's three cars behind the Jeep. Fisk hits an intersection on a yellow light and makes it through. Miller gets through, barely, but I'm a second behind and have to stop. When they get a few blocks farther, I make sure it's clear and then bust the light. I'm driving a beat-up, faded-blue Mustang, and I look like a parolee. This would be a terrible time to get pulled over.

I catch up to Miller as they approach a freeway. He's now only one car behind Fisk.

"Fisk's hitting the freeway, northbound." Miller picks up speed on the approach, but the Jeep suddenly swerves off of the ramp. "He jumped the onramp!" Miller continues onto the freeway, unable to follow him without an attention-getting maneuver. "Take point, Soto."

I haven't committed to the onramp yet, so I remain at surface street speed a few cars behind the guy. He's looking in his mirrors for anyone who pulls off the ramp. "He's checking to see if you follow him off." I hold the mic low and out of view. I'm trying to appear like any other driver, but it feels as if he's looking right at me. "Smitty. You and the sarge close enough to take point?"

A tedious silence and then, "Trying to get through traffic. Coming up on you now." Smitty's voice brings a sigh of relief. "Drop back at the next intersection and I'll take your spot.

I drop back, and then pull off altogether when Smitty finally catches up in the van. I listen to Smitty broadcasting their path as I jump on the freeway to parallel them. "He's turning under the freeway," Smitty's words are barely understandable with the pipe in his mouth. "Getting on the freeway, southbound!"

Fisk had been headed north, and now he's getting ready to go back in the opposite direction. I pull off at the next exit and whip around the cloverleaf so that I'm at least going the right way.

Smitty comes on again, "We got any idea where this jackass is headed?"

"He told a guy named Doug that he'd be there in ten minutes." My spinning tires almost drown me out. "The connection has to be fairly close."

There's an unsettling lull, and I strain to see them up ahead.

"This fucking van might as well have *police* written on it. We're right behind the shitbird." Smitty's garbled transmission makes me laugh. I see Miller's car streaking up the next onramp and he pulls onto the freeway just ahead of me.

"Me and Miller will be coming up on you in thirty seconds." The Mustang's tired engine sounds like it's about to blow up as I race toward them.

"We're in the number three lane now. Which lane are you guys in?"

"The number two," Smitty barks. "We're burned up; gonna pull out at the next exit."

Miller slides into position just as the van with Smitty, Sarge and Salami pulls away.

Roberts, who has been relatively quiet up to this point, must have grabbed the mic from Smitty. He suddenly comes over the air. "Did someone say Fisk's connection's name is Doug?"

"That was me, Sarge." I cut around a slow-moving truck. "That's what Fisk called the guy he was on the phone with."

I'm right behind Miller and we're both a few cars behind Fisk. His Jeep slows and speeds up, and then slows down again.

"He's playing games, Soto."

"You think he's picked us out?"

Miller watches a few more seconds before answering me. "Nah, I think he's just paranoid. Looks like he's headed back to where he started. He may have had the dope at his house all along. Telling the CI he had to trip for it could just be a precaution." I hadn't even thought of that.

Roberts comes on. "Are you sure he called the guy, Doug?"

"Sounded like it."

The freeway is starting to thicken with rush hour traffic. We've all slowed and cars are changing lanes back and forth, as if the maneuver is going to get them out of this gridlock any sooner. Miller finds himself right behind Fisk in stopped traffic, and there's no way to drop back or change lanes. A bus finally gives Miller a break and he slides into the number-one lane. Unfortunately that lane starts moving again, and now Miller is ahead of the suspect.

The sarge comes on the air again, this time talking to Van Kirk. "Hey Kirkie, this connection could be Doug Stowers."

I've never heard of the guy, and the silence over the radio tells me that no one else has, either.

"He's probably one of the biggest PCP connections in the Bay Area," Sarge says. "Feds have been after him for years."

Fisk steers his Jeep to the right side of the freeway, and I'm far enough back to follow without drawing attention. Miller is stuck in the fast lane and can't get over in time. I hang back as Fisk drops off the freeway, down the off-ramp. The suddenness of the new information only adds to my angst. I broadcast the fact that I'm now the only one in a position to follow, hoping that someone is close enough to help me out.

Smitty comes on. "The van is too hot. You and Miller are going to have to do it."

"Miller?" One of my sweaty hands clutches the mic while the other grips the steering wheel.

"Sorry, Soto, I'm out." Miller says. "Can't get off the freeway."

Fisk makes a left turn at the bottom of the ramp onto a street that parallels the elevated freeway. I'm rolling slowly down the ramp, trying to keep Fisk in sight without being right on top of him.

Van Kirk, a hyper guy under normal circumstances, comes over the radio like a kid who's been allowed too much candy and soda. "Stay on him, Soto! You gotta make the house!"

"I'll do the best I can," I tell Van Kirk. "He's off the freeway now, and he may be tripping back home."

I inch my way to the bottom of the ramp. The roadway is barren except for the Jeep. I catch the name of the street, Liberty, and broadcast it over the air. I take my time making the turn, and now I'm about a block behind him. Right now mine is the only other car in sight. The raised freeway stands to my left, and on the other side of the street are deep, garbage-strewn lots. Without warning, Fisk abruptly pulls to the curb. I hold the mic down by my leg as I pass, keeping my eyes straight ahead. In my periphery I see the guy's head twisting every which way as he checks for a tail. There's nothing I can do but continue down the road. I slow down considerably, keeping an eye on my rearview mirror.

The Jeep suddenly starts moving again, and makes an immediate right. I'm certain there was no side street there, and now I have no idea where he went.

"You still got him, Soto?" Van Kirk's pleading voice calls out. I pull over and jump out on foot, not even giving myself enough time to answer or put my location out over the air. I'm probably three hundred yards or so past where he ditched in, and I'm running all out. Somewhere between here and the bottom of the off-ramp is the best I can do to approximate where I should be looking for him. There's no Jeep.

A few long driveways run off to the side of me, and I can only guess Fisk turned down one of them. I keep running, looking, and running some more. Still no Jeep.

Shit! I blew it. I stop with my hands on my knees, sweating and panting like a dog. *I lost him.*

"Soto!"

I look up and see Miller on the freeway, leaning over the concrete sidewall waving his arms. His little Toyota is pulled off to the side with its emergency flashers on. He calls to me again and then points to a driveway I had run past in my delirium. I suck in another labored breath and take off down the dirt drive, staying close to a stand of trees so I won't be seen. A house comes into view and I throw myself to the ground behind a pile of leaves. I see the Jeep stopped in front, and Fisk is standing next to it. He's still on high alert. After a minute of making sure he hasn't been followed, he steps to the door and is let inside. I make a mental note of the address, repeating the numbers over and over so I won't forget.

He's out of the house in under a minute, and back in his Jeep. I lie still as he passes me on his way back up the driveway. I'm hoping that by now Miller has directed Smitty and the sarge into the area, so they can tail him back to the CI. I let a few seconds pass before finally crawling out of my lair. I hoof it back down the street to my car and turn up the radio volume. Traffic on the channel sounds good—they're positioned behind the Jeep, following him underneath the freeway and back to his house. Van Kirk picks him up from his fixed position across the street, and eyeballs Fisk all the way to his front door.

Fisk's voice is suddenly heard over the CI's wire, and it's evident that the quarter-ounce PCP sale was successfully accomplished.

Back at the police department, Van Kirk dances into the office with the good news: the utilities for the house on Liberty come back in the name of Doug Stowers—the PCP Godfather of the East Bay. Van Kirk now has enough evidence for search warrants for both Fisk's and Stowers' houses.

The bad news is my heroin search warrant for Clifford Foster's place didn't make today's batting lineup. Sarge assures me that I'm first up tomorrow.

11

Open Mic

I drop my daughter at pre-school on my way to work. The other parents see me coming and hurry their kids into the classroom. My little girl wraps her arms around my neck and nuzzles into my stringy hair to give me a kiss—completely innocent to how I'm perceived by the world around her.

On my way to the station, I swing by Foster's house on Miami. No activity to speak of, and the tan pickup is still parked in his driveway. The whole way back to the office I'm thinking of the enormous charge I got from my big lab case. Nothing in police work has ever affected me like that. I want to do more labs. I want kilo dealers and kingpins. Hell, I'd interdict a Colombian mothership in the bay if I could find one.

I get into the office and nobody is there yet. I drop down to the jail and thumb through the in-custody bookings, looking for anybody with a Columbian-sounding name. The closest thing to a kingpin I can find is a 28 year-old white guy named Craig Johnson. He's charged with possession of a gram of methamphetamine. Not exactly what I'm looking for, but let's hope he knows a major trafficker or two.

I have the jailer pull Craig out of the cell, and he walks sleepily upstairs with me. He's a slow, easygoing type, and we seem to click right away. We talk for about twenty-minutes and he runs down how he gets his dope, and from whom. We're not talking about huge amounts though, and it doesn't sound like he knows about any meth labs.

He's trying hard to come up with something for me, yet he hasn't mentioned what he wants in return. He's not pushing to get out of jail or have his charges dropped.

"So, what is it you want me to do for you?" I finally ask. "Help on your case? Money?"

Craig laughs, then shrugs his shoulders. "I got bail money." He's not boastful, just matter of fact. "And I'm not all that worried about my case." He leans back on his chair and gazes out the window. "When I was a kid, I always wanted to be a cop."

His answer, though not what I expected, gives me a little insight into the guy. Whether he wants to do the right thing for a change, or maybe just have some fun with the whole double agent thing, he's motivated to help me out. I press him a little more about what he can do, and he tries to think.

"Oh yeah, I got something." He whacks the table with his hand. "But it's not drugs."

I urge him on with a nod.

"I know these black dudes who sell machine guns."

Sweet! Whether he cares about the case against him or not, I need to get Craig out of jail.

I bring him back downstairs and hand him off to the jailers. Back in the office, Sarge has called an ad hoc meeting with Van Kirk, Salami, Miller and Smitty. They have apparently just started, and Sarge quickly brings me up to date.

"Smitty's been working an organized crime angle against Hog Heaven, the motorcycle dealership downtown," Roberts says. "Lou Sessions is the owner of record, but it's been a front for the Hell's Angels for years. Smitty's put together a shitload of intelligence for the feds, but we need to tie their activities to specific crimes."

I'm trying to act interested, but the whole time they're talking I'm slyly going through my desk, pulling out the paperwork needed to get Craig released.

Smitty takes a puff of his pipe. "The scrawny chemist of yours we busted in Oakland wouldn't talk. He got himself a lawyer right away . . . an HA lawyer. And you made that coke buy from one of the salesmen, but the DA won't charge it."

That was the one I did in Walnut Creek. "Why wouldn't he charge it?"

"He thought it was entrapment," Roberts says.

"What? Entrapment how?"

Roberts shakes his head. "The DA said a jury might feel that the only reason the guy sold to you is because he wanted to get in your sister's pants."

"That's ridiculous."

"Be that as it may," Roberts says, snagging a photo from Miller's desk. "At the same time as Smitty's putting all this stuff together, Miller started working a coke investigation on this rich white guy up in the Castro Valley hills. His name is Bryce Feldman." Sarge hands it over to Miller to explain the connection.

Miller swings his chair around. "Turns out that Feldman's cocaine business has gotten so big, that he's now got a bodyguard. According to my CI, the bodyguard is a heavyweight Hell's Angel. The HA's wouldn't provide protection for someone unless he was dealing their dope."

"As of right now, we're going to have to put aside all our other cases so we can focus on this investigation." The sarge looks directly from me to Van Kirk, since we are the two most impacted by the hasty change of direction.

I can't help wondering why the sudden urgency. *Could it be one more effort to prop up the beleaguered Vice/Intelligence unit? Or even more likely, is it a thinly veiled attempt to pull our reputation out of the toilet and impress the accreditation suits?*

"You remember I have that signed search warrant for Clifford Foster's place," I say with just a whiff of sarcasm. "It dies at the end of the week."

"Would the judge grant an extension if you updated it with some fresh information?" The sarge's question is a legitimate one, but I have no intention of busting my ass to try to get *fresh* information. I was lucky enough to see the transaction at the Quick Stop, and then be able to ID Foster's source through his phone call to the San Francisco guy. Besides, I've already been screwed out of hitting Foster once, just so I could look like a fool with a bag over my head.

"There's no way to freshen it," I say with a phony sadness. "Wish I could, but it was a stretch to get it signed in the first place." Then, remembering Sarge's worries over the accreditation debacle, I try a different approach. "If we hit Foster at the right time, we could get lucky and catch him with a fat load. I'm sure we could use some good press about now."

Roberts stands silent, caressing his chin. "Hmmm. Lieutenant Preston is giving those accreditation stiffs a tour of the night operation later this evening. The timing might be just right to impress them with a good seizure." He turns to the board and puts me down for 6 o'clock.

In the meantime, I fill out the release forms and walk them over to the DA's office. I return an hour later and give Craig Johnson the good news: he'll be released during his afternoon arraignment.

By briefing time, everyone in the unit is milling around with their raid gear on. I run through Foster's information, and let everyone know that the warrant includes his house, the Toyota pickup, and anything on Foster's person. The San Francisco connection is of little consequence to anybody in the room, but bringing it up in the briefing is my way of showing that I've done my homework. Maybe too, it's a little guilt trip I'm laying on Miller and Smitty for getting me bumped for their organized crime case. Now all I have to do is find heroin. Otherwise I'll have provided more rationale to be passed over next time.

Sarge keeps opening the office door during the briefing. I finally figure out that he's checking for the accreditation guys. I hope to God he didn't invite Preston and those boobs to come along.

I wrap up the briefing quickly and we all move to the back lot. It's gotten dark and the temperature has dropped significantly. There are no uniforms available to assist with entry, so we all head out. Miller and the sarge are in the van, and the rest of us are stuffed into Van Kirk's car. We're at an intersection a few blocks from Foster's house when I see a tan Toyota pickup drive past.

"I think that's our guy," I say to Van Kirk. We pull out of the turn lane and accelerate after him. I get on the radio and let the sarge know what's happening. In the mirror I see the van lumber through the intersection behind us.

We pull up close enough to read the license plate, and I confirm it with the DMV printout in my case file. I'm thinking about how much easier it will be to stop Foster out here on the street. We could grab his house keys and detain him here while we make entry. With Foster in handcuffs, there's little chance of someone arming themselves or flushing the evidence. And with any luck, maybe Foster's just met with his connection and we'll find all the dope on him.

Sarge's voice comes over the air. "You want to try following him, Soto?"

"We could give it a shot, but he'll probably get heated up pretty quick." Again, we should have thought to take more cars in case of a rolling surveillance. I look back at the unwieldy blue van and realize Smitty was right. It might as well have *police* painted across it. "We probably ought to take him down now. Let's try to block him in at the next intersection."

"We'll pull the van in front of him, and you guys pinch him in from behind." Miller says.

"Ten-four." I feel the hot surge of excitement as the van speeds past us and pulls in ahead of Foster. Salami is hunched forward between Van Kirk and me, and we're all grappling for our flashlights.

"Coming up on a red light now," Sarge says, an octave higher than his normal voice.

The van is in front of Foster's Toyota. Two men are silhouetted in the little pickup, apparently unaware of what's about to take place. The signal light turns green, but instead of going the van's backup lights come on and it rolls slowly backward. I hear Foster's horn blaring.

"Move up!" I yell to Van Kirk. "Get up on his ass!"

We pull forward, but not quickly enough. By now Foster has sensed something amiss, and his pickup is backing toward us. A smashing jolt nearly propels Salami into the front seat as Foster's truck slams into the front of Van Kirk's car. Horns honk from cars on either side of us—some stopping to watch the chaos and others trying to scurry clear. The yelling inside our car is deafening, as me and Salami yell directions and Van Kirk curses the son-of-a-bitch who wrecked his car.

Foster manages to pull free of the pickle, but now other cars have stopped in his way. Van Kirk pulls around to the side of him and I roll down my window. I've got my badge in one hand and my gun in the other.

For whatever insane reason, Van Kirk decides to switch the radio from our car-to-car narc channel to the police dispatch channel. He keys the mic just as my passenger window comes abreast of Foster.

"Pull your fucking ass over!" I yell out at the top of my lungs. Not only does Foster hear me, but it also broadcasts into the dispatch center and over the radios of every cop in the city.

We manage to pin Foster's pickup in place long enough for Salami and I to pull his door open and drag him out. His passenger, a man about Foster's age, sits there with his hands in the air. He is also placed in handcuffs until we can sort out who's who and if there are any drugs on either of them.

We've got the two men seated on the curb, and we're trying to move all the cars out of the street. A couple of marked units come flying up with their lights on and sirens wailing, apparently having been dispatched to a vehicle accident and fight in the middle of the street. We wave our badges and call out that we're *Code-4—no further assistance needed.* I glance around at the disastrous mess I've caused. Sergeant Roberts stands there rubbing his temples, and the rest of the crew looks thankful this wasn't their case. *Please let us find dope.*

We turn the two guys upside down and tear the pickup apart, but there are no drugs. Foster isn't talking, though he doesn't look smug. I'm hoping that means there's plenty of heroin back at his house. We hustle through the search out on the street so we can hit his place before someone sees us and tips off his family.

We have one of the marked units stay there and hold the two guys, while we take Foster's keys and head over to his house. One of Van Kirk's headlamps is smashed, and the bumper is askew, but it'll get us there. Smitty and the sarge follow us in the van. Dispatch is calling for Sergeant Roberts to switch to an auxiliary channel for an important message. Van Kirk flips to that channel so we can also listen in.

A haughty voice comes over the air. "Roberts? This is Lieutenant Preston."

"Go ahead, Lieutenant," the sarge answers weakly.

"I had just taken the accreditation committee members into the dispatch center when one of your narcs embarked on a profanity-laden tirade over the radio."

Roberts doesn't respond, and all I can think of is that he may have swallowed his tongue. I throw a pissed off look at Van Kirk.

He smiles back impishly. "How did I know you were about to yell out the window?"

"Roberts, are you there?" Preston barks.

"Yes, sir." Sarge goes into his overly submissive mode. "We are looking into how that might have happened. It appears there may have been an equipment malfunction, sir."

"Equipment malfunction! Your entire unit is a malfunction!" The lieutenant is obviously playing to the crowd, and I'm betting all the committee stiffs are standing right there next to him. He finishes his little show of power with the words, "Captain Evancheck and I would like to see you when you get in."

"Fuck that windbag." Van Kirk flips off the radio speaker.

I feel like a total loser for all that I've caused. Though he's a little bit brash sometimes, Roberts is an exceptional boss with a hell of a mind for trickery. I'd hate to see him get into trouble over some screw-up of mine. I could apologize to him when we get to Foster's house, but I know that won't really help. *We gotta find drugs*!

I pound on the door and a woman opens it just as I start to slip the key in the lock. She seems equally as perplexed that the narcotics unit is there as she is that we have the key to her home.

I give her a copy of the search warrant. "We're here to search for drugs, Mrs. Foster."

"Drugs? There are no *drugs* in this house."

I point to the warrant. "Specifically, heroin."

"Heroin." She has a genuine look of confusion. "That's impossible."

Mrs. Foster's two children have wandered out of their rooms, so we seat them with their mother in the living room while we search. I listen as Mrs. Foster does her best to explain to them that there has been some sort of mix-up. She picks up the warrant and studies it's face sheet. I'm certain that by now she's seen the references to her husband and his vehicle. I see a look in her eyes that tells me the wheels are turning inside her head. *Could she really be oblivious to her husband's heroin enterprise?*

Roberts sits glumly on an ottoman in the living room. He's keeping an eye on the family while we preen through all of their belongings, one-by-one. We search the house from top to bottom, and there's not even a hint of drugs. I'm afraid to look the sarge in the eye.

It's been nearly two hours and the kids are starting to squirm. The patrol watch commander has come on the air asking when we're going to release his patrolman from the scene of the car stop. I pull Miller, Van Kirk and Salami together and ask about each location again; the bathrooms, the garage, the attic, the backyard, the workshop on the side of the house, even the crawlspace beneath the house—all searched, and all clear of any drugs.

I finally break down and go out to Roberts. "Any suggestions?"

"I've seen it hidden in waterproof bags inside a fish tank before."

I glance around. No fish tanks.

"I've also seen them burry it in flowerpots."

No flowerpots, either.

"How about the tops of the doors?" Roberts motions to the coat closet. "I once saw a dealer drill down into solid core doors and slide rolled up ounce baggies inside the holes."

The other guys and I check every door in the place—no drilled holes. I'm about to admit defeat. I look around at my buddies and I see they're exhausted. The streets are busy and the radio chatters with traffic. I'm a minute from telling dispatch that the uniform cop can release Foster, when I notice the look of dread on Mrs. Foster's face. She's no longer questioning whether or not we have the right house. Instead, she looks like a woman who's come to the realization that she's been lied to. I think back to what Maria told me about Foster: he doesn't do any business out of his house because of his kids. But I followed him from his house to meet the connection, and then back again. It has to be here. And if his wife and kids are truly in the dark, then it must be somewhere that they would never find it. Somewhere they don't go.

I grab my flashlight and walk into the backyard. It's an open, grassy area with a few pieces of lawn furniture. Around to the side is a small, covered workshop pinched between the house and the wooden fence. A piece of plywood has been cut to act as a door, and hinges attach it to the fence. I push it open and walk onto a row of wooden slats that have been laid on the dirt as a makeshift floor. There is a workbench, a few tools, and a fluorescent light powered by an extension cord running into the bedroom window. *Someone's gone to a lot of work.*

I stand in front of the workbench and I feel in my bones that this is where he weighs and packages his drugs. But Salami has already searched it, and he didn't find so much as a scale or a baggie. Still trying to place myself inside Foster's head, I walk, pivot, reach up to the light, and rub my hand along the shelf beneath the workbench. I can almost smell it. It has to be here. It has to be within reach.

I kneel on the floor slats, and stare down at them. I lift one and it comes up easily. The dirt below it is dry and hard-packed. I stand and put my weight into the toe of my boot. Stepping systematically from one end to the other, I try to gauge the support beneath the wood. At about the middle of the floor I feel a little give in one of the slats. I step back and then forward again, bouncing slightly as it flexes. I drop to one knee and lift the slat. A perfect rectangular hole has been dug directly beneath it, and I can see a green trash bag protruding from it. I pull it up to find a gram scale, dozens of balloons and baggies, and a notebook filled with handwritten transaction records. I pull up the rest of the wooden slats and find another hole about the same size as the first. This one holds another trash bag containing thousands of dollars bundled in rubber bands, and a glob of raw heroin about the size of my fist.

I take a deep breath and exhale it slowly in thanks. The group grows quiet when I walk back into the house with the two plastic bundles in my arms. Miller and Van Kirk seem happy for me, and Salami looks worried he missed something that he should have found. I assure him that finding it was a stroke of luck on my part.

Roberts comes bouncing over to the table. "What'd ya find, Philly?"

He seems relieved when I show him the dope. He radios the patrol cop and tells him he can release the passenger, and he can transport Foster to jail. My hope, and I'm sure Sergeant Roberts' hope, is that Preston and his accreditation minions monitored that transmission as well.

Back at the station, Lieutenant Preston and Captain Evancheck are waiting in the lieutenant's office. I grab the drug evidence envelope out of the larger bag and follow Roberts across the detective floor. Roberts looks surprised I'm behind him, but doesn't say anything. Preston smirks as I enter the office, but nobody tells me to leave.

Preston sets a cassette tape recorder on his desk, and I have no doubt what's on it. "Your narcotics unit is an embarrassment to this department," he starts. Then turning to me, "And I assume that was you cursing over the radio?"

"Yes sir." I try to look contrite. "I didn't realize that there was an open mic at the same time I was trying to get our suspect to . . ."

Preston waves a hand in front of my face. "That's a non-issue."

Oh really? For some crazy reason I thought it might actually be germane to the issue.

Sarge is watching the dynamics, and the captain looks indifferent to the whole thing. I apologize to all three of them for causing any embarrassment, but Preston won't let it drop.

"The committee's perception of the narcotics unit is that you're all cavalier." He turns from Roberts back to me. "This accreditation is an important step for this organization, and not one to be taken lightly."

A thought suddenly comes to me. I smile and nod at Preston in agreement. "I realize that, sir. In fact lieutenant, I think we're both saying the same thing."

I quickly turn toward the captain whose sporting a curious grin. "This is what we seized from Foster tonight, Captain." I hand the envelope to him. "Thought you'd enjoy taking a look at it."

The captain examines the heroin with childlike fondness. "Great case, men. Outstanding job." He launches into a story about a joint heroin investigation he and the feds once conducted. Roberts and I listen intently, as Preston bristles. His big, gauche hand wanting so badly to press the play button on his little recorder, but the fervor of his inquest has escaped him like air from a party balloon. The captain is now more interested in our heroin, and Preston's proof of our cavalier-ness is no longer relevant. A *non-issue*, one might say.

The captain's story dies down and the sarge and I make a quick exit. He flashes a sideways eye as we walk back to our offices. "You stole that from me."

"Stole what?" I reach for the door handle a step ahead of him.

"That line, 'we're both saying the same thing.' You stole that line from me!"

I give him an innocent face. "I don't know what you're talking about, Sarge." I step into the office and quickly close the door.

Van Kirk must have raced out after the warrant, because all his stuff is gone and his desk is locked up tight. Miller asks me if I'm going up to the PBA. He says he and the sarge might stop by, but he doesn't sound real firm on it. I check my watch and it's already nine o'clock.

I log the drugs into evidence and then drop by the jail to make sure they have the correct charges on Foster's booking sheet. I give my prisoner another opportunity to talk and perhaps give up his San Francisco connection, but he declines.

Miller and the sarge are gone by the time I get back upstairs, and I assume they've headed up to the PBA for a drink. I've just locked the office door on my way out when I notice a light coming from Preston's office. He looks out at me as I cross the detective's floor, and I know he'll be holding a grudge. I may have slipped through his grasp tonight, but he's not likely to give up that easily. *I'd better watch myself around him.*

It's a slow night at the PBA bar. Two guys sit hunched over their drink glasses, while Larry stands at the ready. I wave to him as I come in, and then scan the place for my cohorts.

"Any of my guys show up tonight, Larry?"

His brows come together as he towels off his hands. "Detective Van Kirk came in for a few minutes, sir. But the two of them left about a half-hour ago."

"The *two* of them? Who was he with?"

Larry replaces a coaster beneath a customer's drink. "He had the Hawaiian officer with him."

"The Hawaiian officer?" After a half-second of trying to figure out who that could be, it dawns on me.

"Would that be the *female* Hawaiian officer?"

"Why, yes it was. A young lady with long black hair. She must be new on the force because I've never seen her before." If Larry suspects anything he doesn't show it. The epitome of diplomacy and prudence.

I sit down next to one of the guys at the bar and order a bourbon and seven. Larry asks if I'd like a barker to go with that, and I tell him I would, indeed.

After about twenty minutes, it's apparent that my partners are no-shows tonight. It doesn't matter though, because I've struck up a conversation with the guy next to me—a homicide detective with the sheriff's department. Years of senseless deaths and grieving loved ones have made him angry and cynical, but Larry's strong drinks have begun to smooth the sharp edges. We talk about the job, laugh about the informants, and make fun of our bosses. The investigator tells me he's on his third marriage, and that one's coming off the tracks as well. I shake my head as if I can feel his pain, but I'm thinking that could never happen to my marriage.

I've heard about this guy, and I tell him he's got a great reputation. He says he's heard about me, but I can't tell if he's just returning the compliment. As the night wears on, we ease into a melancholy yet brotherly familiarity.

Sometime around midnight the detective's pager goes off. He steps behind the bar to use the house phone and I listen to his half of the conversation. It sounds like the nightshift watch commander at the sheriff's department is passing on some important information to the detective. He returns to the bar and finishes his drink.

"Imagine that," he says with a chuckle. "A deputy out at Santa Rita just came up with a jailhouse snitch who has info on one of your murders."

"One of *our* murders?" The last one I remember was the Bascomb homicide, and we cleared that one. "Was it a recent one?"

The detective shakes his head. "Old one. Happened about five years ago." He wipes his lips with the back of his hand. "Some woman out in Fairway Park apparently shot her husband and then buried him in the crawlspace beneath the house."

I remember hearing something about the case several years ago. The investigator working it suspected the victim's wife all along, but he was never able to get enough evidence for a search warrant. "It's officially a missing person case, right?"

He checks his watch. "Until now." The detective stands up and places a wad of cash on the bar. "Nice talking to you. Gotta go to work."

12

COLD CASE

It seems like we just had SWAT training. My dead hand flops over the top of the clock, trying to find the alarm shutoff.

The girls are eating breakfast on a blanket in front of the TV. I give them both a kiss on the head on my way to the kitchen.

"Got time for breakfast?" Gale asks.

I check the clock. "Better not. We've got to take the physical test this morning, and I'd probably just puke it up."

She gives me a half-nod. "Will we see you for dinner tonight?"

"It kind of depends." I open the refrigerator and take the bag lunch she's made me. "Don't really know what we've got going until I get in."

Gale's head does another half-nod. "Do you think you'll have time to stop by the church? We promised to help them haul away all the donated clothes from the fundraiser."

"We?" I lower my voice so the girls won't hear. "How come it's always *"we"* who gets to haul that shit away? There were two other families running the fundraiser with us. Why am I the one who gets dicked?"

Gale leans her head out to check the girls. When she leans back into the kitchen, her eyes burn into me. "I'm sorry, get 'dicked'?" She takes a measured breath and I know something more is coming. "Maybe I should remind you that we both volunteered to do the fundraiser; it wasn't something I just decided on my own. It isn't just for the church, it's for the school where one of our daughters goes and the other one will be starting next year. If it's too much trouble for you to spare forty-five minutes, leave me the keys to your truck and the girls and I will do it!"

I toss a hand up as if shooing away her point. "Where's all this coming from?"

"Where's it coming from?" She takes a second. "Lately you seem to forget that you have a family. You pay more attention to those losers you deal with on the street, than you do to us."

"What, I'm not home enough? Sorry for trying to make a living."

Gale sits down as if the conversation is exhausting her. "I don't begrudge you the time you spend at your job. But even when you're home, it's like you're not really here. You're either on the phone with work or with one of your informants."

I let out a sigh. "Is there anything else?"

She looks at me for a second and then her eyes drift downward. "I guess not."

I glance at the clock. "I don't have time for this now, I'm gonna be late for training."

Gale does another one of her half-nods as I grab my duffel bag and head out the door. I'm driving to work trying to figure out when I'll be able to stop by the church.

The timed, two-mile run comes after all the other physical tests, and for the first time since joining the team, I'm not sure I have the stamina to finish it. I feel heavy and out of shape.

I stretch my legs a bit, and then line up with the rest of the team. Following the course as it snakes through a neighborhood near the police department, I'm able to hang in there for the first half-mile. After that I start to fade, and I realize that I could be kicked off the team if I fail the test. As we come up to the end of a long block, I dive into an overgrown juniper bush. The team rounds the one-mile mark and heads back in my direction. They're more spread out now, and I wait until there's a sizable gap before jumping back in. I finish the run with only a few seconds to spare, but I'm as tired and winded as some of the guys who actually ran the whole thing. Any other time in my career I would be disgusted with myself, both for being so out of shape and for cheating. But I give myself a pass, justifying the behavior in my mind as just a necessary part of my undercover job.

The SWAT commander passes out new transmitters that connect to our radios. They're consolidated units with a tiny microphone that clips to the uniform. He starts to explain how the on/off switch works and that it can also be set on voice-activated mode. I hear someone paging me over the department intercom, and I leave training without ever hearing the rest of the lesson.

The call turns out to be the excuse I'm looking for to bug out of the remainder of the day's training. The T-NET task force wants me to be their buyer on a big marijuana case. It's hard to get charged up for a marijuana buy, but it's better than sitting in training. I change back into my casual clothes and they wire me up for an intro.

We meet with their informant at a shopping center on Mowry Avenue in Fremont. It's the same Indian kid who intro'd me to a heroin dealer. *What's the deal? They only have one informant?*

The other cops clear out, and I wait there with Sundip for the seller to arrive. He pulls up in a restored Mustang, and I'd swear he's not even old enough to drive. We talk for a few minutes and I get the impression he's not too bright. We haggle over the price a bit and then he sells me a half-ounce of weed. *Some big trafficker.*

I get his number and then he drives off. When the T-NET guys return, I ask them what kind of weight this kid can do. They look at each other nervously and then their sergeant comes clean. "Well, he's not really a heavy-hitter. In fact, the half-ounce you bought probably maxed him out."

"Then why are we wasting our time with him?"

Their sergeant lets out a little laugh. "We had a complaint from somebody who asked that we put a case on him and take him to jail."

"Who's the complainant?"

"His dad." The sergeant holds up his hands in defense. "Apparently he's a friend of our police chief."

I roll my eyes and hand him the dope.

It's about 2 o'clock in the afternoon when we get back to the station, and the other guys are going out to get lunch. I grab my bag and eat mine while driving up to the church. I figure that getting this done will buy me some goodwill with Gale.

Someone has stacked the boxes of donated clothes behind a cyclone enclosure next to the school playground. I pull up the collar of my trench coat to shield myself against the damp wind. The weather has corroded most of the dozen or so cardboard boxes, and now clothes and other donated items are scattered on the ground. I clench my teeth, angry all over again that this somehow fell on me to do. I'm bent over, gathering up the wet clothes, when I hear the clattering of little feet behind me. Scores of children have lined up on the other side of the fence to watch me—their eyes wide with fright.

"He's a homeless person!" one chubby boy yells. "He's a homeless person!"

The rest of the mob surges forward against the fence, pointing at me and telling me to get out of their schoolyard. Soon they've all joined the little fatso's chant. "He's a homeless person!"

One of the teachers finally comes over and the kids scatter. She knows our family, and apologizes profusely.

I eventually get the clothes loaded into the back of my truck and I deliver them to the Salvation Army drop-off.

I return to the station, wet and pissed off. I've worked myself into a lather about all the demands on my time. Between picking up clothes and being the buyer for everyone else's cases, I can't find time to do my own thing. Craig Johnson has been out of jail for a few days now, and I'd like to find out if he's hooked up with the machine gun guys. I'm about to call him when Smitty and the sarge come in. I let out a long sigh as I set the phone back down.

"Smitty just got a warrant signed for Hog Heaven!" The sarge slaps his hands together.

We're all sitting at our desks wondering what they expect to find besides a bunch of Harley Davidson motorcycles. Whatever the point, I can tell from Roberts' exuberance that he's going to want to hit it right away.

Smitty takes the pipe out of his mouth. "With all the intel we've got on the place and that coke buy we made from one of the salesmen a few months back, the judge finally signed off on it."

"What's the warrant for?" Van Kirk asks.

"On paper it's for cocaine, but what we're really looking for is documentation of Sessions' connection to organized crime. This is just part of the bigger investigation that includes Miller's case against Bryce Feldman, his bodyguard, and the Hells Angels."

Their plan is to wait until Sessions and all his salesmen have gone for the day. That gives me the next couple of hours to get other things done. I give Gale a call and let her know that I'll be late. I apologize for this morning, and offer my humiliation at the hands of the school kids as proof of my repentance. She laughs at the image, and tells me to be safe tonight.

Smitty holds a quick briefing and by 6:30 p.m. we're rolling to the motorcycle dealership. The place is right on the main drag, illuminated by dozens of lights. Salami and Van Kirk use the heavy key to bash through the glass front door. It sets off an ear-piercing alarm that sounds even louder once we get in.

Sergeant Roberts advises dispatch that the alarm was caused by us, and not to bother sending a patrol cop. We bypass the showroom, and then split into groups of two to search the offices. I end up in Sessions' office with Salami. I comb through every drawer in his desk looking for incriminating paperwork, but the entire time I'm hoping to find a load of dope. I find neither.

By the time I return to the finance office, my head is pounding from the alarm. Van Kirk stands at a row of file cabinets, tossing folders and all their contents into the air like confetti. The floor is like a sea of paperwork. I stare down at the mess, wondering how they will ever be able to straighten out their billing. We couldn't have massacred the guy's business any worse if we had set the place ablaze.

Lou Sessions shows up in his black Lincoln Town car, and strolls inside like he doesn't have a care in the world. He stands amidst the shattered glass door and surveys the disarray with a steel gaze.

Van Kirk makes no attempt to straighten the mess, though he couldn't if he tried. At least he's curtailed the file demolition. Smitty and the sarge walk over and say something to Sessions, and I see Smitty hand him a copy of the search warrant. Sessions' attorney shows up a few minutes later with a camera. Neither of the men speaks another word to any of us after that.

No drugs are found on the property. And if there was paperwork documenting an organized crime connection, I doubt it could have been found in that trash heap. We finally finish up around nine o'clock, but I worry we haven't heard the last of Lou Sessions or his attorney.

I get home too late to see the girls, but Gale is still up. She tells me that Miami Vice is about to start, and there is some Ben and Jerry's in the freezer. We sit together watching the show and eating ice cream. I decide to skip all the work stories and narcotics jargon tonight.

We plan to attend a wedding over the weekend. One of my cousins is getting married in San Francisco, and I think Gale is excited to get out of the house for a change. Since we are going to be over there anyway, I slip the Foster case file under my car seat.

The wedding is a nice affair, and all my cousins are getting a kick out of my UC look. After the event, I take a drive across the city to Mangels Avenue. Gale crosses her arms tightly as I pull onto the street where Foster's connection lives.

"Honestly, Phil. You're doing this with me and the girls in the car?"

I pull out the file to double check the house numbers. "It's nothing dangerous. I'm just grabbing a license number."

We drive past the house, as if we're any other family on a Sunday afternoon drive. Sure enough, the white SUV is parked in the driveway. Only this time the correct license plate is on it. I run it when I get back to work and confirm that it's registered to Talbott.

* * *

My Monday starts out pretty well. I call the court on the Frank Bellotti subpoena I have for this morning, and I'm told the jury has yet to be selected. The case has been postponed until later in the week, and I now have some free time to spend with my family. I make the girls breakfast and I eat with them while Gale does an exercise video.

As I'm getting ready for work, Gale tells me about a Hall and Oates concert this coming weekend. She says it would be a nice break for us to have a night out together, as long as I don't bring along any of my case files. I agree, and by the time I'm heading out the door she's already on the phone ordering the tickets.

First thing in the office, I sit down and call Craig Johnson. Though he hasn't had any further contact with the gunrunners, he sounds eager to start working on them. I ask about getting together this afternoon so he can point out the house, but he says he has a job interview. Craig agrees to call me back when the interview is done.

Miller is meeting with Alberto next door, and I have the nagging suspicion that they'll want to do another intro. I'm sure The Big A needs more money. Miller walks in and drapes a consoling arm over my shoulder. He doesn't even have to say anything.

"Where am I buying?"

He smiles. "Oakland. Alberto knows a dealer on 35th avenue."

Who doesn't? I pull out my pencil and start touching up my track marks. "Have you noticed that The Big A is looking pretty bad lately?"

Miller says he's seen it too, but I get the feeling he's missing my point. I've been up close and personal with a lot of heroin addicts since coming to narcs, and Alberto is beginning to look worse than most of them. I see a guy whose habit is spiraling out of control.

The Big A and I ride together in my car, and the van follows behind. As bad as Alberto looks, my appearance is probably just as bad. We talk easily along the way, like a couple of dope fiends. Not at all with the stiltedness of our earlier buys. A marked Oakland unit stops at a light next to us, and the two mustached cops inside stare at us with palpable hatred. I find myself averting their stare so as not to attract more attention.

We pull onto a narrow street clogged with parked cars. Mexican music sings out from a purple lowrider as it inches past us. I pull to the curb in front of a weathered, white, two-story house, and read the address aloud into the wire. We walk up the steps and bang on the metal screen security door.

The door opens a couple of inches and a Mexican guy in a black fishnet tank-top peeks out at us. "Hey. Whatchu want?"

"Can you do a hundred?" I see The Big A's eyes light up at my request. *What does he think? He's really going to get some of it?*

The dealer grunts and then opens the security door for us. The place is nearly empty inside, and I wonder if it's some kind of stash pad. He pulls a plastic-wrapped wad from his pocket and pinches off a small hunk between his thumb and forefinger. I gather from his rudimentary measurement that his is an unsophisticated operation. "I give you a fat one."

I smile broadly. "Yeahhhh!" I find it curious that the seller hasn't acknowledged Alberto. It makes me wonder if they've ever even done business before.

"We need to get a taste of this shit," Albert suddenly says. I look at him with eyes that could kill, and he just smiles back at me.

"Okay," the dealer says. "You guys try it."

Now I'm really pissed at Alberto. He knows damn well that I'm not going to touch the stuff, and there's nothing I can do to keep him from doing it, without blowing my cover. He's got me in a catch-22 and he knows it.

The Big A smiles at me again as he pulls an eyeglass case out of his pocket. He opens it up and takes out a syringe, a spoon, a piece of matted cotton, and a book of matches. I scrape him off the tiniest piece I can, and his smile fades. Now we're both glaring at each other.

He lays out the tools of his trade like stations at a salad bar, and then he goes about his ritual with surgeon-like precision. Alberto unbuckles his belt and loops it over his bicep. The loose end is clenched in his teeth, tightening it around his arm like a tourniquet. With the belt still held in his teeth, Alberto flicks the small brown chunk onto the spoon and drools a mouthful of saliva onto it. He lights a match and holds it under the spoon until the slop starts bubbling. The dealer's expression is impassive, as if he just wants us to finish and leave before his next customer comes. I find myself captivated by the show, more curious now than angry.

Alberto uses the end of the syringe's plunger to stir the spoon's contents, and then drops the wad of cotton in the mixture. He takes the needle and draws the grey-brown concoction into the syringe. I'm shuddering at the idea that people actually put that shit into their body. But that's exactly what he does.

The Big A looks at me with a devious grin as he jabs the needle into the bulging vein of his forearm. His eyes flutter as he thumbs the plunger part way down. He holds it there, as if tasting a sip of fine wine, then pulls the plunger back up a bit. A slimy mixture of brownish fluid and blood backs into the syringe, and he holds it there for another second. Finally, he pushes the plunger all the way down. A light sweat breaks on his brow and his face flushes red. Alberto's eyes roll back in his head as his ritual comes to its orgasmic conclusion.

I waste no time getting out of there, damn near pulling Alberto along behind me by the scruff of his neck. He's stumbling down the sidewalk, trying to stuff his injection paraphernalia back into the eyeglass case. I load the weasel into my car and we're back on the road, headed home.

Even thought Miller heard the whole thing over the wire, I retell it in detail. "Homeboy's out of control," I tell him. "You better put a leash on him or we're gonna have problems."

Miller says that he knows Alberto has got a growing habit, but he assures me that as a CI he's still controllable. I remind Miller that he might feel differently if he were the buyer. I log the drugs into evidence and type up my supplement, the whole time thinking that Alberto is a rip-off waiting to happen. I've heard a lot of narcs talk about losing their money during a buy. I can only imagine that it's either because they look like chumps, or they're so eager to make the deal that they front the money and then never see it again. I should probably be more concerned with the safety issues around Alberto setting me up, but in truth it's more about my perfect buy record. *If I ever get taken for a ride, it's going to be by someone a lot sharper than The Big A.*

The board shows a search warrant at 2 o'clock, so I start getting my raid gear together. Van Kirk gives the briefing, and tells us that his CI, Marquita, gave him information about a guy dealing heroin from a motel room in Castro Valley. It sounds like a small potatoes thing.

We roll up in the van and Van Kirk uses the manager's passkey to open the door. A stringy white guy with pimples is lying on the bed, fading in and out of a drug-induced stupor. I get to him first and roust him off the bed. He's standing there with no shirt and tattered blue jeans, and with his bad breath enveloping me like a stale cloud.

"Got anything on you?" I ask before starting my pat search.

"Huh?"

I nearly gag. "Anything in your pockets! Drugs, weapons, needles?"

"No." His arms hang limply at his sides as I start checking.

I've heard the saying that *no means no*. But I guess that doesn't apply to heroin dealers. As I sweep my hand over his pants pocket, I feel the sting of a sharp object. I jerk my hand away and watch a drop of blood ooze from a tiny hole in my palm.

"Son of a bitch!" I squat and aim my flashlight at his pants. "Take the fucking syringe out of your pocket and set it on the table." He had jammed the syringe into his pocket without the cap on, just moments before we hit his room. The used, dirty, disgustingly diseased needle had bent sideways through the fabric of his jeans—just waiting there for me to come along and impale myself on it.

The whole episode is made even worse by the fact that we don't find any drugs. The guy was a nothing dealer to begin with, and had just injected himself with what little he had, minutes before we got there. Van Kirk ends up taking him for under the influence.

I tell the sarge about the needle stick. He tells me to fill out the Worker's Comp paperwork in the personnel and training office. The sergeant there says there's nothing they can do, and that I should just stop by a hospital on my own to get an HIV test. *I'm fairly certain I won't have developed the HIV antibody this soon after being exposed.*

I ask if there's any way we could force the suspect to get tested.

"That's a good question," he says. "But it would take too much work. Why don't you just go down the jail and ask the guy if he's got AIDS?"

"Never mind, Sarge. Thanks for the help."

It's late in the afternoon when Craig Johnson calls. He's finished with his job interview and ready to meet up with me. He tells me his address, which is back in Oakland, only a few blocks from where I bought this morning. I tell him I have a stop to make first, and I'll be there in an hour.

I get to the County Hospital's free HIV testing clinic, and the woman inside the door gives me a number. I'm sitting in the waiting room, checking out the other patients and wondering how many of them will test positive. I find myself sizing them up based solely on appearance, pigeonholing them into groups and guessing at their statistical probabilities. It's not very scientific, but it passes the time.

"Number 61."

I get up and shuffle in behind the Filipino nurse. She tightens a rubber hose around my arm and swabs the skin with alcohol. "The needle stings a little."

"Yeah, I know."

I watch her poke it into my vein and then draw my blood up into the syringe. *When I woke up this morning, I had no idea how many times I'd be seeing this today.*

"Okay, thanks." I start to get up.

"Oh no, you can't leave yet." She unwraps the tube from my arm and slaps a band-aid over the vein. "The doctor has to talk with each patient."

"Hmm." I suppose that has something to do with the *free* part. Probably a federally funded program that obligates them to provide counseling.

A Jewish-looking woman comes in carrying a clipboard. Her glasses dangle from a thin chain wrapped around the collar of her lab coat. She introduces herself as Doctor Levine, and then starts right off by asking if I'm homosexual, an intravenous drug user, or if I've had unprotected sex with multiple partners.

"No to all of them," I say.

"Then why are you here, getting tested?"

"I was accidentally stuck with a needle." I show her my palm.

"What kind of needle?"

"Well, a hypodermic needle. It had been used by someone to inject heroin."

"Uh-huh."

"It was an accident."

She stares at the track marks on my arm. "Uh-huh."

"No, really. I'm an undercover cop."

"Uh-huh." She writes something on her clipboard. "Okay, we're done. Call the hotline in ten days for the results." She hands me a slip of paper with a bunch of numbers on it. "This is your individual code. Just dial that in when you get the prompt. It's all totally anonymous."

It's dark when I come out. I drive the rest of the way to Craig's place, a small house on MacArthur. The light is on inside and I can see him talking with a woman. She comes part way out with him, glaring at me the whole time. He jumps in and we pull away.

"What's going on?" I ask. "She doesn't want you helping the cops?"

"No, it's not that. She just wanted to make sure you weren't a chick." We both start laughing.

Craig directs me to a neighborhood about a half-mile away, and then has me park on a deserted street. "I don't want them to see me driving by their house," he says. "They're pretty bad dudes, and they can get really paranoid sometimes."

We walk a couple of blocks down and then cut into a vacant lot. Craig motions to me and then he hunkers down in the weeds. "Follow me," he whispers.

We crawl toward the backend of the lot where it drops off, down a slope into someone's yard. Craig points to the house below us. "That's where they stay."

It's a two-story, wooden home with a small garage attached to the side. A dilapidated fence surrounds the back, but we're high enough on the hill to see into the window.

"Can we move up closer?" I ask.

Craig nods. "They have pit bulls, so not too close."

We inch down the hill in the darkness, peering into what appears to be a kitchen. I hear the sound of male voices, heavy and serious. A couple of silhouettes move past the window toward the back door and we freeze. The door opens and there's more talking. The door closes again and then it's quiet. I'm hoping they didn't just put the dogs out.

We wait a couple of minutes before climbing back up to the lot, and then we hurry to my car. I tell Craig that I'd like to take a pass by the front in order to get the address. He gets in and lies across the backseat under a blanket. As I drive around the block, Craig runs down the specifics. He tells me that he buys meth from a guy who bought a machine gun from them. Craig says he waited in the car while his dealer went inside to pick it up.

"Could it have just been a one-time thing?" I ask.

"No way." Craig pops his head out of the blanket to see if we've passed yet. "These guys are known for it."

I ask about the drug angle and Craig isn't sure. He thinks they might sell coke or take it as trade for their guns, but he doesn't know for certain. All he knows is that they're notorious for supplying high-powered and fully automatic firearms to high rolling drug dealers.

I jot down the address and drop Craig back at his house. The woman stands on the porch with her arms crossed as Craig comes up the walk.

I run into Miller in the back lot and he tells me that Van Kirk and Salami have left for the day. I tell him about the bartender at the PBA referring to Van Kirk's informant as the *Hawaiian officer*, and we both get a good laugh.

"I'm heading out to meet a new informant," he says, "but she doesn't look anything like Van Kirk's."

I climb the stairs to the second floor and see the sarge still at his desk. He motions me into his office. "Has Detective Fowler talked with you yet?"

I tell the sarge that I haven't seen him yet. Dave Fowler is one of our homicide investigators, but I've never even spoken to the guy. He's been on the police force forever though, and he's sort of an icon around the department.

"He may need you to go undercover on one of his investigations." Sarge has an apologetic tone, so I know he recognizes that I've been pretty busy buying for cases that are not my own. "It's the Samuel Mackler homicide from five years ago."

My eyes light up. "The guy under the house."

Sarge looks surprised that I know the case. I tell him about my conversation with the sheriff's investigator up at the PBA, though I leave out that Van Kirk had brought his informant up there the same night.

"Well you know the background then," Sarge says. "Apparently the sheriff's informant is a friend of a guy who's shacked up with the wife now. The informant doesn't want to intro you directly, but he's willing to put you in touch with the wife's boyfriend by phone."

I feel like I missed something. “Put me in touch with the wife’s boyfriend for what?”

“They’re looking for someone to move the body.”

13

Forty Winks

Sergeant Roberts tells me that a search warrant for an address in San Francisco has to be signed by a judge in San Francisco. I come in early and beat traffic over to the city, in order to find parking at the Hall of Justice. I get the warrant signed without a problem.

The following day I'm on the board for the SF raid, and I take my partners back across the bridge in the van. We meet a group of SFPD narcs in a Safeway lot a few blocks from Talbott's house. Miller and Van Kirk haven't done many warrants outside our city, and I get the feeling that Roberts likes the more global view. We caravan onto Mangels, but when we pull up to the front of the house, the white SUV is gone.

The group trudges up the steps and after a brief announcement, we mash the door open. The house is silent, and I immediately notice a large picture window at the back of the living room is shattered. Shards of glass are everywhere. An SF guy and I both ease over and peer through the jagged opening. A woman lies contorted on the backyard pavement two floors below. He quickly radios for an ambulance.

The team searches the rest of the house, and Talbott is nowhere to be found. Unfortunately, neither is his drug operation. The woman has a head wound and is cut all over her body. But she's conscious enough to tell us what we want to know. Apparently, Talbott pushed her through the 2nd floor window after a drug-fueled rant. According to the woman, he then gathered his drugs and guns, and drove off shortly before we arrived. *Lousy timing for me.*

SFPD puts out a broadcast for the SUV, but it'll be about as easy to find as a specific hair on a barbershop floor. Roberts locates a small packet of heroin in the back of a dresser drawer, apparently overlooked by Talbott in his haste to leave. It's good news for us and bad news for the woman. Since the house is technically under her control, she's charged with possession of the drugs. A felony arrest warrant is also issued for Talbott.

* * *

I call the court in the morning, hoping the Bellotti trial will once again be postponed. Unfortunately, it's a go. I quickly shower and then dress in my usual grubs—one of the perks to working narcotics. Most judges seem to appreciate the dangers we face, especially from being recognized as a cop. Sooner or later though, our cases wind up in court and there's no way around testifying.

It's still early when I stop by the office to pick up the case file. Detective Fowler is at his desk, reading the newspaper and sipping a steaming cup of coffee. He glances up at me as I pass his desk, but he says nothing. Maybe he changed his mind about needing my help on his case.

I open the door to a dark office. The drapes have been pulled, and I can't see a thing. My foot bumps something and there is an immediate groan. Startled, I jump backwards and flip on the light.

"You scared the dog shit outta me!" Miller yells from a sleeping bag on the floor.

I step around him to my desk. "What the hell are you doing here?"

He mumbles something about finishing up last night, too late to drive home. But I gather from this expression that there's more to it.

I give him a knowing laugh as I grab the Bellotti file. "Want me to turn the lights out for you?"

Miller grunts off my sarcasm, and I leave.

I've been in narcs for a year, and all the bailiffs working the metal detector now know me. They siphon me from the horde of court goers, around the device, and into a back hallway that runs behind the courtrooms. I'm left waiting in a small room. The VIP treatment protects me from sitting in an open courtroom full of miscreants—some of whom I may be currently buying drugs from.

A while later the bailiff comes in. "Sorry officer," he says. "The defense attorney wants to voir dire you."

"I hope he buys me a drink first." I say it as if we're talking about an unholy sex act, but I don't think the bailiff gets my joke. Voir dire is actually legalese for challenging a witness's expertise. More than likely though, his client just wants to get a look at the cop he mistakenly sold to. "Who's the attorney?" I ask.

"Tony Fontana." The bailiff heads back into the courtroom.

I roll my eyes as I pull myself up from the comfortable chair. I know Fontana from a couple of cases I had while on uniform patrol. He's a high-priced, private attorney specializing in drug cases.

I step into the courtroom through the judge's access door, and quickly scan the audience for anybody I know. Thankfully, the place is nearly empty. One of the guys who was in the house during the sale is seated a few rows back, and I'm sure he's there as a witness to dispute whatever I say. There's also a young woman, whom I presume to be Bellotti's girlfriend.

I smile politely at the judge, Karen Joya, who's signed a few of my search warrants in the past. "Good morning, Your Honor."

The prosecutor from the DA's office sits at one table and Bellotti and his attorney sit at the other.

His attorney, Tony Fontana, stands up when I come in, and he gives me a sarcastic smirk. "Nice look, officer."

He's a scrawny guy with sharp, rodent-like features and a ponytail that extends down to his shoulder blades. He struts around to the front of the defense table and stops. I notice he's wearing white tennis shoes with a silky gray dress suit that probably costs as much as I make in a month. His pants are way too long though, overshooting that chic, stylish look by a good three inches.

"New suit, Mr. Fontana?" I move toward the raised witness stand at the front of the courtroom. "Very nice. I particularly like the fit."

He glances down at his Bazooka Joe cuffs and then frowns back at me. I give him a wink and then raise my right hand to be sworn in.

Fontana makes a motion to reject my testimony as a cocaine expert, and launches into a series of questions challenging my background, training, and experience. At the conclusion Judge Joya denies Fontana's motion and finds me qualified as a court expert in cocaine,

cocaine possession, and cocaine sales. The jury is brought back in and the trial continues.

The diverse group of men and women look beleaguered by what I imagine has been mostly legal arguments and boring testimony to this point. I take the stand and they visibly perk up. The jurists all lean forward in their seats and watch with wide eyes as I'm introduced as an undercover narcotics cop. I describe the events leading up to the buy, and get a good laugh from them when I joke about using the *"Davy sent me"* line. They devour the testimony about the drug transaction and my subsequent detention, as if listening to an action thriller.

I finish my testimony and the audience slumps back, smiling and whispering to one another. A few of them lock eyes with me and nod approvingly.

Fontana peppers me with questions. The entirety of his cross-examination is built on the scenario that his client was a first-time dealer, and that he only sold cocaine to me because I badgered and begged him. It's a weak defense, and from the jury's expressions, I doubt they're buying any of it.

In the end, they find Bellotti guilty of selling a controlled substance, and the judge gives him an additional weight clause enhancement.

Sleeping beauty is up when I get back. He's at his desk, hunkered over a cup of black coffee. After all my recent screw-ups, I decide to lay off of Miller.

"Where is everyone?" I toss the case file onto my desk.

Miller shrugs. "I think Roberts is in a meeting with the chief." I raise an eyebrow and he raises one back. "I'm glad you're back though. Dispatch just got an anonymous call about some black kid dealing weed at Longwood Park."

"Sure, why not?" I unlock my drawer and grab some money out. Since it's just a kid, I decide to forgo using the wire. We opt instead to have Miller park at the curb and watch me from the car. When I rub my hand on my head, it'll signal Miller to move up and help me make the pinch.

It's a still morning, and the sun hasn't yet broken through the fog. The park is empty, with the exception of a lone black guy in the middle of the picnic area. He's leaning against a bench while straddling the seat of a blue bicycle. He sits there calmly, watching me as I walk toward him. The closer I get, the older he looks. By the time I reach him, the *kid* is over six-feet tall.

I ask him for a couple of joints and the deal goes down quickly. I run my fingers through my greasy hair and I hear Miller's car door open behind me. The dealer's eyes flash panic and I tell him to freeze. He steps off his bike, then picks it up over his head and heaves it at me. It crashes down onto my raised forearm with a painful thud. I shed it off, and the kid is already several strides into the park. The foot chase is on.

He's running like a jackal, and I'm chasing like a guy who has to cheat on the SWAT test. I hear Miller huffing and puffing behind me, but he's still about fifty yards back. We come to a narrow opening at a cyclone fence and the dude gets hung up. It's only for a second, but it's enough for me to catch up to him. I tackle him to the grass just beyond the fence, and Miller helps me hold the kid down while I put him in cuffs. We walk him back across the park, put his bike into Miller's trunk, and drive the weed dealer back to the station.

My 6-foot-2 suspect turns out to be five days shy of his eighteenth birthday—a juvenile, according to California law. I get a patrol cop to transport him to Juvenile Hall for me.

Van Kirk and Salami are in the office when we get back. None of us know where the sarge is, so we all just work on reports. Two guys I know from the sheriff's narc unit call me about helping them serve a search warrant later in the day. I agree to help and I log it on the board for 3 p.m.

Just as I'm sitting back down, the office door springs open. The sarge storms in and slams it closed behind him. The four of us sit at our desks in silence. Roberts looks right at each of us, one at a time. His face is red, but he still hasn't said a word. Then he unbuckles his belt, unzips his brown corduroy pants, and pulls them down around his knees. In another swift motion, he drops his underpants and swings his backside around toward us. We're all just sitting there in shock, staring at our sergeant's hairy white ass.

"Is there anything left back there?" he yells.

"What the hell are you doing, Sarge?" Van Kirk asks nervously.

"I want to know if I've got anything left after the ass chewing I just got from the chief!"

We all ask at once what the ass chewing was about.

"Everything!" He slowly pulls his pants back up. "The accreditation review, the photos on the wall, the cussing over the radio, the names carved into the cement. All of it! But the last straw was the Hog Heaven search warrant. Sessions and his attorney filed a complaint with IA, and they're probably going to sue us."

"For what?" Van Kirk throws his hands up in indignation. We all just look at him.

"Per the chief, we now have a new policy." Roberts yanks the latest Beauty Queen off the wall and slams her into the trash. "The only photos we're going to be taking are before and after shots of our search warrants."

"What!?!?" A collective cry rings out.

"That's right." He swings a hand toward the search warrant board. "Every search warrant we execute now requires photo documentation. We take pictures before we start searching, and we take pictures after we're done."

"What happens if a place gets a little bit messed up?" Salami asks.

"It won't!" The sarge eyeballs each of us sternly. "Every photo gets routed to the chief's office. Got me? No more dumping out drawers and no more tossing things around. If that means we have to straighten things up, then we straighten things up. And goddamnit, there better not be so much as a rumpled bed or a cracked ashtray. Not a speck of damage!"

There's a light knock on the office door and we're all thankful for the interlude. Detective Fowler asks Roberts if this is a good time to borrow me for the Mackler case. I'm already up and putting on the wire, relieved to have a valid excuse to run off. The lecture is pretty much over anyway, and the other guys are all trying to find something to do. I hold my arms up as Miller tapes the harness down, and Roberts sees the bruises on my forearms caused by the thrown bicycle.

"What the hell happened to you?"

Miller and I look at each other. "Nothing." I realize my answer came too fast and was not very convincing. "I got banged up the other day at training." Probably not the best time to tell him that Miller and I put together a half-baked arrest plan, ending up in a bicycle assault, foot chase, and forcible face-in-the-dirt arrest of a juvenile.

Fowler briefs me on the particulars: The guy I'm meeting is the murder suspect's current boyfriend, Mitch Tucker. Though he was not involved in the killing five years ago, he is now helping the killer find a way to get rid of the victim's remains. Tucker asked a trusted friend to find someone, and the friend went to the police.

"Mitch Tucker manages a bicycle shop downtown," Fowler says. "All I want you to do is tell Tucker that a mutual friend referred you to him. Let him bring up moving the body." He shows me a photo of Tucker as we all move out to our cars.

A few other detectives move into positions around the bike shop, and my narc partners watch me from the van parked across the street. I light up a cigarette as I cross the street, even though I don't smoke. Tucker is at the top of a stepladder replacing an outside light when I walk up. He glances down at me and stops what he's doing.

His jaw tightens. "What can I do for you?" he asks, though I get the feeling he already knows exactly why I'm there.

"A mutual friend referred me to you." I don't divert from the scripted instructions, even though it sounds a little stilted.

He looks a little frightened, and I wonder if I've overdone it with the ex-con look. Tucker stutters a bit, and tells me that he doesn't know what I'm talking about. I now have to either repeat the same line, or try to improv. I want to stay in character though, and I imagine that your average body-mover would be at least a little irritated by the brush-off. Especially after coming all the way down here on a friend's referral.

"Hey, I'm just trying to help you out," I say. "Your buddy told me I should drop by, so here I am."

Tucker hasn't moved from the top of the ladder, and I feel as if I'm talking to his feet. I squint up into the sun, trying to see his expression. "I don't . . . I don't know anything." The reality of what he's doing appears to be setting in, and he's obviously having second thoughts. "Just leave, okay? Just leave."

I really wanted this to happen, partly to impress the detective and partly to feed my own ego. But it clearly isn't going to come together with this guy. Still in character, I snarl up at Tucker as I take a final drag of my cigarette and then stub it out on his shoe. I walk away wondering if I did that as part of my act, or because I was pissed off at the guy for not taking the bait.

Back at the station, Fowler and I go over the conversation. He heard most of it over the wire and I fill in the garbled parts, leaving out the bit with the cigarette. Even though Tucker didn't take me up on my offer, Fowler wants to make another run at writing a warrant for the Mackler house.

Sergeant Roberts is in his office when I come in. He's had some time to cool off, so I sit down and break the ice by updating him on Fowler's cold case. He's only half-listening, so I keep it short.

"Sarge. You remember I'm leaving a little early today to go to that concert with my wife?"

Roberts gives me a wave of the hand. "Sure, yeah. You can go whenever . . ."

I look at my watch. "We're helping out on that search warrant at three," I remind him. "I'll just take off after that."

We brief at the sheriff's substation on 150th. They tell us that their suspect is a paranoid meth dealer, with a penchant for firearms. Their informant told them that the guy has a machine shop in his garage, and he's altered a couple of rifles to make them fully automatic. Aside from the obvious concerns about getting shot, the whole gun thing reminds me that I have to give Craig Johnson a call.

Roberts interjects at what seems to be the most inopportune time. "We have a new policy at our department," he says, holding up a Polaroid camera. "Unfortunately, I'll be taking before and after photos of the house we're hitting." He tries his best to explain the rule, but the deputies look as baffled after the explanation as they did before it.

The guy running the case assigns Miller and me to handle the entry key. Most of us are packed into their van, while Roberts and the sheriff's sergeant follow in an unmarked sedan. We turn onto Royal Avenue and the lead deputy points out the suspect's house. Our van hits the curb, and Miller and I are the first out. We heft the key quickly up to the porch, and draw it back as the deputy pounds on the door. In one fluid movement, we swing the heavy ram forward into the strike plate. The door splinters open, and we toss the key out of the way. I lead through the doorway, with Miller right behind me.

I've got a combat grip on my handgun as I clear the empty living room. The suspect suddenly springs into the kitchen from the garage, and then darts away from me down a hallway. I round the corner into a hallway, right behind him. I'm trying to see what's he's carrying, but I can't see his hands. I'm yelling at him to freeze, but he's in an all-out sprint. He bursts through a bedroom door and he hurdles over a bed. Other than a closed window, there's nowhere for him to go. He's still moving fast though, and I'm still right on his tail. In that fraction of a second, I see what's about to happen. I duck my head and tuck my gun against my side. Without even slowing down, the guy lunges headfirst into the plate glass window, and I dive along with him. Our momentum carries us all the way through, and onto the front lawn. The suspect lands on a bed of shattered glass, and I land squarely on his back.

The guy wheezes in agony as I holster my gun and wrestle him into handcuffs. I glance up and see Roberts standing there with his camera, glaring at me. The sergeant's car had pulled to the curb a few second after the van, and then it must have taken Roberts another few seconds to grab the camera and get out. It was all the time it took for us to make entry, chase the guy down the hall, and crash through the window. The sheriffs all think it's hilarious. Roberts looks like he needs a drink.

It turns out the suspect is unarmed, but had grabbed his stash and was stuffing it into his pants while trying to make his escape. I find a couple of ounces of meth in a zip-lock bag, tucked down the front of his boxers. Meanwhile, Roberts is taking photos of the broken window.

Figuring that I've done enough damage for one day, I decide to slide out and surprise Gale by getting home early. She's really been looking forward to tonight's concert, and getting home on time for it is sure to score some much-needed points.

I radio for a patrol unit and bum a ride back to the station. It's my buddy, Ryan Kalani. We worked patrol together and had adjoining beats on the South End. He and I both got our special assignments about the same time—me to narcotics and Kalani to the downtown foot patrol.

"Which one of you idiots smashed out the front window?" he says.

I ignore his question. "What are you doing in a car? Aren't you supposed to be walking around harassing drunks?"

He grimaces. "Hemorrhoids are acting up again."

I give Kalani my views about the possible causes of his hemorrhoid problem, and he gives me hell about how ugly I look. We spar back and forth all the way to the station. I walk upstairs to my office, realizing how much I miss working with him. Life was different in uniform. It seemed so organized, as if we were always applying order to chaos. Working narcs is an insane environment without any rules, and most of the time it's us who create the chaos.

Sure is fun though.

I lock my things in the drawer and straighten up the top of my desk. It's 4:20, and I'll easily be home before 5 o'clock. I head out to my car, a little tired from the early mornings and long shifts but looking forward to a night out with Gale.

"Hey, where are you going?" The patrol watch commander leans his head out the back door. "Aren't you listening to the radio?"

"No, I'm off-duty. Why?"

"Better get back in here," he says. "We got a gunman holding hostages, and we've had to call out SWAT."

I close my eyes and lean my head back. "Mother fuck!"

I rush back inside, hoping beyond hope that the situation will resolve itself before the team gets involved. I stop by the sergeants' offices to get a better idea of what's going on. It started as a domestic violence call on A Street, phoned in by the suspect's wife. When the husband realized she had called, he barricaded the doors and grabbed his trusty pistol. He's now holding the wife and two children at gunpoint inside the house.

I do the walk of the condemned, down the hall and into the patrol report-writing room. With a sick feeling in my stomach, I dial the phone. "Gale? You won't believe what's happened."

"Why am I not surprised?" She doesn't even wait to hear the excuse. "I'll call Donna and see if she wants to go with me."

I try to apologize, but she sort of cuts me off before I have a chance. Apparently, Gale's in the middle of feeding the girls, the sitter is on the way over, and now she has to call her friend at the last minute to see if she can go to the concert with her. I hang up the phone, wishing the son-of-a-bitch who caused me all this grief would just shoot himself.

It takes a good couple of hours for the rest of the team to arrive and gather their gear. Then there are the intelligence briefings, the transfer of command from patrol to special operations, and the unloading and setting up of all the equipment. By the time we formally take over the scene, it's nearly seven-thirty.

The night has become damp and ruthlessly cold. I'm standing in the back of the SWAT van, fumbling with my new tactical microphone setup and trying to keep my teeth from chattering.

One of the team sergeants steps in to brief a handful of us. He unrolls a sewer map and points to an address right on the corner. Though I've never had a call there, I've driven by the tiny house a thousand times. The latest update is that the suspect, a Mexican man here illegally, has started drinking Tequila and shouting threats in Spanish. He's still got his family at gunpoint, but at least no shots have been fired. Just as the sergeant finishes, the commander pops his head in.

"We've commandeered the restaurant on the corner as a command post," he says.

It's good news for us, because it'll be much warmer and there will likely be plenty of food. I can also use better lighting. I've spent the last fifteen minutes fiddling with the new push-to-talk radio transmitter. The mic is pinned to my lapel the way we were instructed, and I've managed to thread the wires down the inside of my shirtsleeve. But in the dark van, I haven't been able to figure out the damn buttons. I probably should have paid more attention to the instructions during the last training.

I flounce into a padded corner booth, warmer now and eyeing the place for something to eat. "I sure could use a little sustenance," I say to nobody in particular.

A couple of the guys laugh at my unpolished demeanor. "I think there's some coffee behind the counter," one of them says.

I get up to check, and the team commander comes in carrying a clipboard. "You, you, and you," he says. "Come with me."

Three of us follow him outside and around the corner, to a cluster of lieutenants, sergeants, detectives, and hostage negotiators. They've pinned a couple of giant sheets of paper on the wall, documenting everything we currently know about the suspect. One of the detectives has a stack of eight-by-ten photographs of the guy, which appear to be enlargements of a booking photo. He hands one to each of us.

"You three are going to replace patrol on the inner-perimeter," the commander says. "We want you in as tight as you can, leaving no possible way for this guy to escape."

An anxious voice comes over the air, followed by a sudden surge of activity. A sniper reports that he sees someone coming out the back door of the house. Everybody tenses. My radio is flooded with garbled traffic as too many people try to transmit at once.

"It's the wife and kids," the sniper says. "Get them out of there!" A small team staged near the fence line moves in and quickly escorts them away from the house.

I assume Pancho Villa lost track of his family momentarily while refilling his shot glass. Lucky for the wife, she was able to grab up the kids and take advantage of the situation. It also makes our job easier, now having only to deal with the suspect.

"He's at the window," the sniper says. "He's figured out that they've split."

The commander turns to the three of us. "Get up there now, and lock down that inner-perimeter!"

We take off on a diagonal course across the street, deploying around the back and on both sides of the house. The exposed front is covered by another pair of cops, hunkered down with assault rifles, behind a patrol car. I end up in a small planter box full of shrubs on the west side of the house. I'm crouched right beneath a bedroom window.

Meanwhile a Spanish-speaking negotiator is on the phone with the suspect, trying to reason with him. My Spanish is primitive at best, but even I can tell the negotiator isn't having much luck. The gunman keeps hanging up on him. With no hostages left and the suspect confined to the house, the process becomes methodical and drawn out.

I'm stooped over, in the same position for what seems like hours. I feel like I'm frozen solid, and the entire time the suspect is drinking and listening to music in a warm room right above me. I adjust myself, trying to find a more comfortable position.

"Negotiations is attempting another call," the commander says over the radio. "Suspect's not answering. Can anybody on the perimeter hear if the phone is ringing?"

I feel around for my mic control buttons and flip a switch that I hope is the right one. "It's ringing," I report. "But all he's doing is singing."

The night drags on. I recline against a bush and stretch my legs out flat on the ground, finally settling into a position of relative comfort. I holster my gun, button the top button of my jacket and tuck my hands under my armpits. Radio traffic has all but ceased, and there's been little activity inside the house for an hour. The suspect puts on a particularly soothing ballad, and I rest my head back as I listen. The gentle sound of the little Mexican lullaby seems to ease the burdens of my day.

I close my eyes. *So soft, so warm, so sweet . . .*

14

Internal Affairs

"Security check!" a dispatcher's voice barks into my headset.

Oh, shit! How long have I been asleep?

I clear my throat. "Nora-forty-six, I'm okay."

"Did you hear us calling you?"

"Uh . . . The suspect's music was a little loud. I must have . . ." My words trail off in yet another sorry excuse—my second of the night.

I scurry to my knees. Then, and at the risk of getting my head shot off, I peek into the window. Thank God, the suspect is still in there. He's passed out on the bed now, with an empty bottle of Tequila lying next to him. I briefly consider what would have happened if the guy had escaped during my lapse of vigilance. *I wonder which one of us fell asleep first.*

I fiddle with the button again, sliding the switch randomly in an attempt to activate my radio. I advise the command post that I can now see the suspect unconscious on the bed. The commander orders me to take aim at the suspect, and cover him through the window while a team makes a stealth entry.

The guy doesn't move a muscle, and he's still motionless when the team rushes in to take him. I'm immediately struck with a new fear now. *What if he shot himself and he's been lying there dead all this time. Could I have possibly missed a gunshot?*

Thankfully, he's only drunk. He groggily submits to handcuffing, and the entry team recovers his small pistol from the nightstand next to him. They drag the guy outside to a waiting patrol car, and whisk him away. We gather our gear and load up all our equipment. Several of us squish ourselves into the back of the SWAT van for our short ride back to the station. I check my watch and see it's close to midnight.

Gale should be back from the concert by now. I hope she's not too upset with me.

Laughter erupts as one of the guys retells an episode from earlier in the night. "You heard it too?" one of them asks.

A couple of the guys laugh some more. "Yeah, we all heard it."

"Heard what?" I ask.

"Snoring over the radio."

A wave of panic hits me. "Snoring?"

"Yeah, some idiot must have set his controls on voice-activated. Every time he snored, it transmitted over the radio."

"Heh." I manage one measly laugh. "The suspect's music was so loud I must not have heard it."

I slowly slide my hand down to my side and grope in the darkness for my control button. While the story moves on to something else, I thumb the button to make sure it's not still on.

* * *

It's Saturday and I'm determined to make it up to Gale. The girls and I pack some snacks for us, and some old bread for the ducks. It's a warm day at the park, and it's the first time in a while that we've done something as a family.

I'm thinking about my investigations while we walk. *I should give Craig Johnson a call about that gun place.* I spend most of our time telling Gale all about work—my failed attempt at moving a murder victim, the heroin buys on Sonoma, the Hog Heaven law suit, and the ridiculous marijuana buys the task force has me making from that dumb kid. Then, in what might be considered even worse timing, I mention to Gale that the annual narcotic officers' conference is coming up. "The whole unit will be going to San Diego for a week," I say.

She lets out a tired sigh. "That sounds like fun."

Her words sound less than sincere. Probably more out of guilt than conviction, I start in with my sermon about the demands of my job. While the girls feed the ducks, Gale and I sit together on a bench—far enough away that we can talk privately. When I'm finished telling her how hard I work, Gale informs me that she's unhappy.

"I feel like I don't know you anymore," she says.

"Fine. I won't go to the conference then."

"It's not about the conference." Gale stops to tell the girls not to get too close to the water. "And it's not about missing the concert."

"Then what is it about?"

She takes a breath. "I spend all day with the girls; watching Sesame Street with them, playing Barbie with them, fixing their meals and bathing them."

"You wanted to be able to stay home," I say. "We talked about it and you chose to be a stay-at-home mom. You should be glad I have a job that allows you not to have to work."

"I am glad. And I love being able to spend time with the girls." Gale's eyes start to water. "It's just that, all day long I look forward to you coming home. Sometimes I just really need adult conversation. I need some quality time with you."

"And?" I lean forward with open hands.

"And, what little time you are home you might as well not even be there. It's like you don't want to be with us. Like I'm boring to you. Like you can hardly wait to get back to work."

I can't believe she's ruining a nice day with this stuff. I've never said anything to make her feel that way. "So, you're jealous that I enjoy my job more than you enjoy yours."

Gale looks away as a group of women pass. Neither of us says anything. They walk up the steps of the community center, chatting happily and carrying their arts & crafts supplies.

"Why don't you do like them?" I motion toward the building. "Join a club or do some activity with other moms."

Gale rolls her eyes as if I don't get it.

"You can't lay all that on me," I tell her. "I worked hard to get into narcs. I've waited a long time to get my shot. I'm trying to make a name for myself... move up in the department and make a decent life for us. You're just going to have to find your own happiness."

Neither of us says anything more. We sit there for a long time, absorbed in our own thoughts. When the last of the bread is gone, the girls join us on the bench. They describe each of the ducks by name as we walk home.

Even though I've gotten into my defensive mode, I know some of what Gale says is right. I need to stop with all the work stories. Maybe take the girls to the park more often or give them their baths once in a while.

* * *

I walk into a somber office on Monday morning. Van Kirk, Miller and Salami are sitting at their desks, and the room is unusually quiet. Sarge and Smitty follow me in, and I see they have the same troubled look on their faces.

"Somebody die?" I toss my duffel bag on my desk.

"We got a leak." Miller says.

I look around the room at each of them. "A leak. How do you know?"

"My CI told me," Miller says. "Somehow Bryce Feldman found out we're tracking his calls. He disconnected his phone and his attorney filed some kind of an injunction."

"Who's your CI on the case?" Sergeant Roberts asks.

Miller stammers for a second, as if he'd rather not say. "It's the mother of Feldman's fiancé, Lisa Molinari."

We all start laughing. Though it doesn't take anything away from the seriousness of the information leak, the image of Miller meeting secretly with the suspect's soon-to-be mother-in-law is comical.

"What's her motivation?" Roberts asks.

"She doesn't want her daughter to marry the guy," Miller says. "Everybody knows he's a drug dealer, but he's never been caught. She wants us to put a case on the guy so he goes away to prison."

We all laugh some more. "I can see it now," Van Kirk says. "Mrs. Molinari down in the barrio, making a drug buy with The Big A."

I chuckle along with the rest of them. Then I look around at my cohorts and consider the possibility that the leak may have come from someone in the room. Without being obvious, I gaze from one person to the next.

The sergeant? Smitty? Nah, they've both been around long enough to know not to talk. Salami? He hasn't learned enough to even know what to blab. What about Van Kirk? Maybe he's told the Hawaiian officer a few things he shouldn't have. Then I look over at Miller. He wouldn't intentionally derail his own case, but then again I could see him trusting the wrong person with a secret. After all, he did spend the night on the office floor last week, and I know there was more to that. Come to think of it, wasn't he meeting with an informant the night before? Now my thoughts have taken off in another direction. Could Miller be banging the old lady—Mrs. Molinari?

A knock at the door rattles me from my suspicions, and Roberts leans over to open it. Sergeant Clawson asks if he can speak with Roberts and me in his office. Clawson used to be one of my nightshift sergeants on patrol, but now he's the head of Internal Affairs. The whole way across the building, I'm trying to figure out what thing I did that has gotten me into trouble. Could someone have identified me by the sound of my snoring? Gale is the only person who is capable of that, and the way she's been feeling about me lately she might have.

"Close the door." Clawson squeezes behind his desk, and Roberts and I sit down. "You've been named in a formal complaint," Clawson says to me. "And I'm obligated by policy to notify you that I'll be looking into it."

I can feel Roberts' eyes burning a hole in the side of my head. "Can you tell me what it's about?" I ask.

Clawson says that he wasn't the person who actually took the complaint, so he hasn't read it yet. "All I know is the boy's family came in and contacted Lieutenant Preston," he says.

I can't even look at the sarge. We both know Preston's been licking his chops to find something he can use against us. Now, it seems *that something* has fallen right into his lap.

"What boy?" Roberts asks.

I perk up. "Yeah, what boy?"

Clawson checks his notes. "Some kid you arrested at Longwood Park."

I feel as if a weight is suddenly lifted off me. "Oh, that. There's nothing to worry about." I assure them. "It was a straight forward buy-bust." *Whooo!* I let out a sigh. "What's *he* complaining about?"

Roberts jumps in before I get an answer. "Wait! What arrest at Longwood Park?"

I grit my teeth. "Ooh yeah. I forgot to mention it to you, Sarge. Just a little operation me and Miller put together the other morning." Roberts closes his eyes, and I can almost hear him counting to ten.

I raise my arms in a demonstration of transparency. "Anonymous caller, quick hand-to-hand sale, and an arrest. The only thing out of the ordinary was the guy tossed his bicycle at me and then tried to run. Other than that—nothing much to it."

I alternate glances between the two sergeants. Clawson doesn't seem all that concerned, but Roberts gives me a dad-like look that says, *I'll deal with you later.*

"Well, I'll need memos from you and Miller about what took place," Clawson says. "And if that's all there was to it, then you've got nothing to worry about."

I thank Clawson politely, hoping that his assessment is accurate. I really like Clawson, but this is the same guy I watched sucking down a bottle of booze in a patrol car one night. He never knew I saw him, but the incident definitely left me with questions about his fitness for the job. Now, my whole career may hinge on his ability to investigate this complaint competently.

Salami and Van Kirk are suiting up when we get back to the office. Van Kirk is on the board for a search warrant, and thankfully that doesn't give Sarge any time to bawl me out. Miller comes in and while we're putting on our gear, I tell him about the complaint. He snorts it off like it's the least of his concerns.

During the briefing, Van Kirk describes our mission. We'll be hitting an old-time PCP dealer by the name of Laurel Quincy. She's been busted a half-dozen times, and she gets slicker and more difficult to catch each time. The warrant is for a big house up on Grandview, where she lives with her four Pit Bull dogs. According to Van Kirk, the old lady has them loose in the front yard for protection.

"What's your plan to deal with the dogs?" asks Sarge.

Van Kirk shrugs. "Shoot 'em if they attack us."

Roberts shakes his head in anguish. "That's just what we need right now." Then, like I've seen him do so many times before, Roberts comes up with a brilliant idea. "How about getting the animal services truck over here. I'm sure they deal with Quincy and her dogs all the time."

"Then what?" Van Kirk asks.

"Then we all hide in the truck's doggie compartments and we drive right up." Roberts smiles proudly. "She thinks animal services is there to cite her for letting her dogs off leash, so she chains them up. Once that happens, we jump out and raid the place."

Sometimes I think the guy is a genius. Everybody loves the plan, and other than my claustrophobia, I'm onboard as well. I'll just keep my cage door propped open a crack so I don't panic.

We meet the animal services officer a few blocks away, and Roberts describes our plan to her. She graciously wipes down the cages with disinfectant, before we climb inside. Roberts rides up front with her, while the four of us each jam ourselves into the cages. We bark wildly as the truck pulls right up the driveway.

I hear some dialogue, and it sounds like the animal services officer is telling Quincy to tie up the dogs. A minute later Roberts pounds on the side of the truck. Quincy's eyes register sheer shock as she watches four hairy men climb out of the cages.

We run past the tethered dogs, and make a safe entry. Quincy ends up in jail behind a possession for sale charge, and the dogs are taken to the shelter. The successful operation does a lot to loosen Roberts up, but I definitely don't want to do anything else to piss him off. He takes his *after* photographs, and seems pleased that no damage was done this time.

Roberts checks his watch. "Let's move. We gotta get back to the station."

We ask him what's going on, and he tells us there's a departmental inspection at 2 p.m. I remember seeing something about it in my mailbox, but didn't realize it applied to the narcs.

"They want us in uniform?" Miller asks—his beard as long as mine.

"The whole department," Roberts says. "It's all part of that damn accreditation thing. They want to do a formal inspection of each and every employee in the building. That means long sleeve shirts, ties, hats, and Class-A jackets."

Miller and I help Van Kirk unload the van and then log all his evidence. We have just enough time after that to get down to the locker room and change. Had I known about the inspection, I could have polished my brass and shined my shoes. This would have been a perfect time for the unit to rehabilitate it's poor reputation with the accreditation committee.

I throw open my locker and my heart is paralyzed with panic. "Shit! My shirts aren't here." I realize I must have brought them home to be laundered when I transferred out of patrol, thinking it would be a few years before they would be needed again. They're probably still at the cleaners. Neither Miller nor Van Kirk has an extra one, but Salami has a shirt he can lend me. It's twice my size and it's got short sleeves, but it'll have to do.

Salami tosses the shirt to me. "As long as you keep your jacket on, nobody will notice that it's not regulation."

I tuck it in as best I can, and put the formal jacket on to cover the sleeves. Roberts pulls us into a corner of the back lot to go over the commands with us. He says there should only be a few: come to attention, present arms, and present whistles. "You all have your whistles, right?"

We all check our pockets and pull them out to show him. I shake my head in amazement. *A bunch of professional adults presenting goddamn whistles—how ridiculous is that? But we'll all be accredited.*

The command staff comes out the back door with the blue ribbon accreditation committee on their heels. They pause to look at the two hundred or so employees—many of whom are here on paid overtime to present their beloved whistles.

I see that Lieutenant Suckass Preston is leading the inspection, and I hear Van Kirk mumble something under his breath. Roberts gives him a dirty look, and then shoots one at me for good measure. I'm standing like a military honor guard, determined not to screw this up.

The drill goes off without a hitch, and I execute all the commands perfectly. Just as I'm putting my whistle back into my pocket, I notice Preston working his way down my line. With the commanders and the accreditation committee following closely behind, Preston comes to a stop right in front of me.

He gives me a sly grin and I know something bad is coming. In the elongated preparatory order he barks, "R-e-e-move jackets!"

That dirty son-of-a-bitch. There's no inspection command to remove jackets! He overheard us in the locker room! He knew I didn't have a long sleeve shirt!

The rest of the police employees are baffled. Just the same, they unbutton and remove their jackets. I slowly work mine off, trying to quickly figure something out. Nothing comes to me. With hundreds of eyes now on me, I pull my jacket off and stand there at attention. My floppy short sleeve shirt, half untucked, hangs on me like a Halloween costume. I'm staring straight ahead, and without even seeing him I know Preston has a massive smile on his face, if not a burgeoning tent in his pants. I hear Roberts let out a child-like whimper behind me, and I feel terrible.

Damn that Preston. This time he's gone too far. He obviously doesn't know who he's messing with.

There's no wind left in our sails, and the rest of the day is pretty much shot. We hang around the office doing paperwork, and Roberts leaves early. Van Kirk and I scheme about different ways we might get back at Preston, but it's all just talk. He's a lieutenant—one of only eight in the department, and he's three ranks higher than either of us.

We spend a couple of hours surveilling Bryce Feldman's house, grabbing a couple of new license numbers from visiting cars in the process. It'll be harder, now that he knows we're watching him.

It's dark when I finally leave the building, and the last of the swing shift cars are pulling out of the back gate. One of their sergeants, a guy I don't much care for, sees me and makes a hurried effort to get to me before I drive off. He's Evan Casey—a used car salesman of a guy who's cut from the same mold as Preston. Casey slows his roll and swaggers up to me, still wearing his formal inspection uniform.

"Hey, Phil," he extends a hand and I hesitantly shake it. "Glad I caught you."

"What's going on, Sarge?"

"I can't say where I heard it . . . but rumor has it there might be some changes in the narc unit soon." He gives me a wink and I nearly puke. "Hypothetically, if Roberts was to be transferred out, what do you think about me taking his place?"

If I took a dump on your shiny shoes, it wouldn't even begin to describe what I think. This guy went behind my back one night on patrol, and released one of my prisoners from jail—a suspect who had fought me and tried to grab my nightstick. Casey even drove the dude home!

"Can I count on your support as Roberts' replacement?" Casey stands there eagerly.

How can I be diplomatic? "Well 'hypothetically,' Sarge, this whole thing is kind of catching me by surprise. Besides that, I'm only one guy in there, and none of us would even have a say about who the new sergeant would be."

"I know, I know." Casey looks around to make sure we're alone. "But you're kind of the big fish in the narc unit now, and I think the commanders will listen to you."

This guy's gotta be kidding. Hello? Were you not at the inspection today?

I stay non-committal, and squirm my way out of a firm answer. I drive out of the lot, amazed at Casey's arrogance. This guy wouldn't bother to piss on me if I were on fire.

I take a detour downtown on my way home, hoping to see my buddy, Kalani. He should be out here on foot patrol somewhere. After driving past the most obvious spots, I finally give up. I pass the adult bookstore at Mission and A, and remember that the clerk, a Fijian guy named Aaron, gave me information once in a while when I was on patrol. I park in the back and find Aaron working behind the counter. We talk for a while and he catches me up on what's going on in his life. Though I was hoping to hear some information about a kilo cocaine dealer, he's got nothing for me.

"Hey, you haven't seen Kalani tonight, have you?" I ask Aaron.

He smiles. "Yeah, he's here."

"What do you mean, here?" I look around.

Aaron lets out a laugh. "Yeah, he's back there in booth number four."

I walk behind the curtain to a row of rickety black stalls, covered by flimsy plywood doors. I get to number four and push the door open.

There's Kalani, slouched back against the worn seat, smoking a cigar and watching one of the films.

We leave the bookstore together and talk out in the lot for a good hour. He tells me about the goings on downtown, the politics of the walking beat, and the latest scandals on patrol. I bring him up to date on the rumor about Roberts leaving and the craziness of the narc unit. Once I've gotten it all out, I feel spent and ready to head home.

* * *

I get the feeling Miller has also heard the rumor about Roberts' position, and for all I know it could have been from that weasel, Casey. He's probably making the rounds, pandering for the spot. We tell Van Kirk what we've heard and he thinks Preston is behind the whole thing.

I want to get my own investigations moving again, and hope to squeeze in a decent case before we take off to the conference. I've left a couple of messages for Craig Johnson, but I haven't heard anything back. I call again, but hang up when his recorder comes on.

The guys are trying to talk the sarge into a night of barkers and bones at the PBA, and even with everything that's happened it looks like he's up for it. I figure it's a good night for me to take a pass and spend some time at home. They all take off around 7 p.m., while I stick around to finish up a report. I'm about to lock up my desk when someone knocks on the office door.

It's Clawson, the IA sergeant. His face is red and I can't tell if he's knocked back a couple or he's pissed off. He wants to talk privately and I tell him that the rest of my unit is gone. He steps in and closes the door.

"You didn't tell me that the kid was black," he says.

"The kid I arrested? Yeah, he's black. So what?"

Clawson grimaces. "It complicates things. It could get political: white cop, black youth, brutality allegation . . ."

"Whoa, whoa, hold the phone. He's claiming police brutality?"

Clawson nods. "And to tell you the truth, I haven't been able to find any witnesses."

"What about Miller? He saw the whole thing."

Clawson shakes his head. “Another cop? That means nothing in a case like this. It boils down to your word against the kid’s. He’s saying that you smashed his bicycle and beat him up.”

I can feel my blood boiling. “I had bruises on my arms to prove it.”

“Did you charge him with assaulting a police officer?”

“Well, no.”

“Take evidence photos of your bruised arms?”

I shake my head. Now I feel like a total idiot. “Sergeant Roberts had been pissed off at us for drawing so much negative attention to the unit,” I tell him. “I just didn’t want to make a big deal out of it.”

Clawson looks like he doesn’t believe me.

“Besides,” I say, “he was only a juvenile. So he tossed a bicycle at me and ran. So what? We chased him down and drug his ass back to the car. There was no nightstick, no pepper spray, not even a slap on the back of the head.”

“Well, I don’t know what to tell you.” Clawson scratches his head. “I’ve done my best to find you a witness, but . . . you may want to contact the police association and get yourself an attorney.”

I walk back to the office in a daze. I’ve done a few stupid things in the heat of anger before, but this wasn’t one of them. I can’t believe my whole career could come unhinged behind something I didn’t even do. I sit down at my desk, thinking that this night couldn’t possibly get any worse. And then the phone rings.

“Narcotics,” I answer flatly.

“This is Sergeant Shibata with the Oakland police department. Did you leave a message on Craig Johnson’s home phone?”

“Yeah,” I say. “A couple of them.”

“Can I ask why you were calling him?”

I pause for a second, wondering if this guy is legit. “Can you first tell me what this is all about?”

“He’s dead,” the sergeant says without emotion. “Craig Johnson was gunned down on his front porch yesterday.”

15

Sample This

I make pancakes for the girls and watch TV with them while we eat. Gale catches an extra few minutes of sleep, though I'm guessing she's wide-awake and listening to everything we're doing.

She comes out of the room stretching and yawning, and then thanks me for letting her sleep in. As I offer her some pancakes, I wonder when raising the girls became all her responsibility. *Probably when I stopped doing my part.*

While the girls sing along with their show, Gale and I talk at the table. I describe the phone call I got from the Oakland sergeant. "My informant was killed," I tell her. "At first I thought the gunrunners he had told me about found out he was a snitch, and killed him for talking to me."

Gale picks up the plates and brings them to the sink.

"Turns out it wasn't that." I wipe the sticky spots of maple syrup from the table. "His girlfriend shot him with a shotgun."

"Oh my God, why?"

"I guess she caught him with another girl or something." I guzzle the last of my milk, and then bring the glass over. "She seemed kind of jealous anyway. Always checking to see who he was leaving with. The detective that called me said she blasted the poor son-of-a-bitch as he was walking in the front door."

"Do you feel bad?" Gale leans against the counter.

"Well yeah, sort of." I put my glass in the sink. "I mean, I didn't know him that well or anything, but it's still sad. Not to mention, now my gun case goes down the shitter."

When I get to work, I gather all my files on the machine gun dealers and copy them. I'm about to bring the whole packet up to Oakland when I get a phone call from Becky Cranson. She sounds excited, and wants to meet me as soon as possible. I ask if she's got another meth lab for me and she just giggles. I tell her I'm on my way to Oakland, but that she can ride with me and we'll talk on the way.

I pick Becky up at a bus stop on Mission. Her fifty-something year old mother is sitting on the bench with her, and I remember Becky telling me that they often whore together. Still can't get my mind around that one.

"Let's stop for ice cream," Becky says as she climbs into the car and waves goodbye to Mom.

It's 10 o'clock in the morning and she wants ice cream? I can tell she's already had her morning fix. I stare into a mouthful of rotting teeth, knowing exactly how they got that way. The heroin she shoots is probably cut with powdered creamer or baby formula—something with high sugar content. They get as addicted to the sugar as they do the heroin.

"Got yourself a little sweet tooth?" I say, looking at one particularly gnarled eyetooth in front. She giggles again. We stop at a little market and I buy her a Klondike Bar.

Becky drags a long tongue along the chocolaty siding and then thrusts the ice cream bar at me. "Wanna lick?"

I decline her generous offer. While we cruise north on the freeway, I steer Becky back to the purported reason for our meeting. She tells me about a guy she recently met who told her he makes crank. "His operation isn't as big as the guy I gave you in Oakland, but he's always got some."

I park in a red zone in front of the police building, and toss my business card on the dashboard. My gun case packet is left with an Oakland detective who's part of a federal weapons task force. He seems interested in taking over the case, and maybe a little surprised that I'm handing it over so readily. When I tell him that my only informant on it is no longer with us, he gets it. If he and his task force are aware of these suspects and are already building a case against them, the detective doesn't say. He thanks me for the copied file, just the same.

I return to find Becky slunk down in the passenger seat of my car. "All these cops around here make me nervous."

I remind her that I'm a cop, but she just laughs. "I can't imagine you all shaved up and in a uniform."

I return to my own city and she directs me down Santa Clara Street. Becky points to a small house at the end of a driveway and I jot down the address. No cars are parked out front, and the place looks abandoned. "So, how long ago did you meet this guy?" I ask.

"It wasn't that long ago," she says. "Maybe a couple of weeks, or a month at the most."

She tells me that meth dealer's name is Todd, and she describes him as "big and fat." I drop Becky back at her bus stop and tell her I'll be in touch if anything comes of the information.

Grandma Cranson, apparently busy somewhere with a customer, is no longer waiting on the bench. As I pull away, spontaneous imagery appears in my head of the old lady giving some guy a blowjob. I do my best to shake it from my mind as I drive back to the station.

The board has me down for another buy in Fremont. It'll be my fourth one from that pathetic kid whose own father set him up. The board also shows *B&B @ PBA*, which I'm certain means another night of drinking at the police benevolent association bar.

I sit down on a chair in Sergeant Roberts' office. "Sarge, I gotta tell you, I'm feeling a little kicked around by this Fremont case. It's bad enough that it's only a weed case, but four buys? What are we trying to do to this kid?"

He holds his hands up. "I know, I know. I can't argue with you on this one. You probably have more important things to work on, and this case has dragged on long enough. I'll give their sergeant a call."

I thank him and return next door to my office. He comes in a few minutes later and gives me the good news-bad news: They agreed to wrap up the case today, but they want to do a final buy and then bust the kid out.

As if to light a spark of optimism in the unit, Roberts grabs a grease pen and goes to the board. In big letters he prints, *NARC CONFERENCE IN SD NEXT WEEK!*

I call the kid to set up another half-ounce buy. The wire is taped in place, and I follow the van down the freeway to Fremont. We meet with the T-NET guys in the same lot where the other buys took place. They ask what the bust signal will be and I tell them, "Klondike Bar."

As soon as they pull the van out of the way, the kid drives into the lot. He waves me over and I get into the passenger seat. We talk for a minute or so, and then he slides out a baggie from under his seat. He hands it to me and I hand him the cash.

"You know what I feel like?" I tell the kid. "I feel like one of those Klondike Bars."

"I love those," he says. "Especially when I've got the munchies."

Just then the other unmarked cars pull up and the cops run up with guns drawn. I close my eyes and shake my head. They take the poor kid out of the car and sit him on the curb in handcuffs.

I get out with the baggie of weed and grab a flashlight from our van. With a pen and evidence envelope from the raid kit, I package the drugs and begin filling out the evidence tag. The kid watches me from the curb, but says nothing. When I finish, I hand it to the task force sergeant and we talk about getting together at the conference. He wants to buy me a drink for helping them on this case.

Meanwhile, one of the other cops is searching the kid's car to see if he has any more drugs stashed inside. I walk over and hand him my flashlight so he can check under the seat.

The kid watches in confusion, and then he finally calls out to me. "Wait a minute. Hey Phil, you know these guys?"

All the cops break into hysterics. A little jabbing pain hits me in the gut, and I suddenly feel for the kid. Dumb as a rock, and now squashed under four separate felony counts, the poor sap doesn't even know that he was setup by his own dad. Ashamedly, I laugh along with the rest of them.

The task force guys meet us up at the PBA after work, and we have a spirited game of liars dice. Miller gets pissed off and accuses Van Kirk of cheating, and I nearly spit out my hotdog. The place is crowded with police types, court clerks, and the like. Even Judge Joya has decided to stop by. She's drinking at the other end of the bar with a group of bailiffs. It's the first time I've seen a judge at the PBA. I give her a friendly wave, just to keep on her good side.

A few drinks later, I pull Van Kirk off to the side and bust him with the Hawaiian officer story. He denies he ever brought her up here, but he's laughing so hard that I know it's true. We work our way back up to the bar and Van Kirk asks Larry if he has any *straws*. Larry reaches into the refrigerator and in all seriousness, hands Van Kirk a bottle of Stroh's. We laugh until we can't breathe. I wonder to myself if it's really all that funny, or if I've just had too much to drink.

Sarge asks if I've heard anymore about the brutality complaint against me, and that effectively kills the night's buzz. I give him and the other guys a rundown on what the IA sergeant told me, including the fact that without any witnesses it's the kid's word against mine. That gets everyone pretty steamed up, so of course we order another round.

"I wonder how hard Clawson looked for witnesses," Miller says. We all nod our consensus as our fresh drinks arrive.

A new dice game starts up and I sit it out. Miller's comment has got me thinking, and I realize something about this whole IA investigation has gnawed at me from the beginning. The original information came as an anonymous call into dispatch about the kid dealing drugs in the park. But when we arrived, the streets were deserted and the suspect was the only one in the area. So who called it in? If there was nobody around, the call had to have come from someone who lives there. Probably some nosey old retired lady who watches out her window all day. *I'll bet I can find my witness.*

My judgment partially clouded by frustration and the rest clouded by alcohol, I decide that 10 o'clock at night is an appropriate time for a bearded drunk to investigate a brutality complaint in which he is the accused. I leave the PBA on a mission.

I pull to the curb at the exact spot we stopped on the day of the arrest. The park is empty and dark, and the surrounding neighborhood is quiet. I glance around at the homes, trying to figure out which would have the best views of the park. I turn up my radio volume until it's blaring, and then I just watch. It takes less than a minute before a hand lifts the blinds in a house across the street, and someone peeks out at me.

As I get to the front door, I hear that the TV is still on. I knock and an elderly man peeks through the blinds again. "Yes? Can I help you?"

I hold up my badge for him. "I'm an undercover police officer, sir. I'd like to speak with you if it's not too late."

He pauses and then turns to say something to another person inside the house. I can't hear what it is, but I hope he's not telling them to call 9-1-1.

The door opens and the old guy stands there with his wife in the background. A look of recognition slowly appears, and he smiles. "You were the officer who arrested that drug seller in the park a few weeks back," he says. "I thought you looked familiar."

"You saw it!" I accidentally spit the words, and then wonder how badly I'm slurring.

The old man introduces himself as Herman Klingerman, a retired postal worker. He and his wife admit to calling in the report that morning, but say they didn't want to give their names for fear of retaliation. I explain about the citizen's complaint against me for brutality, and they laugh. "We saw the whole thing. He's the one who hit you with a bicycle when you showed him your badge. We watched you and your partner chase after him and put the handcuffs on him. There was no brutality."

I ask if they'd be willing to contact the internal affairs sergeant and give him a statement to that effect. They are more than agreeable. I thank them profusely, and then get the hell out of there before my luck runs out.

My house is dark and warm when I come in, and I lean into the girls' room to see if they're still awake. They're not, so I just listen to their breathing for a few minutes.

I get into bed and curl myself against Gale. She says I smell like the PBA, yet she snuggles with me despite the bouquet of booze, hotdogs, and cigar smoke. Since she's awake, I tell her all about the mishandled IA investigation against me, and how I sniffed out an exonerating witness on my own. She doesn't say it, but I know she's thinking that I'm lucky I didn't make my situation worse. I'm nearly asleep, but I can see Gale staring up at the ceiling.

* * *

A couple of days before the conference Roberts calls us all into the office. He wants Miller to finish up the warrant on Bryce Feldman. "We've been following the guy for months now, and it's time we close this thing out."

I agree. The case has taken up a ton of my time, and it would be nice to finally hit the little prick. For some reason though, I have to wonder if Roberts is under some pressure to make something good happen. We've screwed up a lot lately, and Preston and that damn committee are always breathing down his neck.

The day we decide to hit the place turns out to be unseasonably warm. We put Feldman's house under surveillance about 11 a.m., and then sit there in the blazing sun all afternoon, waiting for him to show up. I'm wearing a tee shirt, shorts and sandals, but I have my vest and gunbelt on the seat next to me, in case we actually do it. Miller comes by and he's got a cooler full of beers. He's driving around to each of us, distributing the drinks. I would have passed on the offer if it weren't so hot. Instead, I go ahead and take a couple of them. No sooner do I down the beers when Bryce Feldman and Rocky Samford, his biker bodyguard, show up. I barely have time to throw on my vest before Roberts comes over the air. "Let's move in!"

Van Kirk and Roberts haven't even gotten out of their cars, but somehow Miller and I are already up the steps and at the screen door. I don't see Feldman inside, but his bodyguard is sitting on the couch right in front of me. He freezes for a second, attempting to process what's going on. The moment I rip the door open he takes off running down the hall. I've just about caught up to him when one of my sandals catches on the carpet, launching me into a nosedive. I lunge forward and wrap my arms around the biker, taking him with me to the ground. Though it may have appeared to be a well-executed maneuver, it was nothing more than an alcohol-inspired belly flop.

We find some drugs and money, and a lot of hand-written records. Because of Feldman's fastidious transaction notes, we're able to put additional criminal conspiracy charges on both of them. The best part is, the case is over with and I'll now have more time to work my own investigations.

* * *

We're taking off for the conference tomorrow, and the rest of the unit has decided not to come in. I want to follow-up on the info Becky gave me about the meth cook, and I'm hoping the office will be quiet for once. I pass Preston's office and see him in there talking on the phone. I scurry by before he sees me.

Once I'm in my office, I phone a guy I know who works for PG&E. We became friends when I was on patrol and investigated an assault on one of his meter readers. In the past he's told me whatever I needed to know, off the record. I'd normally need a search warrant for the information, but he saves me a lot of time by tipping me off as to whether or not writing one would even be worth the effort.

In the case of Becky's dealer, it sounds like it'll be worth writing. The resident of record at the Santa Clara Street address, Todd Harvin, terminated utility service three weeks ago. My friend tells me that PG&E went out to the house after he vacated, and found that Harvin had bypassed the electric meter. The practice is common to meth labs, helping the cook avoid detection because of excessive electricity usage. The fact may come in handy when building probable cause in a search warrant affidavit.

I then check with the post office, and learn that Harvin is having his mail forwarded to an address in Sacramento. *Thank you!*

Another phone line is ringing, so I get off as soon as can I write down the Sacramento location.

I switch over to the next line. "Police narcotics."

A long silence follows. "Officer Miller?"

I tell him I'm not Miller, and I ask for his name.

"It's Richard . . . well, Officer Miller calls me Cone Head."

Miller's crazy informant—the one with Geppetto in his backyard. So glad I rushed off the phone for this lunatic. "Is there something I can help you with, Mr. Head?"

He chuckles, and I'm glad at least someone gets my humor. "I want to put a lawsuit against the USDA," he says. "I think I've been eating tainted spam."

I look at my watch. *I really don't have time for this . . . or do I?*

"Tainted spam, you say." I smile as the idea takes shape in my mind. "Have you had it tested yet?"

"Tested? No. I can't trust the government to do a test on it."

"No, no, I agree. This has to be done in the utmost secrecy." I can't believe my good fortune. "We can test it for you here at the police department."

"You can? Should I bring the spam down to you?"

"Oh no," I say. "Once the spam has been opened, it's of no use for testing. But we can test a stool sample to see if the tainted meat has gone through your digestive system."

"Stool? You mean you want a sample of my own manure?"

"Yes, but it doesn't go to me." I lean my head back in utter ecstasy. "Your sample goes to the lieutenant in charge of investigations. His name is Preston."

"P-r-e-s-t-o-n," Cone Head says as he writes down the name.

"That's right. Now I want you to go find a clear glass jar with a lid." I can barely keep from laughing. "You need to take a shit into the jar and then screw the lid back onto it. Once you've done that, I want you to put it in a plain brown bag and write Lieutenant Preston on the front of it."

"Okay, I'll do it right away."

"When you get off he elevator, tell the secretary you have a private and personal delivery for the lieutenant. He'll be expecting it. And whatever you do, don't mention that you talked to anybody in here."

"Ten-four. I'll be there in less than an hour."

This couldn't have worked out better. First off, the Cone Head doesn't know who he's been talking to, anyway. And even if he did tell someone that it was a narc who told him to bring a jar of shit to the lieutenant, nobody even knows I'm here today. I'm the invisible man.

It's been about 45 minutes since Cone Head's call, and most of the second floor is out at lunch. Rather than get hemmed in inside my office, I take advantage of the empty floor to hide inside a telephone switching closet near the stairway. From there I have a perfect view of the elevator, Mrs. Sasaki's desk, and Preston's office. The big windbag should be back from lunch any minute, so I stand rocking in the dark, with giddy anticipation.

I hear voices coming up the stairwell, and Preston crosses the floor with a group of detectives. Mrs. Sasaki is at her desk, talking on the phone. The elevator light goes on, and after a minute the elevator door opens. Cone Head stands there holding a brown bag like he's a UPS deliveryman. I'm hoping nobody hears the stifled laughter squeaking out of me.

Cone Head leans down as if repeating something to Mrs. Sasaki, but the expression on her face doesn't change. She steps around the desk to take possession of the bag, and then turns and scurries into Preston's office. Cone Head lingers a little, and I'm telling him in my mind to hurry up and get the hell out.

Preston leans back in his chair, loosening his belt after what was probably a gargantuan Chinese lunch. He talks glibly with the secretary as she sets the bag on his desk. I glance over at Cone Head, and the dumbshit is still loitering near Sasaki's desk. *What's he waiting for, the test results?*

Mrs. Sasaki motions to the bag and then pinches her nose. I'm worried that the gig might be up. Nothing gets by that damn Sasaki! But Preston, more curious than intelligent, pulls the bag onto his lap and sweeps the jar up in his big, clumsy hand. He fiddles with the top and finally unscrews it, never considering taking a second to examine the contents through the glass first.

Sasaki must be telling Cone Head to take a hike, because he finally heads for the elevator. Just then Preston flies out of his office wiping his thick hands on his suit pants. He's gesturing like a spastic, and yelling something I can't make out. The elevator doors close just as Preston rounds the file cabinet to the secretary's desk. He might have taken the stairs to find out who left the package, but Preston sprints straight down the hall to the second-floor men's room. I imagine he's either washing some of the *sample* off his hands, or he's throwing up his moo shu pork.

While he's indisposed, I manage to slip out of the utility closet without being noticed, make my way downstairs, and out the back door.

I pack a suitcase after having dinner with my family. I play around with the girls for a while, building a huge dollhouse out of blankets draped over the dining room table. When they finally go to bed, Gale and I have some ice cream while watching a TV movie.

We get into bed and I try to avoid talking about my cases or the conference. My willpower deteriorates after a few minutes, and I describe the ingenious payback I inflicted on Preston. She laughs a little, but it's the kind of laugh that tells me she's grossed out by the story, and doesn't really get the whole payback concept.

After waiting an obligatory few seconds before transitioning, she turns to me. "I got a call from a girl I went to high school with," she says. "They want me to help organize our class reunion."

I cough out a little laugh. "You hated high school. You didn't even go to the first reunion."

"I know, but I've been thinking about something you said."

I'm lying there, wracking my brain to remember something I told her about her reunion.

"That I have to find my own happiness." A long silence follows. "I think getting involved in something like this would be good for me. Good for us."

How would Gale, working with a bunch of people—probably guys—on her class reunion, be good for us? I think she missed my point. I meant joining a knitting club or something, not this. I consider how I might rephrase or even take back that comment, but it's too late. For one thing, she's already asleep.

Tonight it's me who's lying in the dark, staring up at the ceiling.

16

Spiderman

"They never hold these conferences at the same hotel twice," Roberts says as we approach the resort's circular driveway.

I derive my own meaning from the statement. With hundreds of squirrelly-looking narcs from throughout the state, I can only imagine why they wouldn't be welcomed back.

I sign up for a few workshops that appeal to me: meth labs, phone record analysis, organized crime, and major cocaine investigations. I mark down a few others, but I won't mind missing them. Besides attending the workshops, my main objective here is social. I hope to connect with someone from Sacramento, so after the conference I can track down Todd Harvin. And with a little luck, it'll mean taking down another lab.

"Hey!" a voice calls out as we're signing in. "You're that UC who's buying heroin all over the place, aren't you?"

He's a tall, smiling redhead, with a bushy beard. He introduces himself as Kyle Gallagher, sergeant of the Berkeley police narcotics unit. I tell him my name and introduce him to the sarge. They seem to have met before, and they talk briefly about whatever case it was they worked on together.

"I'm glad I ran into you," he says to Roberts. "I've been wanting to work out a trade of some kind, ever since I heard about your Mr. Soto."

They talk a little more about the particulars, but even though the discussion is about me, I'm just a bystander. Roberts knows how I've been feeling about buying for so many cases, especially for other agencies, so he tells the guy that I'm indispensible right now. "Soto's right in the middle of some pretty big investigations," Sarge says.

Gallagher seems like a guy who's been around and who doesn't give up that easily. He flashes his big, Irish grin and turns to me. "I'm not done with you, Soto. We're going to be working together, even if it's the last thing I do."

The entire encounter has taken me by surprise, leaving me elated. It kicks off the conference nicely for me. Truth be told, I'd jump at the chance to buy for Gallagher and his crew in Berkeley. But Roberts was trying to help me out, and I thank him for that. Miller, Salami and Van Kirk whisper among each other then crowd around me asking for my autograph. *Funny.*

I get up early for a tactical entry workshop, but most of the other conference attendees are still in bed. The class is small, but it turns out to be interesting, and worth getting up for. The presenter plays a clip of a police shooting that took place somewhere in Riverside County. It's a reenactment of an actual incident during which a cop was shot in the face. He survived, and was later interviewed on tape as part of the presentation.

As I watch, I can't shake the feeling I've seen the cop before. On the video, his face appeared to have healed well, leaving only a few scars along his jaw line. I glance over at the guy on my left, and notice he's got the same features. His hair is a little longer now, but otherwise he looks the same.

I lean over and nudge him. "Hey," I whisper. "Is that you?"

"Yeah." He leans his head to one side, showing me the extent of his scar. "It happened two years ago."

"You look good." I slap my hand in his. "Glad to see you got through it okay." We talk for a while after class, and then exchange business cards.

A couple of days into the conference, and I find myself at a banquet table with a couple of narcs from Sacramento County's Clandestine Lab Task Force. We get to talking and I tell them about my case. They don't know Todd Harvin, but they seem like great guys and they're eager to help me. I'm invited to come up anytime, and they offer to provide whatever resources I need.

I run into them again later in the evening at Monte Carlo Night, and we have a couple of drinks together. They introduce me to their boss—a supervisor with the State Bureau of Narcotics Enforcement. He and I exchange business cards and he writes his personal number on the back. "Call us after the conference," he says. "We'll be glad to help."

That night I'm bursting with excitement over the connections I've established. I make my nightly call to Gale, but I've missed saying goodnight to the girls by about three hours. *Duh!*

I tell her about the guy shot in the face, and of the potential trade agreement with Berkeley. I decide not to go into my upcoming jaunt to Sacramento however, at least for the time being.

I'm on the phone and Miller is in bathroom, when I hear a raucous commotion in room next door. Miller sticks his head out. "What the hell is that?"

"Can you hear that?" I ask Gale. "It's Roberts and Van Kirk in the next room."

She laughs. "I'm glad you're having fun."

"We have a nice room on the fifth floor, overlooking the bay," I tell her. We're about to hang up, and I apologize for having called so late.

"That's okay," she says. "I just got home anyway, so I was still up."

I look at my watch. "Got home from where?"

"Remember? I told you . . ." The rest of her sentence is obscured by a thunderous crash next door.

"What did you say?"

Gale repeats herself, but there's so much noise I can only make out a few words. It's something about the reunion committee. "We'll talk tomorrow," she says.

We say goodnight, and I get off the phone steaming mad. Mad at all the noise those two dumbshits are making next door, and mad that I couldn't hear what Gale was telling me about her meeting.

Miller and I storm into the hallway just in time to see Van Kirk come flying out of their room. He tells us that Roberts had somehow captured a huge spider and let it loose in Van Kirk's bed. They're laughing and yelling back and forth to each other, and Miller and I just shake our heads.

We're about to go back to our room when the elevator door opens and some guy staggers off. He's hairy and holding a beer bottle, so I'm assuming he's another narc. He stumbles a little, and then straightens up to focus on us. He suddenly runs toward us with wild eyes and a yeti-like growl. The drunk pushes past Van Kirk, and bursts into their room. I hear Roberts yelling at the guy to get out. Miller, Van Kirk and I just look at each other in shock, and then run into the room behind the guy.

By now the lunatic has jumped onto Roberts' bed, and is bouncing up and down on it. Roberts is in the bed, coiled back against the headboard and holding the blankets tightly, like a scared kid. "Who the hell is this guy?" Roberts screams.

None of us have ever seen him before. The guy does a couple of trampoline bounces before jumping off and running over to the sliding doors. He throws them open and then rushes out onto the balcony. "Spiderman!" he hollers. "I'm Spiderman!" The nut climbs out onto the railing and hangs there, five floors up, flailing his free arm.

Monte Carlo Night has just concluded, and now a small crowd has gathered beneath the high wire act. But instead of trying to talk the imbecile down, the group of onlookers starts singing. "Spiderman, Spiderman, does whatever a spider can . . ."

This charges the guy up even more, and now he's trying to do some kind of monkey swing to the next balcony.

"Quick, close the sliding door," yells Roberts. "Lock it!"

By now my stomach hurts from laughing so hard. I step onto the balcony and look down. It would be a deadly fall. But the Great Wallenda still clings precariously to the adjoining railing, waving wildly to the crowd.

The drunken onlookers have stopped singing, and now they've joined hands in a big human circle. "Jump, jump, jump!" They're positioned around an imaginary landing net, but there's nothing there. "Jump, jump, jump!"

I head back inside, and right away I hear police radios squawking below. I assume that by now, someone has called hotel security or San Diego's finest. Miller and I go back to our room and we make sure the door is locked. *No wonder it won't be held here next year.*

Two weeks after returning from the conference it's pretty much common knowledge around the department that Roberts is going to be replaced. Rumors are circulating about a couple of other sergeants who may be interested in the position, and as far as I'm concerned any of them would be better than that complete waste of skin, Evan Casey.

Roberts has entirely lost his fervor for the job, and seems resigned to a fate of going back to patrol. I sit down in his office and lay out the Harvin case file. In the past week I've been able to come up with a couple of vehicles—one registered to Harvin at the old address on Santa Clara Street. The other car is registered to someone else, but Harvin was pulled over in it. And that vehicle happens to be registered to an address in Sacramento. The sarge is only half-listening, and barely acknowledges when I pitch the idea of going up there for a couple of days to work on it. Not that Sacramento is all that far away, but I'd be working on my own, in another county, and submitting my search warrants to DA's and judges who know nothing about me.

"You'll have to get a city credit card from the captain," Sarge says. "And don't do anything dangerous by yourself up there. Make sure you team up with their task force." I assure him that I've already got that part set up.

As I head across the floor to see the captain, Lieutenant Preston steps out of his office and motions me over. He starts making small talk about my cases, as if he really cares, but I can see he's working around to something bigger. He finally asks me about that "informant" that he's seen around.

I know he's talking about Cone Head, though I doubt he's ever seen the guy. The description had to have come from the secretary, Mrs. Sasaki. Preston is undoubtedly been doing his own little investigation to find the mastermind behind the stool sample delivery. I play dumb about Cone Head and throw the lieutenant a confused frown.

"There's a Hawaiian-looking gal that Van Kirk's been using."

Annoyed, Preston waves off my response and describes Cone Head to a tee.

I give it a thoughtful nod. "If it's the guy I'm thinking of, I may have met him once."

Preston asks about the conference; where it was, what the dates were, and who went. He's particularly interested in who might have come in to work the day before we left.

I tell him that we were all off that day, answering his questions in the spirit of earnest cooperation. Whatever he may suspect, he'll never be able to prove it. *Quite simply, I was never here.*

Captain Evancheck is just leaving for a meeting when I get to his office, and he gives up the card without even asking for particulars. All the ex-narc had to hear was that I was going to Sacramento on a lab investigation, and he was all for it.

Gale may have been a little less enthusiastic when I told her, but she didn't seem too upset by it. Maybe just exasperated that I'm leaving so soon after being gone for the conference. I swing by the house to kiss her and the girls before leaving.

* * *

The CLTF is housed in an office building on Marconi Avenue. The directory downstairs lists it only as, *STATE OF CALIFORNIA*. It's on the second floor, and might have otherwise been a dentist office if not for the coded keypad entry. I'm staying at a downtown motel, a block off the freeway and about 10 minutes from the task force.

There are a lot of reasons to go home. The biggest is probably that I've been up here four days already, and tomorrow is my birthday. On the other hand, not only have I been able to identify the duplex where Todd Harvin is probably staying, but I inadvertently came up with an arrest for Sacramento PD when some fool tried to sell me LSD. I had just left the courthouse downtown when the guy approached me. I knew what he was going to do before he asked me. I had him wait while I supposedly got money from the ATM. I used a pay phone to call it in, and came back with a couple of uniforms.

I've been helping the task force with other cases too, completely unrelated to mine. I even went up in the sheriff's helicopter, searching for a meth lab in the foothills. These Sacramento guys have taken me in as one of them. *So I stay a few more days. So what? There will be other birthdays, but how often will I be able to do this?*

I go back to my motel and have a western burger and onion rings at the Denny's next door. My room is dark and empty when I return, yet I'm still too keyed up to sleep. I walk back out to my car and take a drive past Harvin's duplex. His car is parked under a carport a few spaces from the back of his unit, so I back into a visitor's space, turn off the motor, and settle into my seat. After about an hour, a huge figure waddles out. I immediately recognize the guy from Becky's description. *Big and fat? This guy looks like the freak'n Hindenburg.* He backs his gargantuan ass into the car, and then wedges the rest of himself in. *Oh, the humanity . . .*

I follow him out of the complex and onto a main thoroughfare. It's a loose tail since I'm only one car, and I'd hate to heat the guy up at this point. Anyway, the blob is probably going to get ice cream or something. Or worse yet, a western burger and onion rings. *Fawwk, I gotta get back into shape.*

Harvin turns into an industrial area and I drop back further. I see an orange, lighted sign, and contentment percolates up like a wet dream. It's a storage locker facility. Harvin punches in a code and the gate opens. I park in the shadows outside and sit tight for a half-hour until he comes out. The time and address is recorded onto my notes.

First thing in the morning I'm back to get copies of his rental agreement and locker number from the manager. Turns out, the unit is listed under the name, Todd Harmon, but the renter gives an address that matches the duplex where Harvin is staying. The names are similar enough, and I can't find any record of Harmon, which leads me to believe it's a bogus name. Harvin must use it to conceal whatever he's keeping in the locker. With any luck, it's a piping hot meth lab. At my direction, the facility manager slaps one of their locks on the locker and he gives me the key. I tell him, "I'll be back tomorrow with the signed search warrant."

I spend the day in the task force office, putting together a warrant affidavit listing the residence, the storage locker, and the two vehicles associated with Harvin. It's late afternoon when I finally make it over to the courthouse. The judge glances up at me several times as he's reading the warrant, but doesn't utter a word. When he gets to the end of the last page, he sets it on his desk and takes off his glasses. "This is a fine affidavit, detective."

I smile and thank him. He signs it and I thank him again. "It's been my pleasure to read it," he says.

Back at the task force office all the guys are getting ready to leave. After a 14-hour day, the narcs all go home to their families and I drive back to my dark motel room.

I sit at the end of the bed, staring at an image in the mirror—a man I barely recognize anymore. His beard is a tangled rodent's nest, and his slicked back hair accentuates eyes devoid of expression. He's sloppy and ugly, and all alone. I turn away and roll onto my feet. A brief thought goes through my mind that I should search out the motel's exercise room for a short workout, but the notion passes as quickly as it came.

I grab Harvin's case file and walk down to my car. It's after seven o'clock, and the freeway is still jammed. I drive to the storage locker, and find the second lock still securely fastened. Harvin's duplex is quiet when I get there, and I find Harvin's car parked near his place. I get out on foot and make my way around the complex, like any other low-functioning Section-8 resident, out for an evening stroll. As I pass Harvin's unit, I see a couple of people inside watching TV. I can't tell who they are without going right up to the window. It's not worth it at this point, especially since we're going to hit the place tomorrow either way.

I get back to my room around nine, and the phone is ringing as I walk in. "Hello?"

"Happy Birthday to you . . ." Gale and the girls are singing to me. I toss my case file onto the table and lay back on the bed to listen as they go through the whole song. " . . . Happy Birthday to Daddy, Happy Birthday to you."

We talk for a while and I tell them I'll be home in a couple of days. Gale tells me to be careful and I assure her I'm being safe. I hang up the phone and let out a long sigh. I lie in the dark, wondering where this is all going. I ask myself what I'm really after—Promotion? A better marriage? Happy kids?

All I can come up with is the distinction of being the best. The whole concept is tangled up with fame, respect, and self, and I haven't the motivation to delve into it any further. I sweep my fingers through my greasy hair as I turn to check the clock. I've been lying here for two hours. I get up and head for the door, careful to avoid my reflection in the mirror.

At 11 p.m., Denny's is a police lineup of night creatures. I slip past a couple of men in drag and take a seat at the end of the counter. My club sandwich arrives and I'm pissed at myself for not ordering the coleslaw instead of fries. I hunker over my meal like an alley dog.

Two uniform cops come in and sit at the opposite end of the counter. They both eye me suspiciously. I nod out of habit, and they glare back. I leave a tip when I finish, and then use my napkin and water to scour my beard. The cops scowl at me, and I would swear they're hoping I leave without paying my bill, just so they can kick my ass and drag me to jail.

They both turn as I pass them, so I stop and throw my hands in the air. "I didn't do it!"

The uniforms shake their heads in disgust. Pleased with my asshole impersonation, I strut out of the restaurant. I have a momentary surge of remorse as I walk back to my room, but convince myself that they had it coming. After all, I don't think I judged people simply on their appearances when I worked the street. *Did I?*

We pony up in the morning, and I brief fifteen Sacramento cops. Some are uniformed patrolmen, and I wonder if any of them were in Denny's last night. I split the group into three teams—one for the duplex; one for the storage locker; and one for the two vehicles. I will ride with the task force commander, monitoring the raids over his radio and alternate back and forth between each of the locations.

I decide to accompany the group hitting the duplex, figuring I could best gauge Harvin's guilt by the expression on his face. It's no surprise that the guy is eating waffles when we bust down his door. He pauses for a half-second as we rush in, his face set in a sort of confused frown, and then stuffs another forkful into his mouth.

No drugs or lab paraphernalia are found in the duplex, and it turns out that Harvin is staying there with his mother. She's sitting on the couch, watching TV, when we come in. And though she doesn't say anything to us, she glares at her son with eviction in her eyes. The cars are both clear, and I realize all my hopes are now resting entirely on the search of the storage locker.

While we're waiting to hear back from the other team, I take a seat at the table across from Harvin. He's a hulking mastodon, barely supported by the tiny kitchen chair he's sitting on. We talk casually, and I steer clear of anything related to meth labs. He has yet to figure out that I'm not from around here.

One of the task force guys comes out of the bathroom carrying a hockey stick. Harvin's eyes zero in on it, and he quickly looks away.

"What the hell is this?" the narc asks.

"Hockey stick," Harvin bristles.

"What's it doing in the bathroom?"

Harvin belches before answering. "I use it to wipe my ass."

The narc glowers at Harvin and tosses the stick onto the table. The others turn back to what they're doing, but I sit staring at the stick. I'm wondering if Harvin was being sarcastic, or if he really uses it to wipe his ass. Something about his expression seemed more embarrassed than caustic.

"You're serious." I say it almost like a question.

Harvin nods. "Can't reach back that far." He slides the hockey stick around so the wedge faces him. "I wrap a bunch of toilet paper around this end, and then sort of shove it down between my legs. It's the only way to clean my ass when I take a dump."

I feel sort of sorry for the guy. The task force commander listens in on his radio and gives me a thumbs up. Apparently we struck gold at the storage locker. Now that Harvin's going to jail, I feel even worse for him. We have to use a double set of cuffs because of his size. As they walk him out to the transport unit, the commander fills me in on what was found.

"They came up with a complete meth lab boxed up in his locker," he says. "A couple pounds of what looks like finished product, but it still has to be tested."

We take a drive over to the storage facility, and the hazardous waste disposal truck is already there. Besides the manufacturing equipment, Harvin's got boxes of his personal belongings stacked inside. It takes the team a few hours to inventory all of it. Meanwhile, I sift through his clothing, papers, and other effects. I find a folded receipt in the pocket of a jacket that was at the bottom of one of the boxes. It's for 5-gallons of acetone, apparently purchased from a chemical company in Oakland. I slip the receipt into my pocket with the idea that it may come in handy later.

An unmarked car pulls up just as I'm coming out of the locker. A tall guy in dark glasses eases out, then smiles broadly when he sees me.

"You again?" Mr. Meth says with a laugh. "You're making quite a name for yourself."

The task force guys know the state's lab guru well. They seem mildly surprised though, that he is so chummy with me. We shake hands and I give him a quick rundown on my case.

I stay another night in Sacramento and spend the following day filing all my reports with the DA's office. Though physically tired, I'm energized by the success of the operation, as well as the notoriety that will inevitably come out of it.

* * *

It's bath time when I finally get home. I sit on the floor watching the girls fashion beards on each other out of the soap bubbles. They tell me they look like me now, and we all laugh. Gale seems relieved that I'm home, and I imagine her routine with the girls falls short of the thrill level I've become accustomed to.

17

An Old Friend

"Do you have a girlfriend?"

The notion catches me off guard. Gale had been in the middle of making a point about my lack of familial involvement when her soft blue eyes suddenly turned steel gray and she changed course with the girlfriend comment.

"What the . . .?" A patronizing smirk crosses my lips. "Where do you come off with this shit?"

"Look, Phil." Gale steadies her voice. "I get it, okay? I'm a boring housewife with two kids, and you're some kind of undercover celebrity. You have all your informants, your drinking buddies, and your little prostitutes."

My mind stutters, trying to pick which of her accusations I should address. I end up defending myself with nothing more than a snarling look.

Gale reaches under the bed and shoves a colorfully wrapped box in my direction. "Here. Happy Birthday." She walks out of the room before I have a chance to open it.

A few minutes later I emerge from the bedroom wearing my new leather jacket. Gale checks the fit out of the corner of her eye. I thank her, but she turns away before I'm able to see if she's smiling or not.

"We need a trip to Disneyland," I say with a tender lilt. The girls are so excited they can barely finish their Captain Crunch, but Gale looks at me guardedly.

"I'm serious about this." I want her to think I've given this more thought than the half-second it took me to say it. "I know I've been gone a lot, and my job has kind of prioritized my time."

Gale's eyes are screaming, *NO SHIT!* But true to her natural instinct to avoid conflict at all costs, she doesn't respond.

"How about we plan it next summer, right when the kids go on break?" In the complex world of marital discord, mine may be the idea of the century. It also may have saved us from another argument about how much time I spend at my job. I smile, content with having made a proposition I know she couldn't possibly turn down.

Gale looks like she's about to say something, but a glance at the girls stifles it.

I thought I had hooked her with the family vacation scheme, but her expression convinces me otherwise. With eyes only a husband would understand, she communicates a message to me: *Don't toss out the Disneyland bone as if that's going to solve all our problems. I'm not some pitiable shut-in, too pathetic to resist a vacation.*

She knows I get her silent message. I shake my head like a wet dog and grab my duffle bag. "I'm going to work."

The girls are summoned to the front window and they blow kisses as I drive off. Gale's wave is lackluster, and I know she's just about had it with me. I resolve to follow through with the vacation plan.

I actually left a good hour before I needed to, and now I'm alone in the office. I check the phone messages, and then go down to the jail to see if there are any decent prospects in custody. One name catches my eye: Marissa Cox. The jailers pull her out of the cell for me, and I walk her upstairs to the interview room. She's a painfully skinny girl, with stringy black hair and wild brown eyes. As she ascends the stairs in front of me, I stare at her tiny waist. Her blue jeans are so narrow that I can't believe they even make them that size.

I tell Marissa I remember her from a previous arrest three or four years ago—the one when she escaped from the jail through a phone slot in her cell. She smiles when I remind her that the cops caught her trying to walk through the back gate wearing a stolen police uniform.

Marissa laughs. "I was never charged with any of that." She tells me that she had been riding in a car that day, with an Oakland drug-dealing pimp named Otis Love. The cops pulled them over and found drugs and guns in the car. According to Marissa, Love went to prison and the case against her was dropped.

"Even the theft?" I ask. "My buddy, Gary Clancy, was pretty pissed off about his missing uniform."

Marissa nods proudly. "He was in the shower when I took it."

We talk awhile about what she might be able to do for me, and it's apparent she knows a lot of big names. But she seems ambivalent about snitching on any of them, and more interested in talking about sex.

"Otis had the biggest dick I ever saw." She rotates on her chair and crosses her legs. "I like dick . . . but I like pussy too."

I get her back on track about the gun thing. I'm thinking since she knows Oakland gunrunners, she may know the guys Craig Johnson knew. She gazes up at the light for a second, thinking.

"No, I don't think I know anybody selling guns on MacArthur," she says. I'm about to ask if she knows anybody else selling guns, when she abruptly changes the subject. "When can you get me out? My nipples need sucking."

I've gotten informants out of jail for a lot of reasons, but that would definitely be a first. "Whether or not I can get you out depends on your charges," I tell her, "but I'll see what I can do.

I get back upstairs and notice the sarge's office has been cleaned out; Roberts is officially gone.

I toss the interview notes on my desk and slump into my chair. The unit will never be the same without Roberts. To my mind, he was the Einstein of undercover work.

Two phone calls come in, in rapid succession—one from San Leandro narcotics and one from the Sheriffs. In Roberts' absence, the unit supervisors are calling me for our help on their search warrants. I coordinate the times and list both operations on the board.

Miller and Van Kirk come in looking like they've lost their best friend.

"Did you hear?" Miller says. "Roberts is out."

I nod. "Who's the new boss?"

Before they can answer, there's a racket at the door like someone trying several different keys in the lock. Finally the door opens and

Carl Bradford, our new leader, stands there like a kid on move-in day at the freshman dorm. A cardboard box under his arm is overflowing with crap, and the cord of a 1960's era clock radio dangles between his legs. He nearly trips on it as he steps over the threshold.

"Look what the cat drug in," says Van Kirk with a demeaning sneer. We all probably imagined a similar wisecrack, but neither Miller nor I had the balls to say it.

Sergeant Bradford manages an uncomfortable grin. He sets his stuff on my desk and wipes the perspiration from his forehead. "I would have been here for our morning briefing, but traffic was a bear on the freeway. We do have a morning briefing, don't we?"

We all exchange glances and then Van Kirk turns back to his desk.

Bradford and I worked the same shift on patrol. We even took off early one night to follow a coworker. We discreetly tailed the guy to an illicit rendezvous with a girlfriend he was banging. Bradford called the cops, reporting a sexual assault, and we laughed our asses off when they swooped in on our buddy's car.

Bradford and I haven't seen much of one another in the couple of years since he was promoted and I went to narcs. He's green as far as sergeants go, and he knows nothing about drugs; but even so, he might be a lot of fun as a boss.

We help the other agencies on their searches, and Bradford makes assignments and gives directions throughout both operations. He takes before and after photos like Roberts used to do, but then has me take a photo of him posing with the seized drugs. He says it's for his office. Van Kirk and Miller distance themselves by volunteering to search the backyard.

The Sheriffs sergeant sidles up to me when we've finished. "Who's the doofus?" he asks, motioning to Bradford.

"He's replacing Sergeant Roberts."

The sheriff's eyelids flicker closed. "You're doomed."

Bradford's a friend and I don't want to badmouth him—especially with another agency's unit supervisor. I just give him a shrug. "We all have to start someplace."

His eyes settle on Bradford. "The dude needs to admit what he doesn't know instead of trying to bullshit everyone."

Back at the station Bradford gathers us in the office for a meeting. I check my watch, eager to get out of the building. I want to get up to the chemical supply place in Oakland, and check the clientele. The fact that Harvin had a receipt from the place makes me think it's probably a shoddy, backdoor operation catering to illegal labs.

"I want to start accompanying you guys when you're working on your cases," Bradford says. "I'd like to know more about what you do."

Van Kirk lets out an ill-timed laugh, and Bradford glares at him. I tamp down the coals by offering to take Bradford to Oakland with me. During the ride, we have a laugh about the last time we drove that route together.

As I back in between a couple of trucks, I explain about the receipt for acetone found during the Sacramento search. "It's a long shot," I admit, "but we could come up with some good intelligence."

After an hour or so of watching commercial delivery trucks and janitorial vans come and go, someone pulls up who matches my mind's profile of a meth cook. He's a burly white guy, with long hair and a full beard. The guy parks his flatbed truck and glances around before going inside.

He comes out after a few minutes, carrying a 5-gallon plastic drum. When he starts rolling, I jot down the truck's license number, and then maintain a loose tail onto the freeway. He pulls off at Hegenberger and turns down a narrow industrial street across from the Coliseum parking lot. I stop at the corner and wait a few seconds.

Bradford nearly comes unglued. "Don't lose him! Don't lose him!

I stay out of sight long enough for the driver to scan the street for a tail and then get out to unlock a gate. Timed perfectly, we continue past a warehouse in the middle of the block, just as the flatbed pulls though an open rollup.

"Eight, four . . . " Bradford turns to me in a panic. "I didn't get all the numbers!"

"Eighty-four-seventy-five, Baldwin Street." I pen the address on my notepad.

We return to the office and I begin computer checks of the license plate, registered owner, and of the warehouse address. The truck is registered to a guy in Copperopolis—an old mining town in the Sierras.

I double-check my notes to make sure I wrote the license plate down right. *Copperopolis? What the hell is he doing at a warehouse in Oakland?*

I find no local arrest record for Raymond Sides of Copperopolis, so I call Calaveras County Sheriffs Department and talk to one of their narcotics guys. He takes down Sides' information and says he'll do some research and get back to me.

Miller walks into the office, laughing. "The new boss just went out with Van Kirk."

"What's he working on?" I sit down at my desk.

"Meeting an informant." Miller can barely suppress his laughter. "The Hawaiian officer."

* * *

A few days later I'm invited to a luncheon at a hotel across the bay, hosted by the FBI. Their purpose is to distribute information to local law enforcement about cocaine cartels operating in the Bay Area. It's a chance for me to introduce Bradford to some important people.

The luncheon goes pretty well, and I'm able to score us seats at a table with the head of DOJ's San Francisco office, and the state's lab expert known as Mr. Meth. Having learned my lesson a couple of years ago at my first narco luncheon, I stick with ice tea. Bradford on the other hand, knocks back two gin and tonics. Suddenly he's like a high school kid, a few decibels too loud and laughing boisterously at things that are only mildly funny. We leave the luncheon early and I get him out to the car before he makes a complete fool of himself. I back out of a stall, and then stop for two women walking behind me. As I pull past them, Bradford starts hooting and waving his arms.

"Let's try to pick up on those chicks!"

As I continue toward the exit, Bradford slaps his palm against the car's front windshield. "I'm serious. Let's go back and talk to them!"

Now I stop the car. I ease forward in my seat to inspect my now-cracked windshield. Bradford's drunken blow with a ringed finger managed to damage my new car.

"Oh, shit." Bradford studies the crack with his glassy eyes. "That was already there, right?"

I roll my eyes. "Sure, Boss. It was already there."

I pull into the driveway just as it starts raining. For once I'm home in time to eat dinner with the family, only my wife's car is gone. I find her mom inside, watching the girls. It dawns on me that Gale had mentioned something about another class reunion meeting. My mother-in-law leaves me to a fish & chips dinner and a rousing game of hide and seek with my girls.

I'm actually able to give the girls their baths and get them both into pajamas before their bedtime. They giggle at me throughout the effort, pointing out the many things I do differently than *Mom*. Apparently they're supposed to wear shower caps in the bath, because Gale doesn't wash their hair at night.

Headlights through the curtain telegraph Gale's arrival home. I've just gotten the girls into bed, and I hustle onto the couch in order to appear at ease and in control. I turn down the TV as she comes in, as if I've been watching it for hours. Gale sets down her coat and purse, and gives me a grin—either because of my valiant attempt at fatherhood, or the lame attempt to appear unruffled. In either case, she seems happy.

I bring her up to date on news from around the department. She seems surprised that Roberts was moved out and Bradford was moved in so quickly. "Don't they all have families?"

I'm about to answer her when I realize it was only a rhetorical question—probably more of a general observation about disruptions caused by my job. I change the subject to my new case, and tell her all about my surveillance of the chemical company. "With a little more investigation, I might be able to get into that warehouse."

Later, when we're in bed, I find myself still consumed with thoughts about the case, making a mental list of the investigative steps I need to take. The wind and rain rattles the bedroom window, and I'm glad I made it home early. I wonder how it went with Bradford, Van Kirk, and his little Hawaiian informant.

"Are you going to be home next weekend?" Gale's voice whispers out of the darkness next to me.

"Yeah, I think so."

"Would you mind if I invited an old friend over for dinner?"

"Hey, that would be great!" I close my eyes, happy that Gale is taking my advice and getting involved in something that makes her feel good about herself. "Someone you reconnected with at your reunion committee?"

"Yeah, we used to sit by each other in civics class." She turns on her side to face me. "I was thinking about Saturday night."

"Saturday is fine." I scrunch farther under the comforter.

"Good, I'd really like him to meet you and the girls."

My eyes spring open. *Did she say, "him"?* I lie there for several minutes in the darkness—the silence pounding in my head. Unable to bite my tongue any longer, I finally dribble out a question. "Who was this guy again?"

"Teddy Vargas," she says. "You remember me telling you about him. He was the only jock I even knew in school."

Jock? As in athlete? As in muscular, in shape, good-looking single guy? Jock? "Yeah, yeah, I think I remember." My tongue searches desperately for moisture in a parched throat. "So, yeah, Teddy Vargas is coming to dinner. That'll be great. Yes, I'll definitely be here."

I stare up at the ceiling, wide-awake and with a sudden urge to get out of bed and do sit-ups.

* * *

I'm in early for a court case. The defense attorney has the drug dealer plea guilty as soon as they find out I showed up. The district attorney is happy; it means an easy win for him. He asks me to stick around until the defendant actually makes the plea, just in case he changes his mind at the last minute. Although I agree to, I take off as soon as he hits the courtroom door. I jump on the freeway and head to the Oakland warehouse. From a decent spot in front of a sandblasting firm, I watch the warehouse through binoculars. The place is quiet, though I can see a motorcycle parked in a fenced yard behind the building. I'll have to get out of my car and walk past the place in order to get the license plate. Depending on who the bike is registered to, it might help in my quest to get a search warrant for the place.

I glance at myself in the mirror and ruffle my hair. Stepping out of the car, I glance around to make sure nobody sees me. I head off in the opposite direction, and at the corner of 85th Avenue, I find an old shopping cart with a missing wheel. A dumpster full of discarded cardboard and packing foam sits off to my left, in an empty truck yard.

I stroll in, dragging the shopping cart with me. As I begin cramming the cardboard into the cart, a guy steps out on the dock and yells at me to leave. I give him a tired wave and slog my cart back out to the street. Now, with my disguise fully prepared, I turn right and cross the street toward the warehouse. I tug the cart slowly up the curb then stoop to pick up an aluminum can. It gets tossed in with my collection of junk before I continue on. When I reach the fence, I realize the motorcycle is gone. I pause for a second, glancing back at my starting point to make certain I had been looking at the same place. *Where the hell could it have gone?*

Suddenly the rollup door thunders open. I'm standing face-to-face with Raymond Sides, the bearded dude in the flatbed truck. I hear a motorcycle engine echoing inside the warehouse, and I assume he's opening the door for another guy to leave. I still haven't gotten the license plate, and I don't want the driver to speed past me before I can.

"Excuse me." I position my trash-filled cart in the middle of the driveway as I turn toward Sides. "I'm on disability and could use a few bucks to get something to eat."

The guy brushes me off with a gesture toward the street. The motorcycle emerges, driven by a small guy wearing leathers, and sporting a handlebar mustache. I stumble toward him and start in with the same solicitation, only louder in order to be heard over the motor.

"Get your shit out of the way," Sides says. He's still standing there with one hand holding the door up.

"I can get around him," the guy on the bike says as he weaves his way between me and the cart. He takes off down Baldwin and I study the license plate, repeating it to myself several times. I drag my cart back in the direction of my car, and I hear the door roll closed behind me. *Mission accomplished!*

I call the DA handling this morning's case, just to make sure the defendant pled guilty as promised—he did. I tell him I had decided to wait over at the police department, and he apologizes for not calling me to let me know. "That's okay," I tell him. "No harm done."

Bradford comes into the office, glancing around like he lost something important. "Where is everyone? I came in this morning and nobody was here."

"I had court," I say. "Not sure where the other guys are." I'm sensing that Bradford is a little anal about us accounting for our time. For that reason, I decide not to tell him about my Oakland follow-up. He'd probably have wanted to go with me.

"How did it go last night with Van Kirk and his informant?"

Bradford's eyes drop. "Not too good. Van Kirk said his informant was a little skittish, and he needed to get the information from her privately."

I can feel laughter start, and I clear my throat. "Yeah, some of them can be pretty paranoid."

"I guess," Bradford sulks. "But he sure was in there for a long time."

"In where?"

"Her house." Bradford scratches his head. "He told me to watch the door while he was inside debriefing her. I was lying in the bushes and it started raining. I nearly froze my ass off."

The phone rings in Bradford's office and he runs out to get it. I manage to suppress my laughter until the door closes, and then I let it out. *I'll bet he debriefed her!*

My phone rings and I take a minute to get a grip before answering. "It's Detective Griffin with Calaveras Sheriffs. I couldn't find anything on your guy, Raymond Sides, but he's living in an area where we get a lot of meth labs."

I tell him about this morning's surveillance and he doesn't seem surprised. "We've gotten some Intel that our cooks are being recruited down to the Bay Area to make crank for the HA."

I make a note of our conversation in the case file, along with Griffin's name and number. Then I run the license number of the motorcycle that came out of the warehouse. I jot down the name of the registered owner: William Fry, with only a post office box in Oakland as an address. Running his name for a criminal history, I come up with exactly what I'm looking for. He's got an arrest record for guns and drugs, and the best part is a Hell's Angels tattoo listed under salient characteristics. That, combined with my surveillance notes and the information Detective Griffin provided, might just be enough.

Bradford comes back into the office with the excitement of a kid with a secret. "That was Kyle Gallagher on the phone. He's a sergeant with Berkeley's narcotics unit."

I don't bother telling him that I already know the guy.

"We've arranged a deal where you go up to Berkeley and work with them two days a week, and they'll send us one of their narcs."

I'm rubbing the crease out of my forehead. I'm sure working in Berkeley would be a kick in the ass, but I'm after much bigger fish. My investigative agenda doesn't have room for two days a week doing street buys. Not wanting to alienate the new boss, I try to act enthused. Bradford tells me that Berkeley's sending down a Spanish-speaking narc named Ignacio Alvarez. Then he drops the big bomb.

"They need you for a prostitution sweep this coming Saturday."

Saturday! Fawwk! I tell Bradford that I have plans that evening and I can't get out of them. He calls Gallagher back to tell him I have to be done by 5 p.m. I guess I'll have to live with that.

By Friday afternoon I've finished typing my search warrant. I get it signed and I put it on the board for Monday. Bradford is all excited to do what he calls, *his* first undercover case. I guess in his mind, being a passenger during one of the surveillances qualifies it as his case. *Whatever.*

I drive to Berkeley on Saturday, after promising Gale on my life that I'll be home in plenty of time for the big dinner. Little does she know, my desire to get back on time is solely self-serving. *There's no way I'm letting her have dinner alone with that jockstrap.*

A desk sergeant eyes my ID and badge, then buzzes me through. I'm ushered past a bunch of frowning detectives, and into a tiny office. I sit there while he hunts down Sergeant Gallagher. The only other guy in the office is seated at a desk across from me. He's a stocky cop, about forty, with a mustache that wilts down to his chin. I can't tell if he's undercover or a shabby cop in street clothes.

We make small talk for a few minutes and he seems like a pretty nice guy. Turns out he's temporarily working narcs, but is normally assigned to traffic. He slides open his desk drawer to show me his new handgun.

"Just bought this baby," he says, caressing it like a beloved pet. "Haven't even had a chance to fire it yet." He's fiddling around with the magazine as if it's stuck. Suddenly a loud crack propels me to the floor, and a bullet whistles over my head. He looks as terrified as I feel. I glance above me to see a smoking hunk of lead buried in the side of a metal clothes locker. I slowly glance back at him. His bulging eyes plead with me, as the sound of running footsteps approach in the hall. He throws the gun into his drawer and I climb quickly back into my chair.

The office door flies open and all manner of cops rush in with their guns drawn. They glance around frantically. "What the shit was that?" one of them shouts.

The guy across from me shrugs toward the open window. "Must have been a backfire outside."

A wisp of smoke lingers in the air, and there's an unmistakable odor of burnt residue in the room. The cops look at me and then back at him, then walk out shaking their heads.

"Thanks for not saying anything," the guy says. "That could have cost me my job."

"No problem." *I haven't been here five minutes and already I've nearly had my head blown off. Working in this place is going to be some kind of trip.*

Gallagher finally comes in with his crew, and they brief me on their operation. It's nothing special, just a prostitution roundup. He asks if I've acted as a *John* on solicitation cases before and I tell him I have. They seem to have some concerns, but I can't get a fix on what they are. One guy finally mentions how rough I look. They think I'll do better buying LSD at People's Park.

"It's all the same to me," I tell them. "Whatever you need me to do."

They start with the whores, and the first case goes pretty well. I pull over near a young woman standing in front of University Hot Tubs, and I roll down my window. She offers to take me "around the world" for a hundred dollars. The term means I can use her whole body—every orifice—for whatever I want to do. Few of the street girls offer that, at least not where I'm from. In any case, I was only given sixty bucks.

I open my wallet and show her the bills. "I figure this should get me as far as Liechtenstein."

She gives me a confused look, but gets in the car. I tell her I have a room at the Ramada down the street. In actuality, the op plan is to bring the girls to a vacant lot a few blocks away. They have an arrest team and transport van staged there. Unfortunately, we never make it.

Without warning, the girl jumps out of my car while I'm stopped at a red light. She dashes across the intersection waving her hands at a passing patrol car. The cop stops and I can see the chick gesturing toward me. *Now what?*

The uniform cop is talking on his radio, and then he gets out of the car and handcuffs the woman. Gallagher comes over the air, laughing. He tells me to meet them back at the lot. When I get there he tells me what happened. The woman, who was to accompany me around the world, changed her mind only two blocks into the trip. After jumping out, she ran up to the uniformed cop screaming, "That guy is going to kill me." Apparently, she thought I looked like the convicted killer, Charles Manson. They all get a good laugh.

We disband the prostitution sweep after that. I make a few LSD buys at People's Park, a marijuana buy near the university campus, and a heroin buy from a parolee at a residential hotel near the freeway. We bust each of the suspects immediately after the sales go down, and then I have to write out a statement for each one. I'm worried that it's dragging on too long, and I may not make it home in time for the dinner. I finally have to tell Gallagher that I'm done for the day. I check my watch, and it's already almost 5 o'clock. I think Gale said he's coming over at six.

I hit the freeway, and thankfully there is little traffic. A red light suddenly appears in my mirror, followed by the familiar blast of a siren. I pull off the freeway near the Jack London Square turnoff. It's a young highway patrolman and his female trainee. He gets to the car and tells me I was weaving. *Speeding I would believe, but weaving?* He wants me to get out and do a field sobriety test.

I show him my badge and police ID, and he stares at it in disbelief before finally taking it. I tell the guy that I've been working with Berkeley PD all day, and that I've nothing to drink.

He holds my ID to his flashlight as if examining a counterfeit bill, then looks back and forth between the photo on the ID, and my face.

"You're telling me you're a cop?"

"Yes."

"Are you armed?"

"Yes."

He eases one foot back into a bladed stance and grips his pistol. "Keep your hands where I can see them, and step out of the vehicle."

Though I feel like bitch-slapping the moron, I have enough sense to follow his orders. He pats me down and removes the duct-taped gun from the holster on my ankle. "What is this piece of shit?" he asks.

I don't answer.

He turns away like he's hiding something. "What's the serial number?"

Now I start laughing. His partner chuckles in my defense, and I can tell she's not buying into his attitude either. It occurs to me that he's probably posturing to impress her.

"Not only don't I know the serial number of the gun, I couldn't even tell you the make."

The Chipper looks disgusted. "Any good officer worth his salt knows the serial number to his duty weapon."

"Sorry pal. I guess you're worth more salt than me."

He flips on his flashlight again to check the butt of the gun. "The serial number has been filed off!"

Dirty Harry tells his partner to keep an eye on me, and then he starts searching my car. I'm looking at the time, and I'm getting more and more frustrated. He comes out of the car a minute later holding a roach clip and some rolling papers. "Ah ha! What's this?"

"A roach clip and rolling papers."

"I know what they are. Question is, what are you doing with them?"

I sweep my arms apart, exaggerating a display of my attire. "What do you think I'm doing with them? My job is to go undercover and buy drugs. I don't use the drugs, I buy them. And then I arrest the seller."

He sniffs at the clip before finally handing it back to me. "I guess I just don't get it."

The statement is so obvious that I let my wiseass response die as only a thought. "Yeah, well can we all go now?"

He gives my gun back and I take off like a shot, finally walking through my front door at 5:17. Gale shoots me a look that tells me a few more minutes and I would have been a dead man. She's trying to get the girls fed, and prepare a decent dinner at the same time. I take a quick shower, change into regular clothes, and do my best with a comb to make myself presentable.

A knock at the door heralds the arrival of her special guest. I flash a witty grin. "Guess who's coming to dinner."

Gale smiles back. She looks really good, and sometimes it's hard for me to believe she's had two kids. There's no difference from the young eighteen-year-old I met while working at the theater.

Teddy Vargas turns out to be this tanned guy with dark hair and white teeth. Just the kind of guy a husband wouldn't want his wife sitting next to in civics class. He's very personable though, and after a few minutes I begin to feel somewhat at ease. I get him a beer, and we talk while Gale sets up the girls with a movie in the other room.

The roast she made smells great, and I'm really starting to warm to this guy. It's almost 7:30 by the time the three of us sit down to eat. Just as I uncork a bottle of wine, the phone rings.

Gale gets up to answer it, and comes back with a face of stone. She motions to me as her expression melts to one of utter disbelief. "It's the department." She plops into her seat and pours herself and Teddy each a glass of wine.

I take the phone, still trying to read the look. "Hello?"

"It's dispatch. We're calling out SWAT for a barricaded gunman."

18

Wrong Number

As I speed towards the department, I keep picturing Gale's expression. She was pissed for sure, but she also had the tiniest smile. It could have been a look of embarrassment, or the utter disbelief that I would get called back to work on this of all nights. But that's the bothersome detail I can't get out of my head. The hint of a smile on her face.

"Dewey Meadows," the commander says. "He's seventy-three years old, and legally blind."

"Jesus Christ!" The words come out of my mouth before I can censor them.

The commander's eyes ignite like a flare. "I don't want to hear any shit. This guy has already fired a dozen rounds at the cops, and we still have people pinned down in the inner perimeter. I don't want to be here any more than you do."

Somehow I doubt that. During the rest of the ride out to the staging area, all I can think about is the dinner I'm missing. And I don't mean the food.

We start unloading our gear and I hear shots going off, echoing throughout the neighborhood. We're wedged in a tiny pocket of homes just off a main downtown thoroughfare. Banks, restaurants, bars, a carpet store, and then Dewey's house. It sits beside a large, empty lot with a three-story brick building beyond it. The street has been blocked off, and the barricaded corner is cluttered with cop cars, reporters, a fire engine and an ambulance. I guess they're standing by in case someone goes down. Meanwhile, the bullets keep flying.

I'm told that the whole episode started when a process server delivered papers to the old guy. He chased the server off his property with a shotgun, and then threatened to do the same to the cops that arrived. They hunkered down behind their patrol cars and when they wouldn't leave, Dewey began taking potshots at them. Thankfully, his poor eyesight left the shotgun pellets on a course well over the cops' heads.

The back of the brick building has a loading ramp that drops down about six feet to a dock. My assignment is to relieve the patrol cop who's been crouched there since the incident began. I scutter down the ramp and find Thurmond Morris standing in the darkness with a shotgun in his hands. He's a tall, chubby guy whose pants always seem like they're wedged halfway up his asscrack. He's in full uniform, and I'm wearing camouflage SWAT gear.

I tell Morris he can go, and that we've got this side of the house covered. I motion directly above us to the building's roof and tell him that we've also positioned a sniper there.

Morris starts to unload his shotgun as I ease my head up to take a look at Dewey's house. A shot rings out and I instinctively dive to the ground. I glance up to see Morris standing there with his smoking shotgun pointed in the air and a dumb look on his face. *Why is it my fellow cops are always trying to gun me down?*

"More shots fired by the suspect," someone says over the radio.

I hand Morris my microphone. "Do you want to tell them or do you want me to?"

He transmits that it was his accidental discharge on the perimeter. The boss orders Morris to the command post, and that's the last I see of the guy for the rest of the incident.

The rooftop sniper, my police academy roommate, Timmy, leans his face over the edge of the building above me. "I need to come down and change my pants now." We both laugh.

The loading ramp affords the most protected vantage point, and eventually the operation's staging area migrates there. Soon the entire team is huddled around me. We use the safety of the ramp's concrete side as protection while we continue firing teargas across the vacant lot, into Dewey's house. After a few hours of that, the house is a smoky ruin, yet the old codger still refuses to give up.

As the night wears on, I'm having sporadic worries about what may be going on at home. Images of a romantic, candlelight dinner flash through my mind. *I can see it now: the girls are asleep, the wine is drunk and the husband is gone. Gale's worried about me, so The Jock starts massaging the back of her neck. Cue the romantic music . . .*

"We're out of CS canisters?" the commander barks. "What do you mean we're out?"

The poor equipment guy stands there. "We've fired all the teargas projectiles we have in stock. It's more than we've used in the last five years."

The commander aims a scowl at him and then at the Meadows house. "What else do we have? Smoke? Pepperballs? Flashbangs?"

The equipment guy tells the commander that we actually do have more teargas, but they're hand-operated canisters, and cannot be fired from a weapon. "Given the distance, and the open, unprotected field, they're really of no use to us in this situation," he says.

The commander glowers at him again, and then glances around the crowd of SWAT guys. "I need a couple of volunteers!"

He points to me and I suddenly feel like a guy who accidentally scratched his nose during an auction. *Sold to the man with the beard and ponytail!*

Another poor sap is "volunteered," and we're both furnished a handful of teargas grenades. "Go to it, boys!" The commander slaps us on the back. "Let's flush that son-of-a-bitch out of there."

As I don my gasmask, I'm wondering how it is that old Dewey Meadows hasn't succumbed to the massive amounts of gas we've already fired into his home. The entire block is obscured under a gelatinous cloud, and the air inside his place has to be unbearable. The oxygen level can't be enough for anyone to survive.

With the other guy covering me, I inch my way along the far end of the lot—grenades in hand. I've convinced myself that the hour-long lull in the shooting means the old fucker has finally collapsed. I low-crawl toward the beckoning window—the sound of each breath resonating loudly inside the mask. My view, already warped by the plastic lens, is further obscured by the foggy remnants of our onslaught. The closer I get, the more the uncovered portions of my skin start to burn and the harder it is to breathe. Someone whispers over the radio, but I can't understand it. I'm in range of the house now, and there's nothing left to hide behind. I rush the window like the beaches at Normandy. There's a sudden burst of light followed by an explosion of glass. I'm in mid-stride and I've already pulled out the pin. I see the canister gripped in my raised hand, halfway into its pitch. The cascade of motions has begun—too late to call back now. My hand progresses forward through the remnants of the window screen and into the black maw that once held the glass. There's a release and an explosion deep within the room. Success!

In the second it takes for my senses to catch up to my pumping adrenaline, I'm ecstatic. Then, a minor stinging sensation on my wrist and the feeling of wetness seeps into my consciousness. The sleeve of my BDU shirt pulses outwardly with each beat of my heart, and in an instant I know that I've cut into an artery. I duck against the side of the house and thrust my shirtsleeve back. Blood sprays out in a three-foot arc, rising and falling with each pump.

I grasp my wrist with my free hand, and it's like trying to control the end of a pressure hose. I note the strange sensation of watching my life's blood draining out, yet my only thought is to stop the bleeding and get back to safety without being shot.

I yell to my partner through the smoke, "I cut an artery." The distortion of the mask makes it difficult to differentiate between reality and my fading consciousness. As if in slow motion, my partner reaches out and grasps me by the lapel. "Let's get the hell out of here."

With a tight clasp over the leak, I run straight across the open lot toward the staging area. Gunfire barks behind me, and somewhere in my periphery I'm aware of my partner. His breathy voice pleads over the radio, "Forty-six is injured. Have an ambulance standing by at the staging area."

Instantly, there is a barrage of garbled radio transmissions followed by frenzied activity. I'm wondering if they all think I've been shot. We dive over the concrete barrier to safety, and the unit commander is there, waiting. I tell him that it's only a cut, and he eyes the vice grip I have over my blood-soaked sleeve. He grimaces, and then orders a motorcycle cop out of the intersection to ride with me to the hospital.

I'm loaded into the ambulance, at which time they determine I have a "pumper." The EMT cuts off my outer shirt and applies a strangling grip on the underside of my bicep, stemming the flow at its brachial source.

I'm brought into the trauma unit wearing a frayed black tee shirt, camouflage cargo pants and black boots. A doctor evaluates me with an air of malaise. A nurse glowers at me as she checks my pulse and blood pressure, then walks off without a word.

Leland, the motor cop, wrinkles his brow. "What's her problem?"

I shrug. "Maybe you gave her a ticket once."

We're left alone in the room, and after several minutes I decide to call home before Gale hears something from someone else. I dial from the hospital phone and my first question to her is whether or not Vegas is still there.

"No, he's not still here. And his name is Vargas, not Vegas."

"How did it go," I ask.

"Fine, except for you leaving."

"Hmmm. Sorry about that."

"He seemed kind of nervous after you were called in," she tells me. "He asked if this type of thing happens a lot."

"What did you tell him?"

"I said, 'Only when we have something planned.' So, how did the callout go?"

"It's not over yet."

"It's still going on?" A silence follows Gale's words and I suspect she knows something is wrong. "Are you at the hospital?"

"Yeah, but I'm fine." I hear a weak sigh. "I'm okay, I promise. It's just a little cut on my arm. I'll probably need a couple of stitches." *Technically, I haven't lied to her. The cut itself is only about an inch long. I just left out the depth of the cut.*

Gale has little to say after that. She's probably trying to read the truth in my words. I hang up, relieved that The Jock left early.

The medical staff has yet to come in and check on me, so Lee and I pass the time reminiscing about our nights working patrol together. He reminds me about the night we chased a one-eyed man through poison oak bushes.

"Thanks to you, Gale got a rash on both arms when she took my uniform to the cleaners."

Lee laughs and gives me a playful shove just as the nurse comes back in. She glares at us, and then motions Lee over to the corner of the room.

"I can't believe you're joking around with him," she says.

Lee glances over at me. "Why?"

"We were monitoring the standoff over the police scanner," she says. "After the trouble this asshole has caused by shooting at your officers, I wouldn't be so nice to him."

Lee looks at me again and we both burst out laughing. "He's not the crook," Lee tells her. "He's a cop. He works undercover and is also on SWAT."

The nurse is mortified. "Oh shit. I have to let the doctor know right away."

Things move quite a bit faster after that. They call in a micro-surgeon who puts a tourniquet on my bicep and sutures the nearly severed radial artery back together.

I don't get out until 5 a.m., and even then I have to go back to the station with Lee to get my car. The callout is over by then, and the old geezer is in custody. He had evidently wrapped a wet towel around his face and hid in the basement, below most of the gas.

Gale and the girls are at the breakfast table when I walk in with my elbow-to-thumb gauze wrap.

"Oh, just a little cut, huh?" Gale gets up to fix me a plate. "I knew it was something more when you told me the callout was still going on. No way you'd miss out on that, unless your entire arm was falling off."

* * *

I walk into the office on Monday morning and my partners look surprised to see me. "I got a meth lab to bust in Oakland today."

We hold the briefing in the Oakland unit's basement office. Some of their guys know about my Sacramento lab bust, and strangely, they've already heard Saturday night's SWAT injury. An Asian guy approaches me with a wily smile. "What's with you always cutting yourself?"

I recognize him from an incident a few years ago when I was in uniform. He and I were in a wild vehicle pursuit together, and we ended up blocking in the car on a dead end road. The suspect tried to ram us, and I smashed my handgun through his window. It took a few sutures to close the gashes on my hand that night.

We roll out to the Baldwin Street warehouse like a 5-car funeral procession. Oakland's motors escort us, stopping traffic at major intersections the closer we get. Not only do they hasten our approach, but they also prevent anyone from having time to drop a dime and warn the cook we're coming.

I do the knock & notice on the front roll-up door while an Oakland guy slides a pneumatic wedge under it. They begin pumping and the wedge quickly separates, crumpling the door like an accordion. As they thrust the door open, I see a Harley inside the warehouse and I hear footsteps running toward the back. Miller and Van Kirk are waiting there, and roughly toss the biker to the ground. Nobody else is in the building, but it's definitely a good sign that the guy ran.

We find a lab inside a converted storeroom, just off the shop floor. It looks like the cook was between batches, so unfortunately there's only a little finished product. However, the manufacturing charge and the possession of precursor chemicals will send the biker to prison for a long while. The chemist from Copperopolis is in the wind, and we find no good evidence of his involvement.

I meet with Oakland's criminal Intel guys afterwards and give them copies of my case file. William Fry, the guy we arrested was more than likely the HA courier. The Hells Angels clubhouse is in their city, and I know their Intel guys have been working with the feds on a case against them for years. Maybe my information will help.

* * *

A few weeks later, Miller and Van Kirk are transferred back to patrol. It's suspicious to me that they're bounced so soon after Roberts, and that the unit will now not only have a green sergeant, but two green replacement narcs. Jeff Riggs is an older, easy going black cop who I know will be a breeze to work with. The other new guy strikes me as a young up-and-comer. His name is Kevin Hamm, and I haven't worked with him much.

The sheriff is hosting a countywide narcotics meeting, and I see it as a good opportunity to familiarize my new partners with the larger group. Bradford calls in sick, so Riggs and Hamm ride with me to the meeting.

We're sitting around a long able, drinking coffee and eating. I stuff a hunk of donut into my mouth just as the roundtable introductions stop at me. I stand up, and with a mouthful of glazed old fashioned, introduce myself and then the two new guys. Everybody in the room immediately starts laughing.

"What's so funny?" I ask.

The sheriff can barely catch his breath. "Are their names really Ham and Eggs?"

I realize I must have garbled the names of the two rookie narcs. The poor guys are both chagrined. "Riggs," I say, quickly trying to correct the misunderstanding. But it is too late. A bungle in front of a group like that can never be unbungled. Forever more the two will be known in narcotic circles as Ham and Eggs.

When Bradford comes back to work the following day, he's pissed off that he missed the meeting. He doesn't come right out and blame me, but I get the definite feeling that I'm the focus of his anger.

On top of that, the other unit supervisors around the county keep contacting me directly for everything they need. Bradford senses it and it's beginning to strain our relationship.

The other day I was working at my desk when the patrol watch commander called for a narc to assist at the scene of a marijuana cultivation arrest his guys had made. Bradford was in court and the two new guys were in a training class, so I went to assist as requested. Patrol officers had stumbled on a sizable grow inside a greenhouse, while searching the neighborhood for a lost kid. After helping out with their investigation, I returned to find Bradford fuming. Ham and Eggs had come back from their class, and Bradford decided to dress us all down.

"I'm your sergeant. You guys got that?"

We nod.

"The days of running all over the place alone with an informant is over!" Bradford's eyes flash with anger. "Next time you go out to meet with a CI, I want to know about it."

When he finishes his tantrum, I politely let him know that the watch commander had assigned me to assist patrol on a case, and I wasn't with an informant. Ham then reminds Bradford that he and Eggs had been in a training class that Bradford himself had sent them to. We all look at each other blankly as Bradford huffs out of the office.

It's an odd dynamic, and I have trouble understanding it. Bradford relies on my expertise for everything from UC buys to informant payments, yet he seems angered when anyone else asks me a question. I've achieved a certain status among members of the narcotics boys club, and the bottom line is that Bradford needs me more than I need him. With that in mind, I have no intention of inviting him along every time I do an investigation.

For the time being it seems as if whatever Bradford needed to get off his chest, he got off his chest. But even though I'd like to get back to work, he's still hanging around with his scrutinizing glare. The general office line rings and I'm quick to pick it up. "Narcotics."

Silence on the other end. I should probably repeat my greeting, but I don't. Instead, more silence. I know the majority of calls on that line are picked up by the answering machine, and I can almost envision the reluctant caller, panicked that the phone has actually been answered.

"Wrong number," says a meek voice.

I smile to myself. "Wrong number? I don't think so." There's more silence. "Talk to me, brother." I turn away from Bradford and prop my feet on an open file drawer. "Whaddaya got to lose?"

"I wanna talk to the cop who busted many heroin peoples."

"The heroin dealers?" I'm sure he's talking about the Sonoma Street cases. Five different agencies were involved in the roundup and nearly 100 officers participated. The arrests made a big splash in the local newspaper, but that was over a year ago. "You're talking to him," I say.

Turns out he heard about me on the street, and judging from his poor English, he probably never reads the local paper. "I got something for jou, man."

"I'm listening." I slide my notepad and pen in front of me.

"He name, Pablo Troche. He living at 29765 Orlando Avenue, and he selling heroin and cocaine. Big cocaine."

"You've seen him with it?"

"I see it."

"You've seen it at his house?"

"I see it."

"Does Pablo have a regular job?"

"Pablo make French bread at bakery in San Francisco."

"Why do you want Pablo to get busted?"

He weighs his answer for a beat. "Pablo sell the heroin to my cousin, Javier. The heroin kill Javier. Pablo still selling the heroin."

"Where did Javier live?"

"Javier live Clipper Street in San Francisco."

"Can you tell me the address, and Javier's last name?" I sound a little more beseeching than I intend to.

The caller pauses. "You catch Pablo. I going now."

"Can I ask you one more question? What do I call you?"

It takes him a few seconds to come up with a name. "Miguel." He disconnects as if he's afraid I'll trace the call.

Bradford, obviously eavesdropping, eyes the notes on my desk. I lock eyes, silently daring him to ask me what the call was about. His jaw tightens and he storms back to his office. Only after Bradford is gone do Ham and Eggs chuckle.

I grab the notepad and head out to my car, figuring I'll just do a quick drive-by of the Orlando address where Pablo Troche supposedly lives. I barely stop the car and get out my binoculars when a heavyset Mexican man comes out. I note the time and his description: 3:10 p.m. 5-10, 230 lbs., mustache & bushy black hair.

He's carrying what appears to be a shopping bag rolled into packet. He drives off in a cream colored Ford, and I jot down the license number. Just for kicks, I decide to throw a loose tail on him. He makes a sudden turn onto westbound highway 92, heading for the bridge. I consider radioing for Ham and Eggs to come help me, but I can only imagine the fuss Bradford would make. He'd probably want to be involved, and then try to make decisions about *my* case—which would undoubtedly irritate the shit out of me.

I pass the tollbooth—the point of no return—without making the call. I'm now alone, in a ridiculous one-car surveillance to the other side of the bay. Miraculously, I keep Troche in sight without heating him up. He hits 101 northbound in San Mateo, passes SFO, and heads toward San Francisco. It's usually an act of insanity to follow someone in the city with less than four or five cars, but Troche doesn't seem to be looking around much. He gets into the narrow, congested streets of the Mission District, and I'm sure I'll have to give up the surveillance. One hard look in the mirror and he's spooked; one missed light for me and he's in the wind.

Without warning, Troche pulls into a driveway and jumps out. I'm frantically trying to find an open spot to park, but there are none. Out of desperation, I drive onto the sidewalk at the end of the block and leave my car right there. I jog down the row of densely placed homes and spot Troche on the top step of one of them. Someone is working on a car in front of the house next door, and I just keep my head down as I pass by. I turn around at the end of the block and by now Troche's gone inside. I know I'll need the address, so after waiting a few seconds I start back past. The numbers 183 are visible above the door, and I make a mental note of them. When I'm directly below the steps of the house, the door opens and Troche starts down toward me.

If he hasn't noticed me already, he will certainly recognize now that I'm out of place in this neighborhood. The two legs sticking out from beneath the car being repaired gives me an idea. I quickly stoop down and pick up a wrench from the ground, and then crawl under the car with the guy. As if I've been working with him all day, I belly up next to him and hand him the wrench.

He stares at me with a shocked expression, then blinks dumbly and takes the wrench. "Uh, thanks."

Troche has gotten into his car and driven off by now, so I slide back out. I hustle to the end of the block where frowning pedestrians try to squeeze around my car. I glance up at the corner street sign . . . Clipper Street. *Could I be that lucky?*

I race across the bridge back to the station, and my first call is to the San Francisco Medical Examiner. At my request, they crosscheck 183 Clipper with the first name, Javier.

"We've been there," the ME tells me. "November 2nd of last year. We picked up Javier Baca-Mejia, 23 year-old Latin male. Post mortem showed he died of a heroin OD." It's all the confirmation I need to corroborate Miguel's story.

I stay late putting together a search warrant for Troche's house on Orlando Avenue. Bradford and the new guys are headed up to the PBA for a crack at team camaraderie, and I probably ought to stop by and do my part. I bring the Pablo Troche file and search warrant with me, figuring I can get it signed on the way in to work tomorrow.

After a few drinks and a game of bones, a bailiff I know from the courthouse in Oakland stops by to chat. I introduce him around, and then I happen to mention the warrant I'll be getting signed in the morning. Over my protests, the bailiff steps behind the bar and calls the home of the superior court judge he works for.

He turns back to me after ending the call. "She said to come on up."

I take a barker for the road, and then get on the freeway toward Oakland. I pull up to the judge's woodsy, ranch-style place in the hills high above Skyline Avenue. The door opens and the woman doesn't embody the jurisprudence I'm used to seeing in the courtroom. Her honor is wearing silky pajamas and a lacey wrap, which I hope is covering more than just her skin. Unfortunately, the middle-aged woman can't pull off the *I Dream of Jeannie* look she's apparently going for.

Candles light the interior of the house, and it smells of patchouli incense. I hesitantly follow the judge into her den of iniquity.

"Hope I'm not interrupting." I glance around, half expecting to see someone stretched out in front of the fire on a bearskin rug. "Your bailiff kind of insisted that I . . ."

"Don't be silly." A fruity whiff of wine carries her words straight up my nostrils—competing with the liquor already on my own breath.

Her Honor takes the papers from me with a lazy swipe, and leans so close to a candle that I'm afraid they'll ignite. In the event of fire, I've already decided to save my warrant first, then the judge.

She scribbles her signature and then tumbles onto one of several beanbag chairs. She's below me at this point, positioned on her side, with her meaty, varicose legs awkwardly splayed. "Sit down, officer." She pats the beanbag next to her. "Would you like a glass of wine?"

"No thanks, your honor." I hold up the signed papers. "Got an early search warrant in the morning."

Though I'd like to keep on the judge's good side, there are limits. I beat it out of there in a hurry, hoping the alcohol will blur her memory of the encounter—and mine as well.

When later recounting the story to a buddy, I find out that one of our detectives also ended up at the same judge's home one night for her signature on a search warrant. "He got his warrant signed alright," says my buddy. "Afterwards he found himself in the judge's Jacuzzi, and ended up signing her tits with a foreskin pen."

We hit Troche's place the next morning, breaking down the door and inadvertently scaring his wife and kids half to death. Troche is in the back yard watering his tomato plants, and we handcuff him and bring him back into the house. We seat him at the kitchen table, wearing nothing but his bathrobe and boxer shorts. To spare his family additional trauma, he leads me to a lock-box under his bed. Inside it I find about three pounds of cocaine, a loaded gun, and somewhere in the neighborhood of $17,000 cash. It's the biggest haul in the nearly three years I've been in the unit. By the time we return to the police station, word of the triumphant investigation has already spread throughout the department.

Once his booking process is finished, I move Troche to an interview room where I take a crack at flipping him. He sits stoically throughout my pitch, and I can see he only cares about protecting his family from criminal charges. He's quick to admit that the lock-box and its contents belong to him, but other than that, he doesn't want to play ball.

Troche's eyes evaluate me, as if he's dying to know how I uncovered his operation. Then I wonder if he recognizes me from the Clipper Street surveillance. Before I'm even finished trying to flip him, the jailer notifies me that his attorney, Tony Fontana, is at the front counter to bail him out.

* * *

A week after Troche's arrest, I'm in the office alone when the phone rings. I slide my chair over to answer it. "Narcotics."

"Hey, Pheel. Is that jou?"

I recognize Miguel's voice, and tell him I'm glad to hear from him again.

"Jou arrest Pablo, jes?" He had evidently heard about the raid through his own network. Miguel says he waited to call until after Pablo's first court appearance, in order to see whether I had kept my promise to maintain his confidentiality and leave his name out of the paperwork. Apparently I had done an adequate job.

"I calling to give jou someone else." Miguel sounds more at ease than during our first conversation. "Pablo es only . . . how do you say? A little frog," he says. "Now I trusting jou, Pheel. Now I going to tell you about the big frog."

19

THE FROG CATCHER

Buying drugs in Berkeley two days a week definitely has its upside. For one thing, I'm away from Bradford. Another benefit is how well the Berkeley narcs take care of their guests. When we finish for the day, they wine and dine me in superb fashion. If it's not Spenger's for seafood, it's oyster shooters at Skate's on the Bay. Tuesday was killer Chinese, and tonight, as one of their guys says, "They're slinging corned beef hash at Brennan's Pub." And the best part is, the City of Berkeley is picking up the tab for all of it.

I remind Bradford how well they treat me, and I encourage him to do the same for their guy, Ignacio Alvarez, when he works in our city.

"We bought him a bowl of fish soup from El Tenampa last week," says Bradford. "But he ended up getting sick and we had to send him home. Anyway, I can't justify spending the city's money like that. I think we have some frozen hotdogs in the detective's lunchroom. We'll give him some of those next time."

I'm careful not to roll my eyes at my boss. Besides being clueless about the subtleties of undercover work, he seems to have a hair trigger temper. For the time being, I plan on avoiding the guy as much as possible.

Meanwhile, Sergeant Gallagher and I have become great friends, and I get the feeling he'd like to have me up in Berkeley, fulltime. Unfortunately, after fifteen years with that agency, Gallagher's landed a job with the department of justice. He told me he'll be assigned to the San Francisco office, so I'm sure we'll be running into each other again. *Working as a state narcotics agent. How great would that be?*

* * *

I thought I'd be able to get a few things done around the house this morning, but I have a court subpoena. This one is for a case I worked several months ago in San Francisco. I slide by the office to grab the Talbott case file and then I jump on the freeway. As I sit mired in morning commute traffic, I imagine having to do this every day. Still, to work in The City as a state narc might be well worth it.

I finally find a pay parking lot with space, and then hoof it four blocks to the courthouse. As I'm going through security at the Bryant Street doors to the Hall of Justice, I realize I forgot to bring my gun. I flash my badge to the deputy anyway, and he waves me through.

The courtroom is empty except for two women—the attorney and the defendant. The defendant glances in my direction and looks away nervously. I recognize her immediately as the woman who had been so lovingly pushed through the window by her boyfriend, Luke Talbott.

The DA comes in and motions me out to the hall. He tells me that the defendant has been out on bail since her arraignment, and that the case against her is mediocre at best. His office has decided to go forward with the felony however, in the hopes that she'll testify against Talbott once he's caught. At that point, they won't mind dropping charges against her. *Sounds reasonable to me, though I'm mildly surprised they haven't caught Talbott yet.*

We return to the courtroom just as the judge comes in. The woman's attorney asks for a continuance, and although the judge is pissed off, he grants it. The DA comes over, apologizing for wasting my time. He then launches into a glowing discourse about my search warrant. In San Francisco County, it's the DA's who actually prepare the affidavits on behalf of the police investigators. He asks me if I'd be willing to teach a class on the subject to his entire office. I eagerly agree, and then wonder if he's just stroking me as recompense for wasting my morning.

I watch from the corner of my eye as Talbott's girlfriend and her attorney stroll out of the courtroom. The DA wants to talk more, but I'm distracted by a festering suspicion. The way the defendant's eyes averted mine when I walked into the court seemed odd. She has DV victim written all over her face, and she knows I can read it.

I excuse myself from the conversation, telling the DA that I need to use the bathroom. I slip into the men's room across the hall as the message from my gut takes shape in my mind. The cycle of domestic abuse is a simple one, and it's all based on power and control. If this woman is like other victims I've known, she's already reconciled with a remorseful Talbott. And if Talbott is like other abusers I've known, he's keeping her isolated and on a short leash.

I peek out the door to see the woman still in the hallway, talking with her attorney. I crouch to get a better view as a couple of men squeeze past me. Although I must look like quite the pervert, amongst the clientele here I don't seem to elicit much notice.

The two women finally part ways and the attorney walks off toward the elevators. Talbott's girlfriend pauses a moment before heading in the opposite direction. I strain to see down the hallway, but my view is obscured. I step from the restroom just in time to see her dart through a doorway into the building's stairwell. I can feel it in my bones—Talbott's waiting for her there. *He's got to maintain that control.*

I ease the door open as quietly as possible, and look between the handrails to the landing below. There the bastard is. He's wearing dark glasses and a baseball cap, but it's definitely him. He gives the girlfriend a quick embrace, and then they're out of my sight. I have to assume they're heading for the parking lot.

I back into the hallway, looking for a cop or deputy to help me take Talbott down. I ride the elevator to the first floor, which I know houses the police department's Southern District Station. I finally spot a narc named Simms, whom I recognize from the Talbott search warrant. He looks as grungy as I do, and it turns out he forgot his badge. With his gun and my badge, I figure the two halves make a whole.

By the time we make it to the parking lot, Talbott and the girl are in their car. We race across the lot, trying to make it to the exit booth before Talbott drives out. We get there at the same time, me thrusting my badge over the hood of the car and Simms waving his gun all over the place. The toll-taker ducks into his booth and thankfully, Talbott doesn't have the presence of mind to plow through the gate. He freezes momentarily, but then he tries to fight when we fling open the door.

Talbott holds the wheel with a death grip, as we apply alternating punches, gouges and strangle holds in an effort to pry him loose.

We drag him out of the car, and amidst dozens of onlookers who thought they were witnessing a robbery, we walk the two of them upstairs to county booking.

* * *

A few nights later I make it home in time to eat with the girls and Gale. I tell her about the fracas in the Hall of Justice parking lot, and she listens with the enthusiasm of a toothache. The conversation is constrained, and feels somewhat one-sided. I suppose she's heard more than her share of these anecdotes, and by now one mind-numbing story probably blends into the next.

We put the girls to bed and watch TV together. Gale and I seem to have reached an uneasy but amicable détente—she takes care of the girls and runs the house, and I do my job. I convince myself that our disconnect is just a passing phase, yet I know she's unhappy. The idea of Gale actually taking the girls and leaving is absurd to me. After all, where would she go? Where *could* she go?

A disturbing thought briefly permeates my defenses, and I wonder if my use of manipulation and control is any different than Talbott's. I quickly chase the notion from my mind. I know I love Gale. And when I stop and think about it, I couldn't live without her. The problem is, I rarely stop and think about it.

That night we go to bed without saying much. After lying in the dark for a few minutes, I reach over and take Gale's hand. "I'll make those reservations for Disneyland tomorrow."

She's quiet for a few seconds. "The girls will like that."

I'm about to ask about her uninspired response when I suddenly remember something I need to ask Miguel when we meet tomorrow. I jump up, turn on the light and jot a note to myself. I stuff the notebook back into my duffle bag. Gale turns toward the wall as I climb back beneath the blankets.

I glance over at the clock, almost wishing for the time to pass more quickly. Sometimes I feel like an addict, myself. The high is never high enough, and I'm constantly drawn back to the streets for another fix.

* * *

Bradford has got his eye on me, non-stop, whenever I'm in the office. Miguel is about to hand me something really big, but I can't risk telling Bradford about it for fear he'll want to tag along. He'd probably spook the guy and queer the whole deal.

We all leave at the end of the day, presumably to go home to our families, but it's the only time I can be assured of my space. I meet Miguel in the parking lot of a crowded shopping center just outside the city. I know him immediately upon seeing him, as he looks exactly as his voice sounds. A short, sturdy young man whose eyes tell me he knows both hard times and hard work. He probably knows his way across the Rio Grande too, but I don't ask any of the personal questions I'd normally ask a CI. This is probably a huge risk for him.

After some small talk, I ask if he wants some dinner. That always seems to loosen up my informants. We end up at a family-style café across the parking lot. Over a plate of country fried chicken, Miguel tells me more about The Big Frog.

His name is Agapito Hernandez, and he owns two houses next door to one another, on the same block as Pablo Troche. It's no coincidence that they both live on Orlando Avenue. According to Miguel, Agapito is not only Troche's drug connection, but also his brother-in-law.

While he talks, I try to read between the lines. How Miguel has managed to find out so much about the workings of this operation is a piece of the puzzle that still eludes me. His knowledge of Troche's drug business was reasonable enough, after all, his cousin overdosed on Troche's drugs. But I haven't figured out how he'd know so much about the high-level connection, Hernandez.

My questioning expression transcends our verbal shortfalls, and Miguel abruptly stops to clarify for me. He pulls the end of a chicken bone from his mouth and sets it on his plate. "I was mule for Agapito." Miguel wipes the grease from his chin. "I drive to LA for picking up cocaine for Agapito, and I bringing it back to Agapito house. A lots of cocaine."

I scribble furiously onto my notepad, trying not to miss any detail. About an hour into the interview, he's had dinner, a few beers and dessert, and I've barely touched mine. I'm thinking this is the case I've been waiting for. It could be the investigation that launches me into another galaxy. My handprints will be plastered on the Narcotics Walk of Fame. There is no doubt in my mind; this case is The Big One.

I catch myself, and realize it's going to take a good deal of groundwork. I'll have to slow down a bit, get phone records, take my time with surveillances, and do it right. Although Miguel is now *reliable,* after having given me Pablo Troche, his information about Hernandez is somewhat dated. Miguel delivered coke for the guy over a two-year period, but that ended a few months ago. In order to get a search warrant, judges need to be convinced that the information is current and the evidence sought is likely to be there right now.

Instead of going home after our dinner, I return to the station and start working on a search warrant for Agapito Hernandez's phone records. *I'm not going to rest until I bust this case wide open.*

Gale's alarm goes off and I actually beat her out of the bed. "Got a big case I'm working on," I say, as if she's ever going to feel the same excitement about it as I do.

She gives me a strange look, and I realize I forgot to make the Disneyland reservations. *How did she know?*

I rush over to the courthouse and get a judge to sign the phone records warrant. I've made sure to mark the box, preventing phone security from notifying the subscriber. Otherwise, Agapito and his attorney would have copies of my search warrant affidavit within 24-hours. He would be afraid to make a move and my whole investigation would be useless.

I'm about to leave for phone security headquarters in San Francisco when Bradford catches me in the lot. "Ham just got an anonymous call about a meth dealer over on Hacienda."

Are you kidding? Who gives a rat's ass? I wonder if he can read my thoughts through my twisted expression. I immediately temper the look with a less-than-sincere, "Oh, sure. What can I do to help him?"

I accompany Bradford back to the office where I find out two things: Salami was transferred back to detectives and he's not being replaced, and I'm going to be the buyer for Ham's meth case. *Swell. Let's just get it going so I can get on with mine.*

Ham's information is about a 45 year-old woman named Doris, dealing grams of meth from her house on Hacienda Avenue. It's not even in the city, it's a tiny amount, and we have no informant to introduce me. I slap on the wire and drive over there, cold. Bradford is with Ham and Eggs in the van, and they can barely keep up with me. I give the door a good wrap, and this skinny white woman with a lisp answers. I stare at her crooked mouth for a second and let out a sigh of frustration.

"Doris!" I step in and give her a hug. "Long time no see." I stride past her and throw myself onto her floral sofa. "Got a sweet eight-ball for me?"

The woman stands with the door in her hand, looking in at me. "Do I know . . .?"

"You look good, Doris." I pull a wad of bills from my wallet. "It's been too long. I wish I had more time. We could smoke a joint and get caught up, but I gotta run, babe. How about that eight-ball?"

The woman ambles into the bedroom like a confused dog. She returns with a zip-lock baggie and hands it to me. "Where do we know each other . . .?"

I grab the baggie and throw my arms around her. "Great to see you again." I slap the money into her hand. "Stay good!"

As I pull away, she watches me with the same befuddled look on her face. I speed back to the station and wait in the lot for the guys in the van. They're laughing when they pull in. Can't believe the woman would sell an eighth ounce of drugs to a perfect stranger.

"So, are you writing a search warrant for Doris' house?" I ask Ham.

Bradford jumps in. "We were going to, but nobody expected her to sell to you without an intro. Let's see where this goes."

I know that means I'll now have to go back in a few days and try to buy up. "Yeah," I say with all the enthusiasm I can muster. "Good plan."

I'm ready to take off for SF again, but Bradford wants to talk upstairs. I let out a long sigh and follow them up to the office. He wants to know the dates of my vacation this year, so he can put it on the squad calendar. *My vacation? Thanks for reminding me.*

I pull out the phone book and call a travel agent. By the time I'm finished, the Disney vacation is all set and Bradford has the dates on his precious calendar. The bad news is that Pacific Bell Security is now closed for the day.

* * *

I wake up in the middle of the night and sit straight up in my bed. *If Miguel drove the cocaine up here from L.A., then he might know who Agapito's connection is. He might even know where he lives!*

When Miguel calls in the next morning, I tell him I need his phone number so I can get in touch with him. He gives me his number only after I promise not to put it in the informant files. *I don't even have his real name in the file, for Christ sake. For that matter, I still don't even know his real name.*

I serve the records warrant at the phone company security office, and then hurry back to the police department before Bradford gets suspicious.

We do another meth buy from Doris, and she can't believe I blew through the first eight-ball so quickly. I tell her, "When the shit's that good, everybody wants more." This time I buy a quarter-ounce, and then give the old gal a kiss on the cheek on my way out. She's too embarrassed to ask again how it is we know each other.

Miguel and I meet at our usual place after Bradford finally leaves for the day. We talk a little bit about who Pablo Troche and his lawyer think snitched them off, and we both laugh. A few minutes of that and I jump right into the details. "Do you know where Agapito's dope comes from?"

Miguel's look takes a cautious turn, and his gaze drops to the ground. "Pheel. This peoples kill me for to tell his name. Even Agapito is afraid to him. He is called, El Maestro."

"The Master?" At least now I know Miguel knows who it is. He tries to change the subject, but I guide him back. "What about this Southern California guy? El Maestro. How does Agapito know him?"

Miguel smiles. "Every peoples selling the cocaine come from same place in Mexico. Pablo Troche, Agapito Hernandez, El Maestro . . . all of the peoples, they coming from same city of Las Cuevas, in Nayarit."

He gazes away. "And I also coming from Las Cuevas. This reason for Agapito trusting me to mule for hims cocaine."

"So, El Maestro is living in L.A. now?"

Miguel shrugs. "Him always meeting me en Santa Ana."

"Do you know where he lives?"

He shakes his head. "No way, Pheel. He only meeting me at the Western Shopping Center down there, man. I drive you to there, pero I no remember streets."

On Friday I get a call from phone security telling me the results of my records search are in. I fly across the bridge, pick up the packet, and race back before I'm stuck in a swamp of slow moving commute traffic. We're gong to a party tonight, so I head straight home after that.

One of Gale's old high school friends had invited us after reuniting at their reunion. I've met the little blond tart and her fiancé, and though they seem nice enough, they remind me of yuppie jetsetters. I'm just happy that *this* friend is a woman.

My mom comes over to watch the girls, and Gale starts getting ready. I can tell she's excited to be having an adult night out. Her makeup and clothes are a few degrees hotter than what she would normally wear. In an effort not to stand out, I've trimmed my beard and pulled my hair back into a ponytail. But even in nice clothes, I still look like I don't belong with Gale. *I hope I don't embarrass her.*

The party is at the couple's penthouse apartment on Lake Merritt. Gale knows a handful of the people there, and I don't really know anyone. We mingle around and Gale ends up talking with a couple of old friends. Her face is lit up like I haven't seen in a long time.

I'm thinking about the Agapito Hernandez file downstairs in my car, and wondering when I'll get a chance to go over the phone records. *I bet no one would even notice if I slipped out to read through them. No, I better not.*

I step down the hall into the bathroom, and notice my sleek new image in the mirror. I wonder how many people here know I'm a cop. The couple that invited us knows what I do, and news like that has a way of spreading like a case of herpes.

My eyes drift down to the vanity. A ten-dollar bill is rolled into a straw, and it's laid out on a hand mirror. Also on the mirror is a strait razor and four lines of cocaine. *Shit! You gotta be kidding me.*

I suppose in the host's mind, this is no different than setting out chips and guacamole. *Fucking yuppies . . . I knew it.*

I contemplate for a second about dumping the whole thing in the toilet, but then reconsider. I take a leak and then head back down the hall. As I rejoin the party, I'm thinking about the position I've been put in. I bust people like this for a living, and now here I am partying with them.

Gale is laughing amongst her group of friends when I come out, and it's a visual rendering of what's been missing in her life. The carefree time she's having obviously fills a need in her that I've been unable, or maybe too busy to fill. I can't allow myself and my job ruin this night.

I reason that nothing in my life is black and white anymore. My whole existence has turned into a kaleidoscope of contradictions. I bust a whore one minute and then pay her to buy drugs the next. I take a dealer to jail one day, and then get his case dumped when he decides to work for me, the next. *Nobody really gives a shit, anyway.*

"Are you alright?" Gale is suddenly standing next to me. As I fix myself a drink, I tell her I'm fine. But when she heads down the hall toward the bathroom, I know she'll soon understand the look she saw on my face.

She returns with a disappointed expression. "That's why I wasn't very social when I was in school."

I tell her we'll pretend we didn't see anything. "It's not a problem for me," I say.

Gale frowns. "How could it not be a problem for you? It could cost you your job."

I laugh. "Don't worry about that. Just relax and go have fun with your friends."

"They're not my friends." Gale picks up her purse. "And having a bunch of coke laying around is fucking disrespectful to you. C'mon, we're leaving."

* * *

I use the rest of the weekend to go through the eight pages of calls made from Agapito Hernandez's home phone. There are numbers throughout Southern California, from Riverside to San Diego, and all over Orange County. On Monday, I get a map of the area from AAA, and begin plotting them. Unfortunately, the records only provide the numbers and cities called. Not their names or addresses.

By calling information and then reading the map, I'm able to locate the Western Shopping Center where Miguel used to meet with El Maestro. Though Miguel told me it was in Santa Ana, it actually appears to be right next-door in Garden Grove. I draw a circle around it on the map.

I spend the next couple of days writing a second phone warrant, this time seeking names and addresses on each of the numbers called. It's a little trickier to write, and I have to justify the additional request by including more of the confidential information from Miguel. Still, I'm always careful to check the box that prevents them from notifying Agapito of the warrant's existence.

Bradford has been nosing around enough to know I'm working on something, so instead of waiting for him to come to me, I decide to extend the guy an olive branch. I sit down in his office and give him a sketchy summary of the case. I leave out the part about my discreet meetings with Miguel. Instead, I play it like the whole case is a result of information gained when we hit Pablo Troche's house. I also tread very lightly on the L.A. area connection, giving him only enough to know that's where the dope comes from. What I don't need is Bradford going off half-cocked to the DEA or some such thing.

I can already see the wheels turning as he slaps his desk. "This is going to be huge!" He glances at his calendar. "When do you think we can hit the place?"

I caution him that it may be a little while. Leaving Bradford's office, I wonder if I did the right thing.

The judge signs my warrant and I hit the bridge for San Francisco again. The return trip goes quickly, taken up by fantasies of kilos, cash, guns and headlines. The office is empty when I get back. Ham and Eggs are out with a new informant, and Bradford is at a countywide conference of narco supervisors. I turn on some music, open my bag lunch, and lean back in my chair as I eat my sandwich. *The Disneyland trip is a week away, Gale and I are getting along, and my case is coming together nicely. It's great to be on top of the world!*

Then the phone rings.

I thrash around in bed all night, anticipating the morning meeting. *How did the federal task force hear about my investigation?* I wonder if someone at the courthouse could have tipped them off, or maybe my security guy at Pac Bell. I wouldn't be opposed to sharing the case with the feds; Lord knows they have more money and resources. But they are notorious for taking over, cutting out the little guy, and then gobbling up all the glory once it's over.

We use the detective's briefing room, and I make sure there's a full pot of coffee. Bradford greets the two suits at the elevator and motions me to the room. I purposely leave my file in my office, and come in with only a pen and blank notepad. The two guys seem friendly enough—young and eager, although carrying themselves with classic, federal agent arrogance. I schlep into the room and recline into my seat, playing up the UC character in order to emphasize an important distinction: *I buy drugs on the street and you sit behind a desk.*

After slightly stilted introductions, one of them gets down to it. "We have a confidential informant who's told us of a large cocaine operation in your city. Apparently, this suspect deals significant weight."

I nod, trying to appear both unaware and intrigued. But since they haven't yet asked a question, I'm certainly not going to volunteer a response.

"Do you know the suspect's name or address?" Bradford says.

They confer with their notes. "Our CI doesn't know exactly. That's what we're hoping you might be able to help us with." Now they're both looking at me. "Your sergeant mentioned in the conference yesterday, that you're working on a Mexican Cartel case."

I glance at Bradford, momentarily envisioning myself diving across the table to strangle him. Instead, I shrug. "Hard to say if it's related to your information. What's the guy's name?"

They look at their notes again. “His name is Pepito, or something that sounds like that.”

I silently cringe. “How well does your CI know the guy?”

“They met at an Oakland bar called Three Monkeys. This Pepito character was gambling a lot of money at the time. Our informant doesn’t know exactly where he lives, but he says the house has a palm tree in front of it.” The agent flips his file closed.

Bradford lets out a laugh. “Every house south of Tennyson Road has a palm tree in front of it.” Then he looks at me. “What’s the name of your guy?”

I excuse myself to get the case file, as if I don’t know it off the top of my head. I walk slowly, trying to think of some way to get out of giving up all my information. I get the file and return to the room, unable to come up with anything workable. I look across the table at my boss and the task force goons, laughing and talking together. *I got your Three Monkeys.*

I open the file and slide it over to them. “My suspect’s name is Agapito Hernandez.”

We have dinner as a family, and the girls show me all the things they plan to take along on our vacation. We spread out the Disney brochures and each pick out our favorite ride. It’s a good distraction for me—probably better than anything else. But the sudden turn at work weighs heavy on my mind. I can’t imagine the feds would use any of my information without coordinating with me first. I had made sure to stress the great deal of time and effort I’ve put into the investigation thus far, as well as the fact that I’m much further along than they are. *How do they even call their guy an informant? He met a guy named Pepito at a bar, and he lives near a palm tree? Give me a break!*

* * *

I get to work early and Bradford’s car is already in the lot. *There’s a first.* The division secretary sees me come in and hurries over. “Captain Evancheck wants to see you in his office right away.”

I knock on his office door and see that Bradford is already in there talking with him. They let me in and I take a seat on the trouble side of the big mahogany desk.

"The chief of police got a call this morning from the FBI." The captain swings his chair off to the side and lights a cigarette.

I'm wondering what the feds could possibly want now. I've given them all my case notes, albeit without the phone records and any mention of the Southern Cal connection. So why would they call the chief, unless to complain about me? I take in a deep breath and quietly hold it as I wait for he next sentence.

"What I'm about to tell you is not to leave this room." Evancheck leans forward through the freshly blown smoke. "The FBI came across some extremely sensitive information during an investigation into an outlaw biker gang. It was monitored during a phone tap."

The air surges from my lungs as I realize this has nothing to do with me. I ease back in my seat. "What's the information, Captain?"

He pauses a second to finger a piece of tobacco from the end of his tongue. "Someone has put out a contract hit on you."

20

Double-Crossed

The new set of phone records came in, and I pick them up as soon as I can get across the bridge. I glance through the papers while I'm still in the car, hoping something jumps out. I muddle through an assortment of mostly Hispanic names, and mostly Orange County addresses—all completely unfamiliar to me.

As soon as I get back to the station, I leave a message on Miguel's answering machine. "Meet me at 8 o'clock tonight, at the usual place."

Ham asks me if I'm free to do another meth buy from Doris. This time I call her ahead of time and order a quarter pound. Surprisingly, she has it on hand. Despite the larger amount, the deal goes down as easily as the others. Afterwards, we sit around the office with Bradford, talking case strategy. Considering the amounts she has access to, we figure Doris is getting the dope straight from a lab. However, up to this point there's been no mention of who or where. Having had some luck myself, I make the suggestion that Ham write a phone records search warrant. I give him a copy of an old one of mine to use as a template.

"Just remember to include a request for the names and address of the subscribers," I tell him. "Otherwise all you'll get is a bunch of meaningless phone numbers."

I meet with Miguel after work, and I buy him a meal at our quiet little café. We spread the phone records on the table and I ask if any of the names or addresses look familiar. He studies them with a critical eye, running a grimy finger slowly down each page. He points to a number and starts laughing.

"He calling me, Pheel. This number of my friend, I living there when I working for Agapito."

I make a notation next to it. The call was made three months ago, which matches with Miguel's stated timeline. It's a Southern California area code, and it doesn't appear on any of the more recent records.

"This one, Pheel." He stops on one name.

I flip the page around. It's a number that shows up only seven times in the three-month period. Some of the other numbers were called ten times as often, but something about this one must strike a cord. I take out a pencil and draw a line under it: Benjamin Aguilar, 139 Walnut Avenue, Garden Grove.

A glint of excitement edges into Miguel's eyes. "I pretty sure this guy es El Maestro."

"How do you know?"

"I hearing hims name before." Miguel looks at the paper again. "One person in Las Cuevas say hims name to me."

I pull out the map and squint at the cluster of tiny streets. "Do these places look familiar?"

Miguel nods and points to the circled intersection. "Es where I meet Maestro and I getting cocaine."

The Western Shopping Center is only a couple of miles from the Walnut Avenue address—maybe a five-minute drive at most. It makes sense that the guy wouldn't risk carrying the dope too far.

We talk some more, and I'm so excited I can barely eat. We walk outside afterward, and Miguel suddenly stops and steadies his eyes on mine.

"This guys, they very dangerous, Pheel. They try to killing me if they find out." He walks another step and turns back. "They try to killing you, too."

That would be all I need right now. I reach out my hand and rap his shoulder. "Don't worry, my friend. They won't get us."

I make it home in time to tell the girls a story before bed. Their excitement about the trip is contagious, and I find myself becoming more eager about it. Gale is waiting for me in the living room with a bowl of ice cream. I start off by telling her the good news about my big case. The names and locations spew out of me like a hydrant, and she does her best to keep up. I then remind Gale about the case Miller worked against Bryce Feldman. She doesn't remember, but nods when I describe the long surveillances we all had to work.

"One of the guys we busted was in a biker gang," I tell her. "His name is Rocky Samford, and I kind of tackled him when we took them down." She stares blankly back at me, and I realize there is really no good way to say it. I finally come right out and tell Gale that the guy now wants me dead . . . well, actually I found out he only wants to make me a paraplegic. "They put out some kind of contract to have my legs cut off."

Gale doesn't act particularly surprised. Maybe she's thinking that she's also wanted me dead a time or two. Or maybe she's just worried that the girls might hear me.

I lower my voice and tell her that there was some discussion about putting our house under police surveillance, but that I thought it was an overreaction. She rolls her eyes and lets out a sigh. "What's the bottom line here, Phil? Should I be worried about our safety? Should I keep the girls out of the yard? Is somebody going to drive by our house some night and shoot the hell out of us?"

I press my palms against the sides of my head. "Nobody's going to do that." I realize I have nothing more comforting or reassuring to give her than that. I muster a heartening smile. "These things just happen once in a while. It'll all blow over."

Gale shakes her head, clearly disgusted. "Your ice cream's melting." It sounds like a euphemism for something mean, but I can't figure it out. I eat my dessert and we watch TV in silence for the remainder of the night.

I have a fitful sleep, raising my head and listening whenever a car passes the house.

* * *

I'm at my desk typing a supplement for one of my buys from Doris. It's only two days before our Disneyland trip, and I'm trying to get everything wrapped up before I leave. Bradford comes into the office with a strange look on his face.

"I just heard back from one of the federal task force guys who were here last week." Bradford shifts his stance uncomfortably. "They are going to write a warrant for Agapito Hernandez's houses on Orlando."

A flash of heat courses up through my body, boiling when it reaches my head. Besides ripping my case out from under me, searching Agapito's houses now will completely destroy my entire investigation. The organization will cease operations and everyone involved will go into hiding. The LA connection will probably leave the country. "Give me the guy's number!"

Bradford raises his hands to calm me. He starts into a canned speech about how the feds have more resources and can do a better investigation. *If he thinks he's helping, he's not.*

I finally wrangle the phone number out of him and get the guy on the line. "My sergeant says you're thinking about hitting the houses on Orlando." Before he can answer, I add, "The places I've been working on for the past month and a half."

He tries to tell me that nobody owns the investigation, and unless I already have a search warrant in hand, it's anybody's ballgame. I can feel myself getting angrier and angrier as he's talking.

"My case isn't just about Agapito Hernandez," I say. "I'm trying to put together conspiracy charges on an entire trafficking organization. Why would you guys want to cut that investigation off at the knees?"

The suit clears his throat. "All I know is that we have a CI who can give us enough probable cause to get in there now. We're ready to go."

"What the hell are you talking about?" I push the office door closed with my foot. "Until I showed you my case file, you didn't know any more about the guy than the motherfucking palm tree in his yard. And don't tell me about your stellar informant, either. Some dumbshit who once saw Agapito gambling at a bar? That's your probable cause? You didn't even know his goddamn name until I gave it to you!"

I hear muffled conversation behind a covered phone. He comes back on the line a little less confident, but trying to compensate. "Look, we'll hold off getting the warrant for a week. Unless you can put something together by then, we're sending our CI in, and we're going ahead with our own warrant."

My head drops backwards and I close my eyes. *How can I do anything by then? I'll be on vacation all of next week.*

I must have been sitting in the same position, thinking, for an hour. Ham and Eggs are at their desks working quietly when I finally come out of my stupor. They exchange glances when I struggle out of my chair. I pass Bradford as I exit the office. He had enough sense not to stick around during my phone call, and now he has the sense not to ask me where I'm headed. Regardless of how much he sticks up for the feds doing the case, he has to know he blew it.

I use the phone downstairs in the locker room to call Miguel. Fifteen minutes later he and I are sitting in a coffee shop, putting together the first step in my plan. The plan to destroy the feds' case before they destroy mine.

"Do you know of a bar in Oakland called Three Monkeys?"

Miguel nods. "I hear of it."

"It's a place Agapito goes to gamble." I sip my coffee. "Have you been there? Have you ever seen Agapito there?"

My serious tone makes him uncomfortable. "I don't know, Pheel."

"Think back," I tell him. Not that I give a shit if it's true, I just need to hear him say it. "Do you think you might have, even one time, seen Agapito there?"

Miguel stares into my eyes, trying to make sense of the dialog. Maybe he figures it out, or maybe he just wants to please. "Yeah, Pheel. I think maybe one time I see Agapito en Tres Monkeys."

"Good enough!" I grab my notebook and head back to the station. I'm working against time now, trying to get a search warrant written, signed, and served in less than two days. I finish typing just after the courts close for the day, and there's no possible way to justify bothering a judge at home for a telephone records warrant.

It's Friday morning, my last workday before vacation. I'm in the bailiff's office asking for any available judge. Turns out it's a bad day for search warrant signings; several big trials are underway and a couple of judges are out sick. I end up sitting in the crowded traffic court, waiting for a break. It's lunchtime before he's able to fit me in.

We go back to the judge's chambers, and I stand rocking on my heels while he reads through the affidavit.

"Looks good," he says. "But you forgot to check the non-disclosure box."

"That's okay, Your Honor. I'll leave it unchecked."

He straightens up. "You know the phone company will be obligated to notify this Hernandez fellow that you seized his records."

I nod.

"And as soon as you file the affidavit with the court, his attorney will be able to get a copy of it. He'll read everything your informant told you."

"Yes, sir."

The judge frowns through his reading glasses as he signs it, then shakes his head as he hands it back. "Good luck, young man. I hope you know what you're doing."

I do.

I go straight to my car without stopping into the office. I can't risk getting sidetracked. Any delay now would ruin my plan. I zip over to San Francisco and find a parking spot just off Market. I'm out of breath by the time I reach the phone security office. I serve the warrant, which they keep a copy of, and then I take the original back with me.

It's 4 o'clock when I get to my car, and Friday afternoon commuters have started to pour out of downtown. We're leaving for Disneyland tomorrow morning, and this is my only chance at survival. I have exactly one hour to get back and file my warrant affidavit before the courts close.

I bulldog my way into the procession of cars inching down 8th Street toward the freeway. It takes me ten minutes to travel two blocks. The signal turns red and I pound a fist on the steering wheel. I sit there seething as the seconds tick by.

A bicycle messenger weaves his way through the stopped cars and pulls up next to me. He glances in my window and then edges his bike just ahead of my car. He looks over his shoulder at me with a wiseass sneer, and then props his foot on my front bumper. Now, when the light changes, I'll be behind this asswipe, waiting for him to get out of my way. *I don't have time for this today.*

I roll down my passenger side window. "Hey! Take your foot off my car and get out of the way."

Another over-the-shoulder sneer. "Fuck you."

The light changes and he cuts right in front of me, blocking the lane. He's peddling his bicycle slowly, and glancing back at me with a grin. I look at my watch and then at the messenger—his stupid yellow and black tights and his backpack full of cardboard tubes.

I accelerate right into the back of his bike, and suddenly the grin drops from his face. He's peddling faster now, but it's too late. "Fuck me?" I yell out. "No, fuck you!"

I accelerate again. This time my front bumper catches just right, and his rear tire is smothered beneath it. The force pushes the backend of his bike downward, and his front tire lifts into the air. The kid is yelling bloody murder as he's pushed down the street in a permanent, out-of-control wheelie.

We finally dislodge and I'm able to pull past messenger boy. I see him in my rearview mirror—his crippled bicycle wobbling toward the curb. I jump on the bridge approach at Bryant Street and race back across the bay. I get my warrant filed at the courthouse with less than five minutes to spare.

* * *

It feels like the middle of the night when I get up to pack the car. I stand out front in the dark, scanning up and down the street. When I'm confident that I'm not being watched, I load the suitcases and get Gale and the girls.

We're just passing the turnoff to Los Banos when the sun finally comes up. The girls are asleep in the back seat, and Gale is holding her nose as we pass another cow farm.

Our plan was to get there around midday, giving the girls a chance to rest before heading off to the park. But by the time we check in, they're eager to go. The next few days are a whirlwind of long lines, overpriced meals, and tired kids. It turns out to be worth every minute, and I find myself really enjoying our time. For the most part, I'm able to set aside being double-crossed by the feds, as well as the supposed assassination plot against me. We hit all the major attractions in the area, and by the latter part of the week, everybody is bushed.

We decide to spend the day lounging around the hotel pool. Once the sunscreen has been applied, the inflatables have been inflated, and the towels have been laid out just so, I make an excuse to go back to the room. At the bottom of my suitcase I find the file containing all of Agapito's phone records and my AAA map. *What would it hurt?*

I go back to the pool and sit down on a lounger next to Gale. She's wearing tortoise shell sunglasses and a blue terrycloth cover-up. A relaxed smile crosses her face as she stretches like a cat in the sun.

"Hey, I was just thinking . . ." I scoot the lounger closer. "Since we've got nothing planned today, and the kids are having fun here . . ."

Gale's head turns gradually toward me and I stop talking. She reaches up to her sunglasses and slowly slides them down the bridge of her nose. Peering over them, she says, "Go on."

"I thought maybe I'd check out a couple of addresses."

Without a word, she slides the sunglasses back into place and reclines back the way she was.

It takes me less than twenty minutes to drive to Aguilar's house in Garden Grove. I turn down Walnut, scribbling the description onto my pad as I pass. I continue around the corner to Euclid Park, and back under a large tree to transcribe my notes. In my shady spot, I rewrite every detail about the house; size, color, trim, location of the numbers, and the make and model of a green pick-up parked in the driveway.

I watch the place for a while before driving past it a second time to get the truck's license number. Another short trip and I'm back at the hotel—total time gone, less than two hours. I don't know if the little bit of information I've gathered will be useful, or whether it was even worth the aggravation it caused. In any case, it won't even matter unless my plan to sabotage the feds works.

Back at the hotel, I make up for my gaffe by rubbing oil on Gale's back, and playing a game of water tag with the girls. It turns out to be a great vacation, and other than my one minor relapse, the family was able to escape the weight of my job. The entire eight-hour trip back on I-5 however, I'm in deep thought about what I may be coming back to.

An outlaw biker gang may have ransacked my home, and the federal task force may have ruined my investigation.

* * *

I drive by Agapito Hernandez's side-by-side houses on the way into work on Monday morning, as if I'd be able to tell by looking whether or not the feds raided them while I was gone.

Bradford comes in with a self-assured prance, no doubt cultivated during a week without me there. I ask Ham and Eggs if anything happened while I was gone, and it sounds like it was pretty routine business. Ham has gotten back his records for Doris's phone calls, and Eggs has done an introduction buy for cocaine. But nobody seems to know if the feds hit Agapito Hernandez.

By noon I still haven't heard anything from the feds, so I decide to give them a call. The guy I had spoken with before I left comes on the line. He sounds a little glum, and I can't figure out if it's remorse from having gone ahead with the Hernandez case or if my plan actually worked.

"So, what did you decide to do about the case?" I ask.

The agent lets out a groan. "We're going to have to hold off for a while."

"Oh?" I perk up in my seat.

"Yeah. Our CI got burned somehow, and we had to get him out of town rather quickly."

I suppress a chuckle, and manage to generate concern in my voice. "What happened?"

"We don't know for sure. He went back to Three Monkeys and somebody shot at him."

My glib satisfaction comes to an abrupt end. "Shot at him! Is your informant alright?"

"Thankfully he wasn't hit."

I hang up the phone and slink down into my chair. I knew once the warrant's existence was disclosed by the phone company, Agapito's attorney would immediately get the copy I filed with the court. I had intentionally written the affidavit using the identical facts that the fed's informant had given them—specifically mentioning their having met each other at the bar. Sure, I wanted it to look like the Fed's CI was behind the warrant, and sure, I wanted Agapito and his group to shut the guy out. But I didn't want him gunned down.

My hope now is that the incident won't panic Agapito into closing up shop. Since the warrant was only for phone records, and the guy suspected of snitching is now in hiding, I'm hopeful it'll have little impact on their operation. On the other hand, if they all get paranoid, Benjamin Aguilar and the entire cocaine enterprise from Las Cuevas could go underground. Everything I tried to prevent could end up happening anyway, because of me. *I guess time will tell.*

Bradford and Eggs are gone for the day, and it's just Ham and me in the office. He's a good guy and I think he'll be a good investigator. We end up talking for a couple of hours, and I tell him all about my case. I pull out the file and even show him the map of Orange County, pointing out the Aguilar house and the Western Shopping Center.

It's getting late. I lock the folder in my desk and gather up my things. Ham is staring at one of only a couple of files he has, and I get the feeling he wants to show it to me. I sit back down and he rolls his chair over to my desk. "These are the phone records from Doris' phone." He sets the list on my desk. "If she's getting her dope from a lab, the number might be on here."

Though I've seen more than my share of phone records during the past couple of months, I try to look enthused. My eyes are blurred from the long day, and I give the numbers a cursory glance. I stop midway though the list and begin to laugh. "I recognize this one."

Ham twists to see the number I'm pointing at. "Raymond Sides in Copperopolis? How do you know him?"

21

SNITCHING MY SNITCH

We've decided to make one last buy from Doris, and then push for an intro with the chemist in Copperopolis. It would be one hell of a buy case, starting with a cold knock on the door and gram purchase, all the way to a multi-pound buy straight from the cook.

"Are you sure he wouldn't recognize you from the shopping cart thing?" Ham doesn't want his first real case to get derailed.

"No way, he barely looked at me." I have a mental picture of Sides standing in the driveway of the warehouse. "The other guy, the biker we busted inside the warehouse, might remember me, but he's still in custody. We should be alright."

We test the wire as I'm pulling up to the front of her house. I look across the street and get the okay from Ham. He's parked right in front of the place, and I can't figure out whether we've just become far too complacent with this case or if Bradford thinks that's really a discreet surveillance spot. She could have glanced out the window and seen the whole thing.

I continue up the walk and ring the doorbell. Doris's got another half-pound for me, and I count out the money on her kitchen table. She is a nervous little thing—smoking and gesturing, and all the while talking at the speed of sound. *Probably hooked like a dog on that stuff.*

I ease the conversation around to me meeting the connection, and she starts backpedaling. "I've told Ray all about you," she says. "But he keeps asking me where we met."

I throw my arms in the air. "I can't believe you don't . . ."

"I know, I know." Doris' gaze drops to the floor. "I just have a bad memory. Too much drugs over the years."

"Just tell Ray that we've known each other for years. Hell, I'm like a brother to you."

Doris grins. "Ray's just real careful. He got kind of paranoid after one of his friends was busted in Oakland not too long ago."

I smile to myself. That little comment just gave us enough to corroborate the phone records. Now we have Doris essentially saying Sides is the connection. If the intro doesn't work out, at least we have enough to get a search warrant for his place in the mountains. "Are you sure he can handle that much product?"

"For sure," Doris says. "He's the second biggest drug dealer I know."

My eyes widen with the obvious question nearly bursting out of my mouth. "I give up. Who's the biggest?"

"You don't know him," she says. "He's a black guy named Freddy who sells coke out of the Gas House Lounge."

I give her a playful squeeze. "How do you know I don't know Freddy? I know a lot of people."

Doris laughs. "Because you're a straight-up cranker!"

I drive back to the station with a gut feeling they're never going to go for the intro. I tell Ham what I think, and even though Bradford tells him otherwise, Ham agrees. He starts working on a search warrant for the Copperopolis house, just in case.

Bradford leaves early, and I make the most of it by getting together with Miguel earlier than usual. We get a booth in the back of our café, where I can spread out the case file in privacy.

I show Miguel the map, where I've now circled each of the half-dozen homes that showed up on Agapito's phone bill. I also tell Miguel that I've written a phone records warrant for Benjamin Aguilar's phone at the Garden Grove house. I'm hoping those records will give me more information about the man called *El Maestro*.

"You probably gonna see a lots of calls to Mexico, Pheel." Miguel says. "Maestro's cocaine coming straight across from the border."

I feel my heart quicken. The idea of investigating an international case is unheard of for a local narc. "Who's bringing it across? How does it get to Aguilar's house?"

Miguel gives me a slow shake of his head accompanied by an ominous laugh. "You going to killing me, Pheel. This guys got lots of guns down there. If they find out I talking with the cops, this guys cut my head off and put it in the water for the fishes."

It's a rough narrative, but I get the gist of it. "Don't worry, Miguel. It ain't gonna happen. I'll drop the case before I let you become fish food."

* * *

A few days later, I take a break from my big case and give Doris a call. We tape record it. She's fine with me ordering as much dope as I need, but I'll have to get it through her. Evidently, Sides told her he won't meet anybody new. Ham secures an arrest warrant for Doris, charging her with five counts of methamphetamine sales. He also finishes writing the search warrant for Sides' house in Copperopolis, and I put him in touch with my deputy buddy from Calaveras County Sheriffs.

I'm going over the Maestro case in my head as I drive home that night. Miguel must know a good deal more than he's telling me. Cocaine dealers from Mexico don't work alone. They're supported by entire networks, from the growing fields in South America to the mules who bring it across the border.

I turn onto a street that just happens to take me past the Gas House Lounge, so I pull in and park. Maybe Freddy the coke dealer will be there and I can make a new friend. A few people stop what they're doing to gauge the unfamiliar face as I walk in, and then slowly turn back to their conversations. I scan the place for a black guy, but the only one I see is making drinks behind the bar.

The place caters to a rough crowd, and most of them seem to know each other. I imagine it's a local hangout, and working my way in with anyone will take time. I grab an empty seat, right next to a burly guy with a goatee and black leather jacket. Within five minutes he and I are talking and laughing. I'm listening with one ear the entire time, to see if anybody calls the bartender by name.

"Give me and my friend another round, Freddy." The guy next to me motions to our empty glasses.

I slap some money on the bar. "This one's on me." I figure it's the least I can do for the free introduction he just gave me.

Forty-five minutes into it and we're all chewing the fat and getting real cozy: me, Carl the biker, Freddy the bartender, and some weasely guy sitting on the other side of me. I'm in the middle of telling a good joke when I become aware of someone standing off to the side, staring at me. I stop just prior to my killer punch line, and look over at a young woman with died blond hair and a face that had seen its share of pool halls.

"I know you," she says with a sense of satisfaction. "You're a cop."

Needless to say, it kills my joke like a kick in the balls. "I'm a cop?" I turn toward my new biker friend. "And who the hell's he? The FBI?"

The group around me laughs, but I know some of them might wonder. I'm the newcomer and she's the barroom vet.

"I used to work with your wife at the bank," she insists. Then she announces my wife's first and last name to everyone within earshot.

I laugh and shake my head like she's crazy. I pull a few bills out of my wallet, intentionally leaving it open on the bar—my phony drivers license facing upwards for all to see. She and one of the guys next to me lean over to glance at it as I'm slipping the bartender a twenty. "This crazy bitch needs a drink," I whisper to him, loud enough for my new buddies to hear. "And I definitely need one." They all crack up.

"His license says his name is Soto," the biker says.

The woman takes the free drink and squints into my eyes. "Must be a different guy." She backs away, still uncertain. "But you sure do look like him."

"Good looking guy, huh?" I toast my glass to her. The guys around me laugh hardily. The barfly slinks back to her seat while we all go back to our storytelling.

In the back of my mind, I can't help wondering whether the biker next to me is really convinced. That is, until he turns and offers to sell me a gram of meth. I tell him I was actually looking for some good coke. I had hoped he'd call Freddy the bartender over and set me up, but it doesn't happen. I end up offering to give the biker a lift home. Somehow during the ride, we get talking about weapons. He says he knows a guy on Bluefield with a "shitload of guns."

"I can always use another gun," I tell him. We drive by and the biker points out the house to me. He says the guy goes by Jerry, but he doesn't know him very well. He describes Jerry as a friend of a friend, and says he deals in a lot of specialty guns. I don't ask what that means, but to me it suggests illegal assault rifles or fully automatic machine guns. In either case, it's not only a decent lead, but it's a free one.

After dropping the biker at his apartment, I go back to the bar and sit outside in my car until closing. When the parking lot thins to only five cars, I note their license numbers and descriptions. Freddy the black bartender finally comes out, and I draw a circle around the gray Lincoln on my notepad. I figure I'll run a check on him later to see if there's anything to Doris' comment.

It's nearly 3 a.m. when I slide into bed. I know Gale hears me, but she doesn't say anything.

* * *

Ham and I are going up to Calaveras County to get his warrant signed. We stop by the sheriffs department first to see my buddy, Griffin. Me and Ham are sitting in the lobby waiting, along with a man and woman who are obviously plain clothes detectives. The guy stretches and yawns, and I catch a glimpse of a San Francisco PD star clipped beneath his sport coat.

"Hey, do you guys know Bobby Simms?"

They look at each other. "Yeah, narcotics?"

I introduce myself, and then tell them about the Talbott case that I worked with Simms. They have a good laugh when I describe the fiasco in the parking lot when we took the guy down. "What are you two working on all the way up here?"

The woman inspector pulls a file from her briefcase. "A missing persons case. Sort of a weird deal—some guy arrested for shoplifting in South City managed to smuggle a cyanide pill into the jail and killed himself. What's got us interested is, he was driving a car belonging to one of our missing persons."

The other inspector stretches his arms again. "We're meeting with some woman who knew the dead guy, and then heading out to his cabin in Wilseyville to take a look around."

Griffin comes out and takes me and Ham back to his office. We give him the background on the buys from Doris, and the intelligence we've gathered on Raymond Sides. He makes a call to a judge and we follow him over to the courthouse to get the warrant signed. Griffin needs a few days to gather some task force people to help, so we set up the raid for the end of the week.

It's blistering hot when we return to Copperopolis three days later. Griffin and his guys meet us out on Highway 4, and escort us in to Sides' place. The house is small, and has a detached barn next to it. We split into two teams and hit them both simultaneously.

I'm part of the barn team, along with Griffin and two other guys from Calaveras County. As we're running toward it, Ray Sides comes strolling out, carrying a big cardboard box. His eyes show a flash of panic, but we grab him before he can react. The box hits the ground with a crash, and he follows with a thud. I handcuff Sides and stand him back up. Griffin opens the box and finds an assortment of broken laboratory glassware. Inside the barn however, we come up with the rest of his meth lab.

We take Sides and the evidence back to the sheriffs department while Ham returns his warrant paperwork to the courthouse. I run into the two San Francisco inspectors again, and they've now been joined by a half-dozen other investigators.

"You guys still up here?" I squeeze past him with my several bags of evidence.

The inspector's lackadaisical yawn has been replaced by an intense manner. "You wouldn't believe what we found out there," he says with an ominous shake of his head. "The place is a torture chamber. We've been out at the property for three days straight, digging up bodies. It's a real house of horrors." He walks off, gazing at the floor.

Suddenly our lab case seems insignificant in comparison. Even with all that's going on at his department, Griffin takes us out to a local steakhouse afterwards. We stay there deep into the night, and finish the two-hour drive back just as the sun is coming up.

I stop in at the office to check my messages before heading home to get some sleep. A note is stuck to the office door telling me to call the DA's office. Bill Canaday's name is on the message, and I immediately remember him as a guy who screwed me over when I was a patrol cop. I had an early morning subpoena after working the previous night shift, and Canaday left me sitting in the waiting room all day. I finally tracked him down, only to learn that he knew the previous day that the case had been continued. The prick then got a good laugh from his cohorts when he added that he had a cocktail party to attend, and was too busy to call me.

I'm in no hurry to do anything for the guy, so I leave without contacting him. I get home just as Gale is leaving with the girls for school. I give them each a kiss and then head off to bed.

* * *

I call Canaday the next morning and he clears the phlegm from his throat before speaking. He already sounds as pompous as I remember him. "I ended up getting assigned your Pablo Troche case," he says, as if I were responsible with burdening him with something outside his job description. "And I see you wrote an X warrant, and that's what got you into Troche's house."

"Yeah, that's right."

"Well, I need to know who he is."

For a second I think I heard him wrong. "You need to know what?"

"You heard me, I need to know his name."

I sit speechless, trying to absorb his request. "First off, I never said X was a *he*. And second, why would *you* need to know X's identity?"

"This is a weight clause case," he says, as if telling me something I don't already know. "The CI is a material witness and you're going to have to disclose the name of the informant in court."

I'm dumbfounded for a second or two, and then swallow hard before trying to speak again. "Why would I do that?"

"Because the judge ordered it."

I pause another second. "Then we'll have to drop the case against Troche."

He's silent for a beat. "No. The DA's office isn't going to drop the charges," he says. "Like I said, 'It's a weight clause case.'" Canaday then tells me he's sending over a subpoena for me to appear at the trial next week. "You want the judge to order you in open court, that's up to you."

After hanging up the phone, I remain motionless at my desk. This has never happened to me before, in fact it's never happened to any narc I know. If the judge ordered the disclosure though, I could be in a tough spot. I'd have to defy a judge's order so that I could protect Miguel.

I'm trying to think of who I could call that would pull rank on Canaday. The only guy I can even imagine has enough juice to do that might be the police chief. I pass Bradford on my way to the chief's office, and I don't mention anything to him about my conversation with Canaday. *The less involvement Bradford has with my activities, the better.*

I manage to get an immediate audience with the chief, probably because I'm a narc, and his private secretary assumes anything I've got to tell the chief is vitally important.

The big boss is a busy man, so I do my utmost to pump up the importance of my visit. I lay out the weighty seizure from the Troche search warrant, and the potential for even bigger cases behind the informant. I also play up the danger he faces if anyone were to learn his true identity. "There's no doubt in my mind he'd be killed," I say.

The chief listens with a confident air, as I recount my conversation with DA Canaday. "So, apparently the judge has ordered disclosure of my informant's name," I say. "And there's no way I'm going to do that."

There, I finally said it. It's what I've been thinking all along, and the chief needs to know, without a doubt, where I stand.

I see the tiny crows feet at the corner of the chief's eyes turn slightly upward. It's the beginning of a smile that I'm certain means that he's in my corner. He knows the work I've gone through to protect Miguel; he understands the dangers involved.

"Sure you are." He stands and moves from behind his desk.

Sure I are, what? My heart pounds at the sound of his words.

"You'll give up your informant's name if the judge orders you to." The chief throws a fatherly arm over my shoulder, and pivots me toward the door. "You wouldn't risk your job or risk going to jail in order to save some shitbag drug dealer. You're too smart for that. " He nudges me out the door with the palm of his hand. "Now go do the right thing."

The heavy door closes behind me and I'm standing in front of the secretary's desk like a blind man who lost his cane. *What the hell am I supposed to do now?*

I'm walking like a zombie back to my office when I nearly get mowed down by a bunch of detectives running out the door. I throw myself into my chair and glance around the empty office. I turn on the police radio to find out what's going on, and hear what sounds like a bank robbery. I gather from the fervor that it's one of several attributed to the same suspect.

The door opens and Eggs and Ham come in. Eggs pulls the wire from under his shirt and stuffs it into the drawer. "What happened?" I ask.

"We were about to try to make a buy from the guy I was intro'd into last week," says Eggs. "But Lieutenant Preston ordered us back to the station."

Ham swivels his chair around. "He wants to set up surveillance of all the banks in the city, just in case this guy hits again."

"He just hit," I say. "The dude's home counting his money by now."

Ham shrugs. "Preston says we gotta do it, and Bradford agrees."

"Bradford agrees with Preston? There's a shocker." I get up and grab my keys. "Do me a favor and don't let them know you saw me. I got better things to do with my time."

I drive by the house on Bluefield, where the biker says I can get a gun. In the daylight it looks like any other house on the block—clean, painted, and nicely landscaped. A little bigger than the others though, it appears to have undergone a significant remodel. A four-wheel drive truck is backed into a carport, but there is no front license plate on it. The truck is not painted camouflage green, it doesn't have a gun rack, and there's no NRA bumper sticker on it. In other words, there's no hint that the guy's a weapons provocateur.

I sit on the house for a couple of hours, listening to the police radio and being thankful I got myself out of Preston's enormous circle jerk of a surveillance operation. When it starts to get dark I check my watch, figuring it's now safe to go back to the station. Even though it seems like watching the gun house was a waste of time, sitting in a bank parking lot all afternoon would have been a bigger waste.

"Where were you?" Bradford asks with palpable irritation.

"I heard that everyone had already been assigned posts, looking for this 211 guy," I say, "so I went out and just cruised around the city, checking all the banks. Had I known, I could have been on the front lines like my partners."

Bradford gauges me with his eyes, while Ham and Eggs turn away to hide their grins. Bradford huffs back to his office.

When they all leave for the night, I make as if I'm going home too. Instead, I get together with Miguel. This time I have him meet me in a parking lot behind a movie theater. He pulls up in a car I've seen him in the last two times we've met—a beat-up looking, Ford Escort. His eyes dart back and forth from the rearview mirror to the dark corners of the parking lot, and then finally back to me. I don't know how he'll react when I tell him what the DA said.

Miguel steps from the car with an odd affect. "I hearing about de attorney for Pablo Troche—he gonna find out my name, Pheel."

I shake my head, amazed at the underground pipeline's efficiency. "I'm the only person who knows it's you, and I'm not going to tell the judge. Even in our official files, I have you listed under the name, Miguel Baca."

He smiles. "They know about you, Pheel." Miguel puts a hand on my shoulder. "All of the big cocaine peoples from Las Cuevas—they sending some mans up here to follow you."

"Follow me? Why"

"They follow you so to see what person you meeting together." He points at himself. "They finding out you meeting together with me, Pheel. They coming here to kill me, Pheel."

I rub my hand over my face as the realization of Miguel's words sink in. "You found this out through your family in Las Cuevas?"

He nods. "The big cocaine peoples, they sending five mans across the border. This five mans go to Jimenez Bail Bonds in San Diego to getting from them the cars and the guns." Miguel lifts his dark eyes to stare directly into mine. "Then they coming up here to find us. They coming to kill me, Pheel."

Unconsciously, I glance around the dark lot. The bulk of the moviegoers are parked in front of the building, and other than Miguel and me, it's pretty empty back here. I think of how easy it would be for someone to take us both out right now. Especially trained killers, who would could do it and be gone in an instant. They would undoubtedly blend anonymously into any number of the East Bay's third world neighborhoods, and then be out of the country in a day or two.

"I show you something, Pheel." Miguel motions me to his car and then opens the trunk. "Those mans getting guns, I getting guns."

I peer down at a soft vinyl rifle case, similar to those our SWAT snipers carry. Miguel unzips it and hoists a scoped hunting rifle onto his shoulder. He smiles and nods approvingly. My eyes slowly close and I massage my forehead, applying pressure to my now-throbbing temples. I take in a deep breath and let it out slowly.

There may be other guns in the dark trunk of Miguel's car, but I don't want to know any more than I do. I motion for him to put the rifle away, and as he does, I scan the lot for anyone who may have seen us. My mind spins like a tire in the mud, trying to come up with my appropriate role here. A hundred people would probably give me a hundred different answers, and I know which one my chief would give me: Arrest the scumbag. Like everything else in this job, this is my decision, and one that I alone will have to live with.

He starts his car and I stand there, leaning into the open window. Miguel says he's leaving town, and plans to stay with friends in Los Angeles for a while. I tell him to give me a call when he get's settled. He reaches to shake my hand and I grasp it with both of mine. "Be careful, Miguel."

He goes his way and I finally head home for the night.

After we put the girls to bed, Gale and I stay up talking in the living room. Actually, I end up doing most of the talking, and the subject is one I seem to have a particular affinity for: me. She listens as I tell her about the *piece-of-shit* district attorney and the *piece-of-shit* judge, and all about how my pleas to the police chief fell on deaf ears. And I tell her about Miguel, and his guns, and about the squad of Mexican hit men.

Gale's face doesn't register surprise or anger, or even fear. She just looks tired. "So what are you going to do?"

"Probably start carrying something bigger than this piece-of-shit .38 I have in . . ."

"No," she says. "I mean in court. What are you going to do about disclosing your informant's name?"

Miguel's face flashes in my mind. A guy who has ostracized himself from everybody he knows and who has placed himself in grave danger. Another image edges into my consciousness; it's the police chief, so stern and so sure of himself. I think of the last thing he told me as I left his office: "Go do the right thing."

"I'm all Miguel has right now," I tell Gale. "No. I'm not going to give up his name in court, no matter what. And if that means they put me in jail for contempt, then I guess I go to jail."

Gale nods her head slowly, then lets out a frail sigh as she gets up. "There are leftover fish sticks in the refrigerator . . . I'm going to bed."

22

CLAIMING THE PRIVILEGE

Bradford begins our Monday with a morning meeting; only he's running late so the meeting doesn't start until we've waited around the office for two hours. When he finally gets to work he tells us he's planning a weeklong vacation, and I'm going to be in charge of the unit while he's gone. I know it pains him to turn the reins over to me, but there's no way he can justify giving the acting sergeant job to either of the new guys.

I thank him for the opportunity, but my appreciation is premature.

"I don't want you to do anything while I'm away," he says. "Just take care of the day-to-day stuff, and don't work on anything big until I get back."

A whole week of sitting in the office with our thumbs up our asses? "Sure, Boss. Just the day-to-day stuff." I stand and grab a file. "Sorry I can't stay for your *morning* meeting, but I have to be in court."

As I drive to the superior courthouse, the exhaustion I'm feeling is eclipsed by my anxiety. I've spent the majority of the night going over my old course notes from an informant management class, and reading through the California Evidence Code. I thought, surely there must be something written somewhere about protecting the confidentiality of an informant.

It turns out there is a rarely used privilege that may be invoked by a police officer when ordered to disclose a CI's identity. It doesn't guarantee complete protection, but it is an intermediate step in the process that allows a judge to privately weigh the defense request for disclosure against the dangers faced by the informant. My angst comes from whether or not I'll have the cojones to actually stand up in court and use it. My other option is going to jail.

Troche's case will be heard in Judge Cloris Comstock's courtroom, which has both positive and negative implications. She seems to have a comfort level with my work—which is a good thing. On the downside, she's the tipsy grandma with a penchant for beanbags and patchouli incense. The worse part is, I can't stop picturing Her Honor's manatee body burbling beneath the Jacuzzi's frothy effuse.

Sitting through the parade of afternoon defendants is like watching a sideshow of human oddities. When they start to dwindle down, a tangible eagerness in the room hints that the main event is about to take center stage. As the day wears on, I'm reminded that the *main event* is the Pablo Troche case.

About mid-afternoon, the door opens and in walks Troche and his attorney, Tony Fontana. They both survey me as if expecting my informant, X, to be seated next to me for all to see. Bill Canaday swaggers in, but he's not the tennis-playing jetsetter I remember from my days on patrol. His thinning gray hair, his flabby stomach and his bloated face suggest that he's spent more time with a martini glass than he has studying his cases. I reflect back to a comment I heard him make once when telling a bunch of his DA pals that he was taking his family to Disneyland. He said he didn't think he could survive a place that didn't allow liquor. *Now I know, he wasn't kidding.*

The bailiff swears me in and Fontana comes right at me. The illusion he seems to be constructing is that there is no informant, and that I made up everything in the search warrant affidavit. After forty-five minutes of innuendoes and inferences suggesting my entire investigation is based on fabrication, he figures the stage is finally set. "Who is the person you refer to as X, officer?"

I can feel myself choking, but I refuse to let Fontana think he's gotten me frazzled. I casually glance around the room, as if looking for a waiter to take my calamari order. Then I lean back and slide my fingers through my stringy hair. For some reason, I find a comforting potency in the rogue character I've become.

Fontana rolls his eyes toward the judge. "Your Honor?"

"Officer?" Judge Comstock says. "Did you hear the question?"

I glance over to the stew bum, Canaday. He shrugs as if he's done all he can do for me. I can't figure out whom I hate more, the drunk or the duplicitous defense attorney.

"Yes ma'am, I heard the question." I pause another beat in order to draw Fontana a step closer. Then, without acknowledging him, I turn to face the judge. "However Your Honor, I'm afraid I'll have to claim the privileges granted me under California Evidence Code, Sections 1040 through 1043, inclusive. I hereby refuse to disclose the identity of X on the grounds that doing so will place his or her life in danger."

Fontana scowls like a rookie yanked from the big game, and Canaday looks like he needs a cocktail. My bailiff buddy is nearly wetting his pants in the corner, nodding and grinning in support. The judge appraises me through her bifocals for a second and then pulls a book from under the bench. After thumbing through it, she addresses the waiting group.

"We'll reconvene in this courtroom at 10 a.m., two weeks from today. In the meantime, I'll hold an *in camera* hearing to determine whether X is a material witness to the crimes for which Mr. Troche has been charged."

I feel like jumping up and kissing the judge. She backed my play, and that left the chumps circling each other like two dogs sniffing ass. Her answer isn't the end all, but it buys me time. I'll have to convince Miguel to meet with the judge outside of the courtroom, so we can prove to her that X does indeed exist. Now I just need to find him.

* * *

By the end of the week I've picked up two more sets of phone records; one contains the most recent month's calls from Agapito Hernandez's address, and the other is from El Maestro's phone in Garden Grove.

Agapito's calls have tapered off a bit since my ploy with the feds' informant, but I expected that he'd be more cautious for a while. El Maestro on the other hand, seems to be conducting his business as normal. A couple of addresses in his area appear to be called more frequently than the others, so I make a note to ask Miguel about them the next time we talk.

On my way to work Friday morning, I swing by the Bluefield house, the gun dealer's place my drinking buddy told me about. The truck is still backed into the carport, and I hope I'm early enough to catch the guy driving away to work in it. A half-hour of waiting and the guy finally comes out the front door. He's a white, construction-worker type in his mid-thirties. He gets into the truck and I follow him out of the neighborhood. I'm able to see the rear license plate, so I jot it down on my notepad. He starts to get on the freeway, and I can see that it's a tangle of morning commuters. Abandoning my surveillance, I continue past the onramp and into the station.

Once in the office, I run the license number. It comes back to a guy named Leonard Cole, at that address. He matches the description of the guy I saw leaving the house. When I check his record, I'm rewarded with the blessing of probation. He's on it. And as an added bonus, his conditions require him to submit to a search of his house, car and person, by any law enforcement officer at any time—with or without a warrant. *Sweet Mother of the Christ Child!*

I put myself down on the board for a 6 p.m. probation search. I give Eggs and Ham a rundown of the case, and they can't believe it. "You met the informant on this while doing an after hours investigation?" Eggs asks. "What if something went wrong?"

I think about his question and I know he has a point. Going into a bar alone and trying to meet a drug connection is not something I ever would have done when I started in narcs. I had a different mindset back then. My whole life up to that point was about following rules and doing what everyone else expected me to do. I'm not that person any more. That's part of the reason I didn't get rattled by the chick who knew my wife. She was talking about a different guy—not Phil Soto.

"Following protocol is only going to get you so far," I tell him. "You gotta push the boundaries beyond just doing the *day-to-day stuff,* if you really want to pull off a big case."

Eggs smiles at the reference to Bradford. "I got this buy case I've been trying to . . ."

I hold a finger up to my lips as Bradford walks in. Bradford glances at the board and then turns to me with a tight jaw. "Can you move your probation search up to four o'clock?"

I wrote down six o'clock for a reason. "The suspect works during the day," I say. "It's a better case if we catch him at home. Why? Does six conflict with something more important?"

"I'm leaving on vacation tonight." Bradford looks at his watch. "I was hoping to get out of here at a decent hour."

I tell him that me, Eggs, and Ham can manage the probation search without him, but he bristles at the notion. "No, that's fine. I'll stay."

We set up on the house and wait until Cole pulls up in his truck. Since the search involves guns, we jump the guy before he gets in the door. He is handcuffed and searched, and then seated on the living room couch. Cole has nothing in his immediate possession but a wallet and a ring with a few keys. Mrs. Cole is in the kitchen when we enter, and is allowed to continue cooking dinner. As always, Bradford snaps a few photos before we begin our quest.

Cole appears unaffected by our presence. He's talking calmly with Bradford about the football game on TV, and seems to chalk the whole thing up to his overzealous probation officer. I overhear Cole telling Bradford that he was convicted of possessing stolen power tools a couple of years ago, but that he had unknowingly purchased them at a flea market. He doesn't mention guns.

It must have been a single-story house at one time, like most of the others in the working-class neighborhood. But a lavish remodel had recently added an entire second floor, complete with a master bedroom and gargantuan bathroom. The guy's appearance and the whole tool thing has me thinking he's in the construction trade. I'm guessing he did the remodel himself.

It's been nearly two hours, and I can see Bradford getting agitated. We've gone through the house from top to bottom, and haven't found so much as a pocketknife. Ham and Eggs have finished searching their assigned areas, and now they're watching the game with Bradford and Cole. The dinner his wife prepared is now warming in the oven, and the smell is making me salivate. I'm about ready to give the whole thing up, myself.

Bradford's face is drawn tight as he checks his watch again. I feel him staring at me as I pass, and I'm sure the only thing greater than his frustration about the late hour, is his pleasure over watching me fail.

I walk slowly through the entire house again, looking at everything and trying to envision myself hiding a bunch of guns. *Where would I stash them?*

I'm drawn upstairs to the newly constructed area. If I had the skill of a carpenter, I'd make some kind of false floor or wall. The bathroom has a huge, raised bathtub, with two wooden steps leading to it. I stare at the pedestal beneath it and then get on my hands and knees to inspect it. The base feels solid, and I surmise from the tub's numerous jets that the space beneath it houses pumps and hoses.

I rub my hands along the walls, as I make my way around the bedroom and down the hall. I'm hoping to detect some palpable irregularity, but I come up with nothing.

I hear Bradford downstairs, whining that it's almost nine o'clock. I close my eyes to clear my mind, and I walk back into the bathroom. "Ham!" I call out. "Can you come help me with something?"

My young partner trots up the stairs with a grin. "You better call this thing off, because Bradford's down there pissing his pants."

I wave away the thought. "I know, I know." Then I bend down next to the tub. "Help me move these."

With minimal effort, we slide the wooden steps a few feet over. The exposed floor beneath the steps is heavy plywood, and something odd becomes immediately visible. A small cylindrical hole, about the diameter of a peanut, has been drilled into the floor. I rub my finger over it, and feel what appears to be a metallic sleeve inside the hole.

"What do you think it is?" Ham asks.

"Not sure." I stare at it as my mind flips through the possibilities. "Could it be some kind of a keyhole?"

Ham looks at me and we both go back downstairs to the area where we first detained Cole. His wallet is still on the kitchen table, but the ring of keys is gone. "Where are the keys?" I direct the question to Bradford as much as the prisoner.

I get the same blank look from both of them. Mrs. Cole hustles past me and I reach out and snatch her arm. The alarm in her eyes tells me she's the one who took them. I grab the pocket of her apron and there they are. A small barrel key dangles from the ring, and I know I've struck oil.

The key fits perfectly into the sleeve in the plywood floor. I turn it and hear an electric, metallic clunk. I stand up and take a couple of steps backward, joining Ham in the master bedroom. His mouth is agape as we both stare at the hinged wall that just opened. Cole had constructed an entire room, about the size of a small kitchen, and hid the secret space behind a false wall. We swing the heavy door all the way open and view an exotic firearms collection numbering in the hundreds.

The seizure is so extensive that we have to call for a crew of ATF agents from San Francisco. It takes us until midnight to clear and catalog all the guns, and I stick around for another hour to book Cole into the jail and then get a written statement from him.

I knew that Bradford was dying to leave after we found the stash, but he couldn't bring himself to pass on an opportunity to rub elbows with the federal agents. He finally took off on his vacation at 11 o'clock. *Good riddance!*

* * *

I have a call into Judge Comstock's bailiff, but he doesn't know when the judge plans to meet for her secret hearing. I let him know that it'll take me a little time to find my informant and coax him in.

It's just me, Ham, and Eggs in the office for the next week, and I suggest we all go out to breakfast and talk about our cases. Over a plate of ham and eggs, I give Ham and Eggs the rundown on Miguel and then describe the courtroom drama from last week. "In the meantime," I say, "we're going to have some fun."

Eggs describes the frustration he's had setting up a buy with the cocaine dealer he was just introduced to. His first attempt was thwarted by Preston's Million Man bank surveillance, which by the way, still hasn't turned up a suspect. I have Eggs set up the phone recorder when we get back, and we go ahead and give the guy a call. Fortunately, the dealer still remembers Eggs, and agrees to sell him a quarter ounce for $500. We get Eggs wired up, and me and Ham follow him in the van.

The dealer's house is perched on a hillside, off a narrow road. I've been in this neighborhood before, and it can be difficult to find an inconspicuous spot for the van. We rehearsed it with Eggs, and it's just supposed to be a quick in-and-out buy. But as soon as he meets the guy, I can see it's going to be a road trip.

"Come out in the garage," the dealer says to Eggs. "I want you to take a ride with me."

The garage door opens and out pulls a white stretch limousine—brand spanking new. It turns out they aren't tripping to go get the dope, because the dealer's already got it with him. He just wants to show off his limo to Eggs.

Since the windows are smoked and the guy can't see very well behind him, following along in the van is fairly simple. I'm driving a few cars behind, and Ham is in the back of the van, tape-recording the conversation over the wire.

"How do you like my ride?" the dealer asks Eggs. "I just bought it. Paid cash for it, too. Thought it would impress my customers."

The deal goes down in the back of the limo, and a few minutes later the guy drops off Eggs back at the house. We follow Eggs out of the neighborhood and back to the police station.

We meet up in the office and discuss where to take the case from here. Neither Ham or Eggs realize that the statement we caught on tape plays right into our hands. "Your guy screwed himself," I tell Eggs. "He basically admitted that the new limo is used as an instrument during the commission of making drug sales."

"Yeah?" Eggs looks over at Ham and then back to me. "So, what does that mean?"

"It means we can seize his new ride."

Eggs spends the rest of the day working on the search warrant, and Ham helps me with the massive collection of guns. We have to make certain each one is unloaded, run checks on all of the serial numbers, and then package them safely for storage. I suspect that the Alcohol, Tobacco, & Firearms agents are going to redo everything again if they decide to prosecute the case federally, but it's still got to be done.

Two days later, Eggs has his signed search warrant in hand and five sheriff's deputies on standby to help us with the raid. We bust through the front door as the guy is counting out a few-hundred prescription Valium tablets on his desk. After handcuffing him, Eggs finds another half-pound of cocaine hidden in a footlocker under the bed, along with a few thousand dollars.

The dealer's face is set in a look of mostly surprise, with maybe a hint of aggravation. It remains that way throughout the entire search, until Eggs asks him for the keys to his cars. The expression turns to aching bereavement as the cops drive off in both his new stretch limo and his vintage 1966 Corvette Coupe—both seized under state asset forfeiture laws.

The police parking lot looks like a wedding reception when we arrive. A crowd has gathered, and the only thing missing from the event is the thrown rice. Employees of every assignment and rank want to check out the latest departmental vehicles, and maybe get a chance to pose for photos in one of them. Even Captain Parks is there, shaking our hands and congratulating us on a fine case. I can tell he's already got his eye on the Corvette.

A wicked smile crosses my face when I suddenly envision Bradford. He's sitting out on a beach somewhere, when a discarded newspaper finds its way to him. He picks it up and sees Egg's case bannered across the front page, accompanied by a photograph of the two seized cars. *Poor guy.*

We invite the sheriff's deputies up to the PBA so we can buy them a thank you drink. The place is bustling, but we manage to claim one end of the bar for ourselves. Cops from other departments are there, a couple of emergency room nurses, and a bunch of girls from the courthouse as well. Larry is behind the counter, steaming a new batch of barkers. The jukebox vibrates to *Everybody Have Fun Tonight,* by Wang Chung.

I'm in the middle of a game of liar's dice when my bailiff buddy from Judge Comstock's court sees me and makes his way over. "Did the judge get a hold of you?"

"A hold of me?" I'm tempted to make a joke, but I resist. "Not since I was in court. Why?"

"She wants to set up the *in camera* hearing for Monday morning." He motions Larry over and tells him to bring me another drink. "You better tune up your informant in a hurry."

The activity level wanes as the night wears on, and the smart ones call it quits and head home. I find myself still keyed up from the day's victorious case, and misguided by alcohol and a losing hand, I stay fastened to my barstool. Our group has evaporated down to just me, Ham, and one of the nurses, who sometime during the last hour slid her chair over to join us.

She's murmuring something about being a palm reader. The next thing I know she's grabbing my hand and telling me about my *lifeline.* Ham raises his eyebrows as the woman leans down to supposedly examine my *love line.* I'm suddenly aware of something slimy on my palm, and I realize she's licking my hand.

With my *marriage line* getting shorter by the minute, I see this as a clear indication that it's time for me to go. I grab my leather jacket and bolt for the door. Ham follows me out, and I'm suddenly reminded that we drove up here together. I take him back to the police department and drop him at his car.

It's 2 a.m. and the streets are pretty much empty. When I pull out of the lot, a pair of headlights sweep across my face. At first I think it's Ham's car, but then I'm not so sure. As I follow my normal route home, I become aware that the car is still behind me and it's definitely not Ham.

At a large, well-lit intersection, I slow down enough to make out the outlines of two men. I'm thinking that they must have been parked near the police building, watching for my car. I speed up and make an abrupt turn down a side street, and the car stays behind me. My hand reaches over to the passenger seat, and I grope in the dark for my handgun. I find it under my jacket, and tuck it in the back of my pants. A few erratic turns later and the headlights seem even closer. Now I feel my heart pounding, and any haze from the drinks has pretty much disappeared. I can't go home and let them know where I live, but I can't keep driving in circles either.

I take a turn on two wheels and accelerate the wrong way down a short one-way street. My car hits a speed bump hard as I slide into the parking lot of an elementary school. The lights are far enough behind me that I have enough time to jump from the car. I sprint to a narrow driveway that leads toward the back of the school, and then dive into a cluster of bushes. With my gun aimed directly at the mouth of the driveway, I squat there as quietly as I can, and wait. I fully expect to see two Mexican assassins in combat formation, inching their way toward me. But I wait, and I wait. After an hour or longer, I creep out of my concealed position, and work my way back to my car. The other car and the two men are gone.

My car sits cockeyed in the empty lot, with the driver's door wide open—probably the way I left it when I jumped out. I inch toward it as if someone might be inside, but it's empty. The glove compartment is open, papers are scattered on the floor, and my leather jacket is gone. I jump in, start up the engine, and tear out of the school. Now I'm speeding through the neighborhood, looking for them. Any set of headlights on the barren roadway would be immediately suspect, but I'm unable to find a single moving vehicle.

After circling my block until I'm positive nobody's following me, I finally pull into my driveway. It's 4:12 a.m. when I wobble into our bedroom. Gale sits straight up in bed, and though I can't see her face in the shadows, I know it's not smiling.

"Where the hell is the jacket I bought you?" Her voice is low and even.

She doesn't ask me where I've been, if I'm okay, or if I've been abducted by aliens—she just wants to know what happened to the jacket. Uncanny.

"Somebody stole it," I say.

Gale's murky outline stares at me though the darkness. "You were probably flat out on your drunken ass and they took it right off of you."

I start to say something, and then sweep my numb hand in the air dismissively. "You don't know what you're talking about."

Gale flings herself onto her side, facing away from me. She angrily bunches the pillow under her head, but says nothing more. I stay on the living room couch the remainder of the night, peering out the window whenever a car passes.

I'm up before Gale and the girls, and head into work before the sun even comes up.

23

When the Cat's Away

I've been looking for a bona fide excuse to get down to Southern California, and finally I think I have it. Two things are now working in my favor: Bradford is gone, and the judge wants my informant to appear at the secret hearing. Maybe that's how I'll justify my road trip.

Captain Evancheck is in his office, stacking police journals into a cardboard box. I stop at the door and look around at the empty walls. "Captain?"

He shoves the box aside. "Have a seat, Soto."

I'm certain that the packing means his stint as commander of the investigations division is up, but I don't ask. Instead, I give him a brief rundown about my informant, Miguel. I describe the Pablo Troche case, the issues going on in Comstock's court, and about the potential for even bigger cases against major traffickers down south. He grins wildly, and I know if anybody gets it, he does.

"Cut to the chase, Soto," he says. "What do you want from me?"

"I'd like to fly down to pick up my informant for court," I say. And then I quickly add, "And I'd like to spend a few days down there nosing around a couple of houses that I think may be involved."

Evancheck ruefully shakes his head, as if he's about to deny my request. "Do you really think you'll be able to make this happen?"

I look him right in the eye. "I do."

He holds up a bladed palm and makes the sign of the cross, just as a priest would during communion.

I stare back at him, a little confused.

"I just blessed it," he says with a smirk. "Now get outta here. And make sure you don't get into any trouble down there. Get in touch with the local cops."

I'm just about skipping back to my office. I suspect he may not have been so generous if he hadn't been on his way out, but what do I care? The ex-narc blessed it! The best part is that I can make the trip over the weekend, and hopefully bring Miguel back in time for the hearing on Monday. I won't have to abandon my post as acting sergeant, and I'll probably still beat Bradford back from his vacation. The only problem is that I still haven't figured out how I'll be able to get in touch with Miguel.

A quick phone call and I'm booked on the Friday afternoon flight From Oakland to John Wayne airport in Orange County. I decide not to tell anyone else about my little excursion, except Gale, of course. She isn't thrilled, but at this stage of the game it probably makes little difference in her daily life.

Although my expenses will be reimbursed by the city, I swing by the bank for some cash. Sometimes I forget just how bad I look, but when I walk into the Bank of America on Second Street, I'm quickly reminded of it. I'm standing in the teller line when I see a young woman behind the counter watching me with panic in her eyes. My initial reaction is to check my zipper, but then I realize it's the entire ensemble that's made her uncomfortable—the greasy hair, the goatee, the pierced ear, and the long trench coat. The woman keeps her eye on me as she inches her hand under the counter.

I reach beneath my coat and unclip the badge from my belt. Raising it up so she can see it, I give her a smile. I guess she gets the drift before actually pressing the robbery alarm, because nothing happens. The woman stands behind my teller, watching me throughout the entire transaction. At one point she makes the comment, "You must be undercover."

Ya think? I smile politely; hoping nobody else in the bank heard her. The teller hands me my money, and I'm certain they're thrilled to see me leave.

I'm getting into my car when I notice a familiar face bobbing through the bank lot, and I call out to him. "Alberto!"

The Big A does a double take and then gives me a sheepish nod. Instinctively, I glance round to see who he's meeting. Must be a heroin connection lurking in some nearby doorway. He comes over to my car and we talk for a couple of minutes. He asks about Miller, and I tell him about his transfer back to patrol. The conversation is short and a bit stilted. As I watch Alberto walk back the way he came, I chalk up the awkwardness to his heavy drug use and the fact that we haven't worked together in several months.

I pack a small carry-on with a change of clothes, a Thomas Bros. map, binoculars, and my case file. The patrol watch commander calls a uniformed cop off the street to drive me to the airport. He's a young, wide-eyed cop named Chase. He tells me he spotted a drug suspect down on Sonoma one night during his first week on the job, but his training officer wouldn't let him stop the guy.

"Why not?" I ask.

"The suspect was you." The cop smiles. "My training officer told me you were probably making an undercover buy, and just to keep on driving. I wouldn't believe you were a cop, and I made him show me your employee photo when we got back to the station."

At the airport, I down a couple of pizza slices while waiting at my gate. Good thing, because the flight is delayed an hour. But by 7:30 p.m. I'm merging my rental car onto the 405 freeway in Orange County.

A lighted sign points to a small motel called Four Winds. It's just off the freeway, and looks to be less than a mile from the county courthouse. The surrounding neighborhood isn't the greatest, but what the hell. All I need is a place to sleep. I stretch onto the bed and stare up at the ceiling. *How am I ever going to find Miguel?*

A thought comes to mind and I dive across the bed to the tiny table in the corner of the room. I grab the case file and spread my collection of phone records under the light. "Yes," I say aloud as I pluck a page from Agapito Hernandez's packet. Hunched over the nightstand, I dial the Southern California number with the notation next to it. Miguel had identified it as the place he lived several months ago while he was driving for Agapito.

A recorder comes on with a woman's voice. Her soft tone is heavily accented in Spanish. I quickly get past my amusement about his *friend* being a woman, and realize that I have to decide whether to leave a message, and if so, what it should say. After all, I'm not sure this is even where Miguel is staying, and I still don't know Miguel's real name. In any case, I doubt if he'd appreciate me outing him as a snitch.

I settle on a message that could be easily mistaken by anyone else as a wrong number, but one that Miguel would recognize. "Miguel," I say in a low voice. "Call Felipe." I scramble to flip the phone around to see the motel's number, and I leave it on the message. As soon as I hang up the phone, I regret that move. If any of Miguel's associates are involved in the effort to find me and kill the informant, I may have just handed them my location—including my room number. It was a stupid gamble, but it was the only card I could play.

I turn out the lights and walk into the tiny bathroom. Peering out the mildewed window into the parking lot, I feel alone and vulnerable. This case could potentially lead to be the biggest drug seizure in my department's history, yet I'm finding the stakes much higher than I ever anticipated. I look at the pile of records spread across the table and wonder if this will all be worth it—not that I would turn back now anyway.

I wedge a chair tightly beneath the doorknob and set my gun on the nightstand next to me. I kick my shoes to the floor and pull the stained bedcover over my tattered clothes. Headlights sweep across the ceiling and footsteps scamper up the steps. I hear a woman's muffled laughter in another room and a dog barking in the distance. I lie there in the dark, waiting. Waiting for Miguel to call; waiting for killers from Las Cuevas; waiting for morning to come.

I'm startled by the ringing phone. I flail for it in the dark, and I'm aware that the clock reads 1:30 a.m. before I even realize where I am. "Yeah?"

"Pheel! You calling for me at my friend house?"

My mind's lens comes quickly into focus. I tell Miguel that I am in Santa Ana and I need to meet with him. We agree on four o'clock the following afternoon at the Western Shopping Center, where he used to meet with Maestro.

I spend the morning checking two other homes, both appearing several times on Maestro's Walnut Avenue phone records. One is in Santa Ana and the other is in Fountain Valley—both within a few miles.

Other than their proximity and the volume of calls, I have scant evidence to tie them to the operation at this point. In the afternoon, I phone my department and run a couple of cars parked in front of the Fountain Valley place. Both come back registered to Roberto Aguilar-Castaneda at that address. Based on the name's similarity to Benjamin Aguilar, I make the assumption that the guy is a relative. In any case, I think I can patchwork the facts together in such a way as to get a search warrant for that house as well.

The Santa Ana house might be a little tougher. No cars are visible in front, and being Saturday, there is no way I can access county parcel records. I watch the place right up until my meeting time with Miguel, but I never see anyone enter or leave.

Miguel seems relaxed and in good spirits when we find each other in the lot. Gone is the gun-toting paranoiac I spoke with in the theater lot two weeks ago. It occurs to me that he's more comfortable down here, closer to his family and his friends, and closer to Mexico. The Bay Area is as foreign to him as Orange County is to me. Then again, the source of his calmness could be nothing more complicated than sex with his girlfriend and a good night's sleep.

We leave his car in the lot and I drive him past all three houses. He's never been to any of them, and other than the truck in front of Maestro's house on Walnut, nothing looks familiar. He agrees that Roberto Aguilar-Castaneda is probably a relative, and his Fountain Valley address might be involved somehow. He says that relatives' homes are often used to hide the organization's money. The theory is that if the police bust one place and not the other, they come away with only drugs or only money, but not both. I make a note of it, figuring to rely heavily on that bit of expertise when writing my affidavit.

I finally have to break the bad news to Miguel. When I tell him about the order to disclose, I quickly follow it up by describing my elaborate efforts to block it. He doesn't seem as concerned as I thought he would, nor upset by fact that he'll have to come back with me on Monday. He just nods and says, "Okay, Pheel"

"I've got it all set up at a secret location near the Oakland Airport," I tell him. "Nobody will be there but the judge, district attorney, and a court reporter. The judge just wants to know that you're a real person and that you weren't lying about Pablo Troche."

His expression changes abruptly and I realize the finer details of my explanation didn't translate well. "I not lying, Pheel."

I reassure Miguel as best I'm able, and I change the subject before I gum it up again. I ask how he thinks Maestro moves the drugs across the border.

"I think he putting the drug inside the car." After a few clarification questions, I get that he means hidden or welded within the car's frame. He doesn't know about any car in particular, but says they use old cars that won't draw attention. I make a notation in the file, just in case it comes in handy down the road.

We agree to meet at the same spot on Monday morning. In the day remaining, I hope to make my presence known to the local police departments. Though I doubt I'll find any narcs around on a Sunday, at least I'll have kept my word with Evancheck. I'll also gather the names of appropriate agency contacts for when I return with my warrants.

Miguel leaves and even though it's late, I make another pass by the Fountain Valley address. It's the nicest of the three, and sits in among other upscale homes. Lights are on, but I still see no signs of activity. I drive by the Santa Ana house next, still trying to figure out how I'll be able to justify a warrant for it. The phone calls alone aren't enough, and nothing seems to be going on there.

I drive to Garden Grove last, and park a half-block from Aguilar's place. The house is dark and his truck is parked in the driveway. I sit staring at the house for what seems like hours, straining to make out something through the darkness. My eyes begin to tire, and they rebel against me by playing tricks. A person moving on the front porch turns out to be an overgrown bush, jostled by the wind. Headlights turning into the driveway are merely reflections from a passing car.

I'm tired and hungry and I have to take a leak. I convince myself that Old Maestro has gone to bed, and to stay any longer is just a waste of time. I start the car and pull onto Walnut. As I pass the house, there's a flash of light. *Are my eyes are misleading me, yet again?*

But the neurotic fear of missing something important summons me back. I park the car again, and watch from another angle. When I see another flash, I freeze in place. My whole body hiccups when I see what seems to be a flashlight moving behind the fence, in his backyard.

I get out and walk down the opposite side of the street. Nobody else is out, and I'm petrified I'll be spotted. Now, the yard is dark. I cross over at the end of the block and head back on his side of the street. My chest burns with tension, and I take in a deep breath to soothe it. One bonehead move and my whole case goes to crap.

Slowing as I approach the fence line, I casually glance up and down the street to see if I'm being watched. The thought of a setup crosses my mind, and I wonder if I could have been lured here intentionally. Somebody could be hiding in any one of these cars, waiting to kill me.

I give myself a mental slap in the face. *Don't be such a big pussy! Besides, they wouldn't kill you right in front of Aguilar's house. They would ambush you at your motel.* Strange as it seems, the thought of being killed later is a momentary comfort that keeps me going.

I crouch down to a small knothole, and peer through. The backyard is pitch black, and it takes me a few seconds to differentiate any contrast at all. I slowly begin to distinguish the outline of a car parked there. It's in the yard, behind a hinged wooden gate with a lock on it. I try to blink added power to my fatigued eyes, but I can only make out the car's boxy form. Its interior light suddenly comes on, and I realize that was the flash I first saw. The dim light is enough to illuminate the oxidized, rust-colored Rambler. The car's trunk slams closed and I jump backwards. When I stoop to the hole again, I see a silver-haired man reach through the open driver's door and press down the lock. The yard goes dark again and I hurry away.

I hadn't seen the car prior to this, and the man has obviously gone to some trouble to secure it. As I drive around the corner, I weigh out the scenario in my mind: *Why would he park the car in the backyard rather than in the driveway? Maybe it isn't running. If it doesn't run, why keep it secured behind a fence? And why would the guy be out there at night, screwing around in the trunk? Was he loading something into the trunk? Yes, I think that's what I saw. It sure strengthens my affidavit if that's what I saw. Yes, I'm sure that's what I saw.*

I pull over in the park around the corner and log my observations into the file. I sure wish I could have gotten a glimpse of the license plate. Nevertheless, when I combine what I saw with what Miguel told me about drugs being transported across the border in old cars, I know the probable cause scale just tipped in my favor.

I'm suddenly aware of my growling stomach. I toss the case file onto the seat next to me and take surface streets back toward my motel. I'm watching headlights in my rearview mirror all the way, still conscious of how exposed I am down here. A small green building catches my eye two blocks shy of my place. It has a big plastic chicken on the roof and a sign that says OPEN 24-HOURS. I don't know what it has to eat, but at this point I really don't care.

I turn off the engine and just as I'm about to get out of the car, I see two figures moving toward me from behind. They're wearing dark clothes and walking slowly, looking around the dark lot as if they don't want to be seen. I grasp my gun and untuck it from the belt at the small of my back. I hold it on my lap as I slide down low in my seat. The two guys pass without noticing me, and then pause at the back of the small restaurant. They remind me of The Big A, only these two don't appear to be looking for drugs at the moment.

I watch as they take out black ski masks and pull them down over their faces. *Son-of-a-bitch! Of all the shitty times to stumble into an armed robbery*. I quickly come to the conclusion that any involvement on my part will end up badly. If I were to make an arrest, or even worse, get into a shooting, my case down here is done. Any action I take will end up in the paper, identifying me as a cop from the Bay Area. Even simply going on record as a witness to the crime screws up my anonymity.

I turn on my headlamps, illuminating the two jerkoffs against the restaurant wall. They stop in mid-motion and shield themselves with raised forearms. I see a gun in one guy's hand, and he hastily tucks it behind him. At this point, they probably think I'm a slow-moving driver about to start my car. But at the risk of really pissing them off, I hit the brights. I'm suddenly transported back to a drive-in movie. Thankfully, the would-be robbers take off running instead of firing into my lights.

I pull across the street and call in on a payphone. I don't leave my name, but I tell the police dispatcher that two suspicious men were about to rob the Chicken take-out place on Westminster Avenue. I end up eating a couple of Jumbo Jacks in my room.

Something nags at me as I'm falling asleep, but I can't figure out what it is. I see my case file on the table, so I know I didn't leave it in the car. I check to make sure my gun is next to the bed, and that I remembered to put the chair against the door.

All night I toss and turn, waiting for my alarm to go off. Strange dreams rotate through my mind, overlapping one another like colored hands on a finger painting: Pablo Troche and his shyster attorney, Tony Fontana. A trio of men from Las Cuevas, dressed like Ninjas and carrying guns. Then, Benjamin Aguilar, the gray-haired man known as El Maestro; his rusty Rambler full of cocaine, and Miguel sitting behind the wheel. The two guys in the chicken restaurant parking lot—their faces covered with ski masks. One of them stumbles and his mask slides off. It's Alberto!

I shake myself from the dream and sit up in bed, suddenly realizing what's been gnawing at me all night. The reason those guys in the restaurant parking lot reminded me of Alberto is because they were up to the same thing. Alberto was lurking outside the bank that day I saw him, because he was about to rob it. And that means he's probably the guy they want for all those other bank robberies.

My clock shows 4:30 a.m., and it's still a good three hours before I'm supposed to meet Miguel. I pack up my things and wake the motel clerk so I can check out. The freeway is already filling with cars, so I take side streets into Garden Grove. Walnut Avenue is still and quiet, and Aguilar's house is dark. I sit down the block in my car, waiting for just the right amount of daylight. When the first orange rays make their way through the valley haze, I get out of my car and walk quickly up the street. I stop at the knothole in the fence, and again check up and down the street before looking in. Aided by the faintest amount of daylight, I squint to see the Rambler's license number. I write it onto my palm and quickly return to my car.

I use a public phone to call my department. They run the license number for me, but make me answer a series of questions before giving me the information. Apparently they feel it's odd that a narcotics officer would be calling from Southern California at 6 a.m. to run a license number. The good news is, they do it for me and it comes back registered to the other house—the one in Santa Ana. Until now, I had only marginal cause to search that place. Now that I've seen El Maestro taking what I believe to be cocaine out of the trunk of a car registered there, the Santa Ana house is a slam-dunk.

I nurse a cup of coffee at Denny's until it's time to pick up Miguel. He's waiting there in his classic work attire, but with the addition of jet-black sunglasses. I chuckle to myself at the Hollywood disguise, but make no mention of it to him.

Our plane off-boards at Oakland's Terminal-1 just after 10 a.m. We take a cab the quarter mile up Hegenberger to the Bayside Park Hotel. I coach Miguel a little along the way, reminding him that his name is Miguel Baca. I don't specifically tell him to lie about his name, I just leave it hanging. As far as that goes, I justify it to myself as a necessary insurance policy in the event the judge ultimately decides to order disclosure in open court. Judge Comstock is waiting in a fourth-floor suite, with a wide-eyed court reporter who looks as if she's been asked to do espionage behind enemy lines. We sit in awkward silence for five minutes, waiting for DA Canaday. He arrives looking like he's been on an all-night binge. Judge Comstock and I exchange looks, but the court reporter is off in her own world and Miguel sits in fixed catatonia behind his shades.

The reporter swears in Miguel, and Canaday immediately steps around me as if this is his show. He straightens his rumpled necktie and clears his gluey throat.

"Take a seat, Canaday." The judge thrusts an arm out in front of him as she settles into her chair. "I'll ask the questions here." The DA melts back into the corner.

"Good morning, young man."

"Jes, good morning." Miguel's head pans back and forth between the judge and the DA, and I realize he expected the judge to be the man. He figures it out quickly enough, and then focuses mostly on Comstock.

"Can you remove your sunglasses for me?" The judge asks in an apologetic tone. "I like to see peoples' eyes."

Miguel complies. In the soft light of the hotel room, his expression conveys a genuine tone.

"Can you state your name, young man?"

"My name?" He glances at me, then back to the judge. "My name es Miguel Baca."

I cringe, hoping the look to me wasn't a tipoff. Thankfully, it seems to have come across as a silent exchange of reassurance.

"Do you know a person by the name of Pablo Troche?" the judge asks.

"Jes. I know Pablo."

"Have you ever seen Pablo in possession of cocaine?"

"Pablo, he have lots of cocaine. I see him at Tres Monkeys Bar."

The judge pauses with a confused look, and I have to chuckle at Miguel's effort to anticipate the questioning. The Three Monkeys reference was in a different warrant—the one for Agapito Hernandez's phone records.

Judge Comstock asks two or three more questions, but it's already clear that she's on our side. Miguel speaks in a low tone, and though he doesn't address the judge in proper etiquette, it almost enhances his candor.

The recorder's fingers pad her tiny keyboard as Judge Comstock makes her final ruling on the matter. "I'm satisfied that this informant has no exonerating evidence to provide the defendant. Therefore, X's identity will not be disclosed in future court proceedings with regard to this case."

She thanks Miguel for coming forward with his information, but I'm not sure he grasps it. I thank the judge and the court reporter, then blow past Canaday with a demeaning sneer. *Useless pile of shit!*

I accompany Miguel back to the airport and buy him breakfast as we wait at his gate. I hand him his return ticket to John Wayne Airport and $200 for his trouble. The security office is on my way out, and I stop there to phone the PD for a ride back. Dispatch tells me they'll send a unit right away.

As I leave airport security, I'm reminded of the last time I was here. I was a young uniformed cop and I had been dispatched to pick up the police chief. Just before his flight landed, I had to arrest a loud-mouthed drunk. The security office was all the way across the airport, and after dumping off my prisoner, I had to race back to the chief's gate in time to greet him. I remember thinking at the time, what a big deal it was to chauffeur the chief back to the station. As I emerge in front of the terminal with a bag slung over my shoulder, my ride pulls up in a marked patrol car. The young cop behind the wheel has the same expression I must have had.

I get back to the station and trot up the stairs to my office. I open the door to find Bradford sitting there with Ham and Eggs, about to begin his Monday meeting. He looks at me with a *glad you could join us* look, but he says nothing.

I toss the bag on my desk and sit down. "How was your vacation?"

"It was okay." Bradford glances at my partners—both sitting there in silence. An inquiring frown settles on his face. His eyes sweep around the room as if gauging any changes. "Did anything happen while I was gone?"

Ham and Eggs both turn to look at me.

24

The Final Straw

The three of us stand silently in the back lot, watching Bradford. His jaw is taught as he paces between the limousine and the Corvette. "You took these from somebody?"

"It's permitted by state asset forfeiture laws," I say.

"I know that!" Bradford's eyes flash fury. "I just can't believe you went and . . . Why couldn't you wait until I got back?"

I consider spouting some colorful rationale, but we all know why I couldn't wait. *I simply wanted to do what I wanted to do, and I didn't want to wait for you.*

I remain silent as we march back upstairs past the captain's office. Evancheck has moved out and Captain Parks is arranging a ficus on his new desk. It'll be much tougher for me now that my key supporter has been transferred to another division.

"Nice work on those car seizures," the captain calls out to Bradford, clearly unaware that he was on vacation when it happened.

I smile as Bradford accepts the praise with a wave, then walks into his own office and slams the door. The three of us peel off and sit quietly at our desks. Ham finally turns to me. "Have you even told Bradford about your trip to LA?"

I shake my head. "Guess I better let him know."

"That's gonna leave a bruise," Eggs says.

Before I get up, the door opens and Bradford huffs in. "I got a captain calling me from Santa Ana PD."

I do my best to explain the sudden turn my case took when the judge nearly ordered my informant's identity disclosed in full court. "Had I known, I . . ."

Bradford dumps my excuse like a dirty ashtray. "You went over my head. You got Evancheck to approve your little *yah-ha* to Los Angeles."

"Yah-ha?" I feel myself hunching forward like a possessed gargoyle. "What the fuck is a yah-ha? I brought a confidential informant in for a court-ordered hearing, and I did it on my own time. I blew my whole weekend down there." I'm standing up now, and we're facing off in the middle of the office. "In fact, I should probably submit an overtime slip and get paid for it!"

"Go ahead," Bradford says. "Might as well. It's the last time you'll be going down there on the city's dime."

"Really?" I've completely come off the rails by now. "That's funny, because I'm finishing up five search warrants on a case, and I plan to execute three of them in Orange County next week."

His eyes burn into me as we stand face-to-face. I almost think he's about to take a swing at me, but he storms back to his office instead. My desk phone rings and it's him. "Come into my office, right now."

I slam down the phone without responding. Ham and Eggs are cowering over their paperwork, and the entire investigative bureau has stopped to hear the two rams clash horns. Those who work most closely with us know it's been building for a while.

I plunge into Bradford's office, ready for the second round. "Don't you ever challenge me in front of my men," he says.

"Then don't come at me with your pathetic criticisms," I say. "I'm sick and tired of hearing it."

He's pissed off and I'm pissed off, and I know this conversation is only going to go from bad to worse. I reel back and regard him with icy cold eyes, then turn and leave.

The remainder of my week is spent typing my warrants. Bradford and I pass one another, but we don't speak. I have one search warrant for each of Agapito Hernandez's two homes on Orlando Avenue. The three other search warrants are for Benjamin Aguilar's place in Garden Grove, his relative's house in Fountain Valley, and the home in Santa Ana where the old Rambler is registered. By Friday night, the two local warrants have been signed by a judge and everything is in place for a coordinated assault on one of Southern California's most prolific cocaine cartels.

I'm antsy all weekend, and I spend most of it going over my files. Gale senses the tension, but doesn't ask me much about it. I decide to fly out early on Sunday in order to prepare for Monday's raids. Gale corrals the girls over to the front window and they all wave goodbye, though by now they might as well be waving to the mailman.

* * *

The briefing hall is teeming with cops—some in uniform, some in SWAT fatigues, and some with drug-sniffing dogs. It's six o'clock in the morning, yet they look like they've been up for hours. I glance at their shoulder patches: Garden Grove Police, Santa Ana Police, Fountain Valley Police and Orange County Sheriff. Emergency Services and fire department personnel are also present, along with three helicopter units. A sheriff's lieutenant steps up to the podium microphone and introduces me to the auditorium. The place grows silent.

I stand there in my hooded sweatshirt and ragged jeans, staring into a sea of hardcore soldiers.

"Thanks for coming to help us out this morning." I thumb a strand of greasy hair back behind my ear. "This morning's searches are the culmination of a three-month investigation that started in my city with a single search warrant, and evolved into a statewide trafficking network. We have three search warrants to execute this morning in your county, and I can only hope they pay off and make your time and effort worthwhile."

I then go into greater detail and describe the background of each location. The group is divided into thirds, according to their geographic jurisdictions, and each one is given specific assignments. I supply each group supervisor a clipboard to log names, ranks, and agencies of those participating. I'll need accurate records for my report, as well as for any future court hearings.

As the briefing winds down and the assault teams file out of the auditorium, I check the logs. Fifty-three public safety personnel have shown up to assist me—none of whom I've ever met or worked with before. I watch as they get into their cars and vans and head off to their respective field staging locations. My head buzzes and my stomach churns as I'm struck with the profound responsibility I have in all this.

We may find nothing, and the entire operation could end up as the joke told at narcotic conferences for the next decade. In an even worse scenario, any one of these people could be shot or killed.

Could I have been mistaken? Could I have become so caught up in Miguel's tales that I've strayed from reality? I force the misgivings and self-doubts from my mind and walk out to my car.

"At exactly eight o'clock this morning, police officers fanned out around the state to execute a number of high-risk search warrants." The reporter's voice resonates the magnitude of the day's top story. "Cocaine strongholds hit simultaneously in northern and southern California yielded record amounts of the drug, as well as firearms and stacks of cash that are still being tallied at this hour. Conspiracy and drug possession charges have been filed against 51 year-old Benjamin Aguilar of Garden Grove, 47 year-old Armando Diaz of Fountain Valley, and 39 year-old Agapito Hernandez from the San Francisco Bay Area."

I sit at the foot of my motel bed, transfixed by his words. A dozen glossy photos are laid out on my table—each one depicting either money, or guns, or neatly wrapped kilogram packages, stacked like loaves fresh from the oven. A photograph of the faded Rambler from El Maestro's yard sits at the top of the stack—the car's trunk having contained the majority of the recovered cocaine.

The phone in my room rings late into the night with congratulatory messages, but I don't mind. I fight through the exhaustion, knowing that this is a once-in-a-lifetime event, and one I should bask in. I finally fall into the first sound sleep I've had in months.

* * *

A local newspaper reporter is waiting for me when I finally get through the back lot and first floor of the police building. I give him some savory specifics, making him feel like he's gotten something of a scoop. The downtime in my own office feels nice. I'm thinking about giving Miguel a call to thank him, and right then my phone rings.

"Hey Pheel."

I tell him about the success of the operation and the amounts of cocaine seized.

"Maestro, he was almost dry," he says, using an oddly American-sounding slang.

"Dry?" I sit straight up in my chair. "He had more dope than we've ever seen."

"I know, Pheel. Maestro, he was jus going to driving across to pick up more."

I sigh, imagining that I could have intercepted even more had my timing been different. Miguel doesn't say how he knows all this, but he's been right all along and I have no reason to doubt anything he says now.

"I coming back up there," he says. "Every peoples down here, they asking questions and looking for the snitch, man."

"Alright," I say. "Give me a call when you get up here. I got some money to help you get set up in an apartment."

We disconnect and I feel the guilt of having placed Miguel in more danger. Even with that, I can't resist the draw of putting another string around Miguel and tossing him back in the water. *I know we could hook an even bigger fish next time.*

I see Bradford reading the paper behind his desk when I get to work the next day. He shoves it aside when he spots me, as if I don't know he's reading the article about my case. He hasn't spoken to me much since our blowout, and I had hoped we could just continue passing one another like a couple of bums in a soup line.

"Come in here a minute," he says with a beckoning flip of the hand. "I'm doing the end-of-the-month books and you're sixty dollars short."

"What, my buy money?"

"Yeah. You're short."

I stare at him blankly. I've been given two thousand dollars a month for the past three years, to spend on drug buys and informant payments. *Sure, I've played fast and loose with the funds—an extra few bucks to an informant or a hot dog here and there—but I've always kept my receipts and my books have always balanced to the penny.*

"This could get the unit into a lot of trouble," he says. "Especially if the city came down and audited us."

"Sixty bucks." I continue my mindless stare. "I just counted out forty-thousand dollars of drug money on my goddamn desk, and you think I keister'd sixty bucks from my city-issued funds?" I shake my head and turn away when I hear the phone ringing in my office.

I answer the call from an inspector named Aaron Bettis. He used to be an Oakland narc and now he's with the DA's office. He congratulates me on my big cocaine seizure and then says he would like to ask a favor.

"Sure," I say. My pen is poised in my hand, ready to take down whatever he wants me to look up for him.

"I'd like to have you as a guest instructor," he says. "Myself and Frank Glover teach a search warrant writing course and . . ."

"I know. I took the class when I was a rookie patrolman."

We laugh about the coincidence and he tells me that neither he nor Glover have the expertise of international drug investigations. They would like me to speak to their students about phone record warrants, and preparing multi-jurisdictional warrants. I tell him I'd be happy to do it.

I'm sitting at my desk enjoying the moment, when Eggs walks in wearing a raid jacket.

"Where you been?" I check the board for a search warrant, but nothing's written down.

He shakes his head in disgust. "Bradford has had us on bank stakeouts again all morning. That guy is up to twelve bank robberies."

I rake my hair back. "Yeah, yeah, the robbery guy." I grab my car keys. "I'll be back in a little while."

The local FBI office is on the fifth floor of the city center building. There is no signage out front. A small camera mounted above the heavy wooden door is the only tipoff that it's anything more than a typical business office. I press the buzzer and after a few seconds of silence, I step back and hold up my police badge. After a few more seconds of deliberation, I'm buzzed in.

"What can I do for you, officer?" A man sporting a sixties crewcut and a dark gray suit blocks me at the first counter.

"I'm wondering if you have any surveillance photos of the bank robber who's been hitting all over town."

"Do you have some information about him?"

I shake my head. "Just thought I may have seen him around."

The guy maintains his stance, as if trying to decide whether or not to grant my request.

"Hey, that's cool." I start to turn back toward the door. "If you're too busy . . ."

"No, no. I guess it's alright." He takes a step back and pivots on his heel. I'm led down a hall and into a small conference room. Two of the walls are plastered with photographs—all of differing sizes and print quality. As soon as I take a look at the first one, I know my hunch was right. I step to the next one, then study the third. I make my way all the way to the corner and down the second wall. By then another agent has stepped into the room. Both of them stand with their hands on their hips, watching me.

When I'm done, I turn back to face them. "I used to work with an informant. We bought a lot of heroin together and when we finished working with him, he was pretty well strung out."

"You think that might be him?" the newcomer asks.

I nod. "Pretty sure of it. His name is Alberto Cruz."

They glance at each other. "Oh no, it's not him. We've already cleared Cruz." The crewcut guy has stepped into the hall, and from the corner of my eye I see him write something down.

I nod again. "Yeah well, take care guys. Sorry I couldn't help." I leave the office, knowing that they're both full of shit. They never checked out Cruz. They never even heard of him until two seconds ago. *Goofy shits.*

I trot up the stairs to my office and find Bradford rummaging through our informant files. I toss my keys on the desk and turn to him. "Hey, I had a thought about that supposed missing money," I say. "Have you double-checked the . . ."

"Not now!" He pushes past me with a photo of Alberto Cruz in his hand. "The FBI just called. They think they have a lead on the bank robbery suspect."

Bradford dashes off and I fall back into my chair. "What a stroke of luck," I say under my breath.

I look up to see Eggs eyeing me curiously. "Are you going up for a drink?" I ask.

"Nah. Got a thing at my daughter's school tonight."

A new pack of phone records keeps me busy for another hour, plotting out times and dates and locations called. I'm hoping to spot a pattern that will identify that next, even bigger link in the chain. Eggs leaves for the night, and then I hear Bradford locking up his office. Most of the detectives out on the floor are gone now, and I'm sitting alone at my desk.

Miguel is driving back, so I can't call him. I thumb through my informant files, trying to find someone to meet up with. I eventually phone Maria Cardenas. She moved in with a guy in Oakland shortly after giving me the suspect in the Arnold Bascomb homicide, and we haven't spoken much since. She's excited to get together, and I end up buying her dinner at a coffee shop near Lake Merritt. Sheepishly, she admits that the guy she's living with is sixty years old. Obviously some sort of *sugar daddy*, though Maria never actually says it. We talk comfortably for an hour or so, and then I drop her in front of her apartment.

On my way back, I stop off at the PBA. The place is empty, but I don't know what I expected for a Wednesday night. Larry is standing attentively behind the bar, waiting to take my order. "A barker tonight, detective?"

"Sure, Larry." I glance around, hoping a raucous crowd suddenly comes clamoring through the door. I'm still the only person in the bar. "And I'll take a seven & seven to wash it down."

"Very well, sir." As Larry stoops to grab a glass, I see myself in the mirror behind the colored bottles. "I read about your big case in the newspaper," he says. "You must be very proud of yourself."

I glance at the reflection again and turn away. "Yeah . . ."

25

Apples and Oranges

"An internal investigation!" I pull the notice from my mail slot. "You gotta be shit'n me! Over a measly sixty dollars?"

Mrs. Sasaki and a few of the detectives turn to look, and I storm past them into my office. I toss my duffle bag against the wall and slam my fist into the desk. *Goddamn Bradford is out to get me, I know it! And after all I've done for this unit.*

I glance around, and thankfully I'm the only one in—*that figures.* There's nothing written on the board, but I notice the cabinet is open and the wire is gone. Whatever they're doing, I'm fine with not being a part of it.

I go through my desk again, checking inside every file and under every pad of paper. *My sweatshirt!* I whip it off the back of my chair and check the pockets. No money. I consider simply withdrawing sixty bucks out of the ATM, and telling IA that I found it in the back of my desk. *Bullshit! I didn't take it, and I'm not giving the department my own money.*

I slide open the cabinet drawer and pull out a memo form. I'm about to type my side of the story for the internal affairs investigator, when I notice a bottle crammed behind all the files. It's a fifth of Jack Daniel's—a gift to the unit awhile back, from Bullet Head. I jerk it out of the drawer and yank off the cap. I pour myself a Styrofoam cupful, then turn up the stereo, and sink back into my chair. Kicking my feet onto the desk, I lean back and take a nice long, body-shuddering swig. The whiskey hits my stomach like a fireball. *Fuck you! Fuck all of you!* I take another hard shot.

I think about giving Miguel a call, but I don't trust the phones. I wouldn't put it past Bradford to tap mine in order to find out what I'm up to, or more likely, try to get something on me.

A knock at the door forces me to slide my feet to the floor. I lean as far as I can without getting up, and turn the knob. The door opens and Lieutenant Preston, stands there looking down at me as if I should stand up and bow. I don't.

He winces at the music. "A young lady is here to see you," he says. "Everybody is at lunch, and it's a good thing I just happened to be walking by."

I guess the inference is that the young lady, whoever she is, would have had to wait out by the elevator until Mrs. Sasaki came back. "Yeah, good thing." I drain he last of the cup.

The lieutenant eyes me, then the cup. Too incredulous a scenario for him to even imagine an employee drinking alcohol in the building and while on duty. Preston frowns and walks off. All he'd had to do was glance atop the file cabinet, and he would have seen the bottle.

I saunter out to the waiting area, and find Marissa Cox looking at wall photos of former police chiefs. I recognize her bony ass before she even turns around. The last time I talked to her, all she wanted was to have her nipples sucked. I'm afraid to even guess what she wants now.

"C'mon back," I say with a lazy wave of the hand. I motion to the interview room. "Sit down in there. I'll be right back." I step into the office and grab a pack of cigarettes, then pour another cup of Jack. I return to the room with it.

She buries her fingers in her straight hair and flings it all around. "I wanted to come by and see you. How have you been?"

I tilt my head sideways. *What kind of horseshit is this? You didn't come in here to find out how I've been.* "Tell me you got something more than that for me; A drug dealer? A bomb maker? A jaywalker? Something?"

Marissa rambles on about some meth-user car-thief she knows, but it sounds like she hasn't seen the guy in months. I recognize his name, Reggie Cuthbertson, from a meth buy I made with Linda. When I went back to buy a second time though, he had moved again. *It's been the story of my life with that guy.*

I try to get directions to Cuthbertson's new place, but Marissa is talking fast and jerking all over. I have to wonder what the hell she's on.

"We got busted together in a stolen Corvette," she says. "And I gave him head in the back of the police car."

My face remains bored and unresponsive. "Where was the cop?"

Marissa shrugs. "Outside taking the report, I guess. Or maybe he was watching."

I take a sip from the cup, but say nothing.

"I like to do it in strange places." She scans the tiny room.

I had taken a cigarette out of the pack for her, but now I find it dangling numbly in my hand as I listen. A light is starting to come on in my head. *She just happened to stop by? And everybody in the unit just happens to be gone? Now she wants to "do it" in the interview room? This smells like a pathetic attempt by Bradford to set me up. The trumped-up missing money charges aren't enough for him?*

"I guess you could say I'm a nymphomaniac." Marissa flashes a mischievous grin. "Just talking about it makes me horny."

I light the cigarette for Marissa, but she doesn't take it. I hold it out toward her in an effort to divert the conversation from her runaway hormones, but she just stares at me contemptuously. I casually glance around the room, trying to spot a hidden camera or wire. I see nothing obvious, but I'm convinced, at the very least, I'm being recorded. I decide not to say a word—*I refuse to give Bradford the satisfaction. At best, he'll have a one-sided tape of this schizoid nymph talking about how horny she is. Nothing else.*

She rotates her sinewy body on her chair. "Mmmm!"

I hear detectives on the floor returning from lunch, and I look over at the unlocked door. The entire bureau sits only feet away, yet I do nothing besides take another sip of whiskey.

Marissa leans back, straddling the chair so that the seat edge fills the gap between her thighs. She starts slowly sliding her body up and back against it, staring at me the whole time.

I remain motionless for a few seconds, and then lean back as if watching a juggling unicyclist. I prop my feet on the desk and take a drag of the cigarette I had lit for her. *Go ahead, knock yourself out.*

By this time, Marissa is in a world all her own. She's undulating rhythmically on the chair, and her pants are grinding so hard that I'm afraid their heat will set off the fire alarm. I'm laughing to myself at the depth Bradford will go to get rid of me. *Who would believe this?*

Marissa glances toward the door and feigns a fearful look as heavy footsteps pass outside. She slows for a second then continues in mocked bashfulness. I take another drag and blow the smoke sideways, as if I were a real smoker. I toss my head back as her pace increases again. Her movements have evolved to waves against a rock, hard and angry. Her crotch, warped onto the edge of the seat, slides back slowly before lifting and crashing down again with gusto. She jerks and bucks to a pulsating buildup, and then moans loudly and slumps into the chair. I raise an eyebrow as a trembling aftershock sends her body into momentary spasms.

Now that's what I call an interview. I stub out the cigarette and hold the door open for her. I still refuse to utter so much as a word. We walk out of the interview room to a floor full of detectives—every one of them trained to pick up on the slightest nuances. I'm certain that someone would have heard Marissa's moans or notice her flushed face and languid posture. But none of them even look up. I deposit Marissa at the elevator—never saying another word, in case she's actually wearing the wire. She gazes back at me with a bewildered expression, just as the doors come together. *Nice try, Bradford.*

A note stuck to my phone hadn't caught my eye before. I stuff the whiskey bottle back behind the files, before slumping into my chair. I whip the note off the phone. It says: CALL KYLE GALLAGHER AT DOJ.

Eggs and Ham come into the office and I stuff the note into my pocket. "Where's Bradford?" I ask.

Eggs motions with his chin. "In with the captain." My two partners are both trying to appear like they're busy with something, but I know how that goes. Nobody wants to get close to a guy who's circling the drain. Afraid they'll get sucked down with him.

"I gotta get the hell outta here." I grab my keys and leave. Bradford is now back in his office, and I could swear I detect a smirk as our eyes meet. Neither of us says anything as I pass.

I pull out of the back gate with my head on a swivel. I stop halfway into the street to see if any cars have followed me out of the lot. I wait for a line of approaching traffic and then quickly pull out in front of them. A couple of the cars skid and honk, as I accelerate through the intersection and onto the freeway. I weave my way into the fast lane, and then suddenly swerve back over to the breakdown lane and stop. When I'm confident I'm not being followed, I continue on. I call Miguel from a payphone a block from our usual meeting place, and have him meet me at a different spot. Halcyon Park backs up to the tracks in an isolated area with only one way in, off 147th Avenue.

I arrive first, and back my car into a private driveway near the park entrance. Miguel pulls into the lot and parks, but I continue watching until it's clear. The weather is damp and overcast, and the park is empty. Anybody who shows up now will automatically be suspect.

I park next to Miguel and he quickly jumps in my car. "I calling to my friend en Las Cuevas," he says. "He say Maestro jump from bail and go back to Mexico. He say Maestro getting the cocaine from one man. He name es Oscar Chapa."

"Does Oscar live here in the U.S.?"

"No, Pheel. Oscar living in Las Cuevas." He scans the park. "This man. He have warehouse in Tijuana to keeping the kilos of cocaine."

"A whole warehouse? How do you know this?"

"My friend, he tell me." Miguel pulls a crumpled piece of paper from his pocket and strains to read his own writing. "Oscar Chapa go to La Flor, and all big cocaine mens, they making the deals there."

"Wait, La Flor?" I squint at his paper. "What does that mean? The Flower?"

"Yeah, Pheel. Es a bar in Tijuana—La Flor de Nayarit."

"The Flower of Nayarit."

All the way back to the station, my mind is racing. I'm trying to figure out how I'm going to get down to Mexico. There's no way it would ever be sanctioned by the department, in fact if it hadn't been for Captain Evancheck, I wouldn't even have been able to work the cases in Orange County. *Any investigation I do into Oscar Chapa and The Flower of Nayarit will have to be off of the radar and on my own.*

I trot up the stairs, my keys jangling in the pocket of my torn, greasy jeans.

"Can you come in here for a moment?" Captain Parks calls out as I pass his office.

I take a seat, and look straight across the desk at his somber face.

"The narcotic unit assignment is from one to three years," he says as if reading it straight from the policy manual.

I nod.

"I just realized you've been up here three and a half years." Parks peers down at his notes. "It would appear it's time for the department to make some changes."

My head is suddenly throbbing with rage. "Does suddenly realizing I've been here too long have anything to do with the missing money?"

"Oh no, not at all." Parks forces a smile meant to convince me. "That's apples and oranges."

"Apples and oranges." I stare back at him. "I saw my sergeant in here earlier. Did he happen to bring this to your attention?"

Parks hesitates. "Uh, no. It's nothing like that. We were just going through the records . . ."

"Just going through the records." I look away, focusing my eyes on a wall photo of a much younger Parks in uniform. I take a deep breath and let it out slowly. "Listen captain, I don't think you understand."

"Oh, don't I?" Parks looks into my eyes without blinking. "I think I do understand. I think maybe I understand better than anyone else."

An old rerun flickers in my head. It's hard to see and the sound quality is poor, but I vaguely remember the original version. Parks is in the lunchroom eating a hardboiled egg, and warning some young sap about the dangers of the undercover narcotics job. "Never forget who you are," he says to the kid. It seems like years ago.

Parks doesn't say it, but I suspect the same film is playing in his head. He leans back and studies me from across the desk. Watching with detached pity, but saying nothing.

I'm suddenly choked with emotion—a muddled mess of all the highs and lows, personal transformations, and career aspirations. I try not to let the captain see it, but my cracked voice reveals the hurt. "So when are these *changes* going to be made?"

"Let's see." The captain runs a finger over his desk calendar. "Today is Thursday. Tell you what. You can have tomorrow to clean out your desk, and then take the weekend off. You'll start graveyards patrol on Monday night.

I walk in the house and throw my stuff onto the couch. Gale sits cross-legged with the girls at the dining room table, working on a school open-house project. "I saved a plate for you if you're hungry."

"Thanks." I walk past them to the bedroom and kick my boots into the closet.

I eat my dinner alone in the kitchen, listening to Gale and the girls in the other room. Awhile later, the girls change into their pajamas and kiss me goodnight. Gale puts them to bed and then comes out to join me. Neither of us says anything, we just sit at the table.

"I'm getting kicked out of narcs." I fork the last piece of chicken into my mouth without looking at her.

Gale is silent.

"That fucking Bradford thinks I stole sixty bucks, and now he's got the captain convinced I've been in there too long." I twist in my chair to face her. "And this is after everything I've done for that unit. In fact, I'm working on a lead right now down in Tijuana. It's a huge case. A goddamn warehouse *full* of cocaine."

Gale's head drops into her hands, shielding her eyes from me. "Now you want to work cases in Mexico? What's next, Phil? Cocaine fields in Colombia?"

I point at her, too furious to even respond. "You don't even know what the hell you're talking about," I finally say. "You're as bad as Bradford and Parks. I don't know why I bother talking to you."

Her blue eyes stare back, their shimmer dulled by the last 3½ years. "Do you ever listen to yourself?" she asks in a tired voice. "Do you realize what you've turned into? You can't leave the house without circling the block a half-dozen times to see if you're being followed. The Hells Angels and the Mexicans want to see you dead. And who knows who else is after you? You hate your bosses, you don't trust the district attorneys, and you even think your own department is tapping your phone. What's happened to you?"

I jump to my feet, thrusting the chair against the wall. I'm standing there with frustration and rage coursing through me. My harsh tone, my bearing, even the pitch of my stance, all strike a sorrowful cord. I'm transported back to the earlier confrontation in Bradford's office. "What the hell do you know?" I finally say, then I turn away. "You don't know anything about my life."

"How could I not know? You've drug the girls and me right down into the sewer with you." Gale takes my plate and turns to put it in the sink. "Honestly, Phil. I'm glad you're leaving narcotics. I don't think our marriage could last through much more of this."

I storm into the bedroom and grab my keys. The phone rings, and I pause for a second deciding whether or not to even answer it. I finally pick it up. "Yeah?"

"Phil, it's Kyle Gallagher at DOJ."

"Hey, Kyle. Sorry I didn't get back to you earlier. It was a bad day at work."

"No problem," he says. "Just thought I'd take a chance and try to catch you at home. I'm calling with some good news."

I sit down on the bed and let out a long exhale. "I could use some good news today."

"You got the job, man." Gallagher's says. "We'll be working together over here at the San Francisco office."

My mouth is open, but nothing comes out. I'm bombarded with thoughts about everything from a permanent vacation from Bradford, to what Gale is going to say.

Gallagher lets out chuckle. "You still there?

"Yeah, I'm here." I stand and cradle the receiver tightly up to my face. I continue in a low voice, barely above a whisper. "Are you sure? I really got the department of justice job?"

He laughs again. "Hell yes, I'm sure. You're going to be working undercover narcotics for the rest of your career!"

I slowly rotate my head toward a noise behind me. Gale's outline is framed in the dark doorway. She stands there for a few seconds, saying nothing. I see her head drop as she turns and silently walks out.

I slam the bathroom door with force that shakes the house. The cold water soothes my face, still hot with rage. I cup my hands under the faucet and splash myself again, running my fingers through my stringy hair. It soaks my shirt and drips onto the counter and floor.

I tilt my head back and close my eyes. I finally landed the dream job, and I have the dream case to take along with me. It's what I've been working towards since I first came to narcotics. I tell myself it's no coincidence that the chance of a lifetime fell in my lap right when I needed it most—a time when I can't do anymore under the conditions at my current department. This opportunity is divine providence. It's karma. I've gone as high as I can here. I need to take the job. I need to move forward or I'll whither and die.

I look up at the reflection in the mirror, and then look away. I force myself to turn back and bear the image standing in front of me. The eyes staring back are uncaring and cold. He's someone I don't know anymore—Gale was right. *What happened to him?*

I sit on the side of the tub—my face buried in my hands. The life I once knew is gone. My entire existence has become an insane carnival ride, spinning and diving, jerking this way and the other. It's both thrilling and terrifying, and it makes me sick to my stomach. Yet, I can't get enough of it. I'm unable to get off the ride. I won't get off.

My hand is balled into a fist and I want to slam it through the wall, but I'm not sure who to blame for all my rage. *Who is it I am I really angry at? My bosses? The feds? Is it the people who are trying to kill me? Is my wife to blame for the position I'm in?*

I walk out of the bathroom to find her sitting alone at the kitchen table. The weathered smile she's fought to keep on her face has all but vanished. The past 3½ years have taken a visible toll. Her trademark optimism has crumbled into bitter disappointment.

I hear the girls whispering in the darkness of their bedroom, and I realize they've suffered too. I'm suddenly struck with a sad reality: In my current state, my family would be much better off without me.

I sit down at the table across from Gale. "We need to talk."

Her soft blue eyes come up to meet mine, but she says nothing.

"I've made a decision . . ."

Epilogue

I drive to the station on Sunday so I can pack up my desk in peace and anonymity. I keep my head down as I hustle up the stairway to the second floor. Thankfully, none of the detectives are working the weekend.

I carry a load of files and personal effects to the locker room and I find a yellow note stuck to my locker. It bears a cryptic message: MISSING MONEY LOCATED—BOOKKEEPING ERROR.

* * *

I walk into the graveyard shift briefing Monday night, clean-shaven and with my hair neatly trimmed. The new uniform I'm wearing is starched and pressed, brass buttons are polished, and my leather is buffed to a waxy sheen. The visual transformation back to a patrol officer startles my coworkers, yet inside I haven't come down from the *narcotics high*. I may look the part, but my heart is simply not in it.

I scan around the room, feeling like a battle-hardened veteran returning home from war to work a desk job. My patrol partners all seem so much younger than I remember. The challenge of riding a beat again eludes me, yet I know it's the job I have to do. I hit the street with the notion of taking the first night slowly, allowing myself to ease back into the other role I used to play so well.

A couple of hours into the shift, a yellow van passes me going the opposite direction on Mission Boulevard. Something about it compels me to turn around and find a reason to stop it. I notice a bald tire, and pull the van over. A huge grin stretches across my face when I see that the driver is Reginald Cuthbertson. The nemesis had eluded me as a young patrolman, and though I was able to buy meth from him once undercover, he had packed up and moved before I could go back and arrest him.

Cuthbertson's eyes are a little bloodshot, but he otherwise appears responsive and sober. I lean in the window and sniff the inside of his van. "Hmm," I say with a wink. "Sure smells like weed in here."

"What's the fine for weed?" He tosses me a surly look. "Less than a parking ticket, isn't it?"

I call for a backup unit and have Cuthbertson step from the van. The self-assured expression drains from his face, and I know I've got him by the balls. "Something else in the van, Reggie?"

The search is ostensibly for the source of the marijuana odor, but in truth I'm hoping for something much better. I find what I'm looking for hidden beneath a wool blanket in the back of the van. A mobile methamphetamine lab, precursor chemicals, glassware, and a small amount of finished product are assembled inside three open cardboard boxes.

My first arrest back on uniformed patrol christens my long voyage toward career restoration. I realize of course, my real reconstruction work will have to take place at home.

The narcotics business had taken a heavy toll on my family, but perhaps not as bad as some. Two of my informants never made it out. Linda the hooker died from an overdose, and RR Express succumbed to the blood clot in his nose. A dirty heroin needle had caused the initial infection, and the poor guy never got proper medical care for it. Both people passed within a year of my departure.

My high school classmate, Aldean Harris, was eventually arrested for the PCP sales he made to me. When he and his attorney got copies of my reports, Aldean finally figured out who I was. He apparently spread a warning amongst others in my class that I was now an undercover cop. According to Aldean, I was so hard-up for cases that I had taken to targeting my old friends. His attempt to save face was so pathetic, it was almost funny.

Alberto Cruz was convicted of eight armed bank robberies, and was sentenced to twelve years in federal prison. In another ironic twist, Bill Canaday prosecuted the case for the district attorney's office. But after two failed attempts at alcohol rehab, The Big A's conviction turned out to be Canaday's farewell effort. The drunk who had screwed me twice, once on patrol and once in narcotics, finally got what he had coming. He was canned from the DA's office.

Maria Cardenas seemed to have better luck at rehabilitation. We kept in touch during my career, and even met a few times for coffee. As far as I could tell, she cleaned up her act and never returned to jail.

Miguel Baca relocated back to Southern California, and though he called a few times, we eventually lost touch. In due time, I learned his true identity, but contrary to department policy I never logged it into the informant files. My fear was that some sleazy attorney would be able to con a judge into disclosing it, long after I was gone. A short time later, we learned through the FBI that the source of the leak in the Feldman case was actually a corrupt courtroom clerk. The news allayed any lingering guilt about hiding Miguel's identity, even from the judge.

As far as I know, Miguel was able to elude detection by the cocaine kingpins. The gang of killers from Las Cuevas never figured out who had informed on their operation. I suppose they eventually gave up and went back to Mexico. Like them, I ultimately gave up and went back home. I would abandon my quest to reach the top of the cartel's pyramid. Oscar Chapa would be relegated to a tattered file stuffed in the back of my locker, and I would never make the journey to Tijuana. The Flower of Nayarit remains a sanctuary where international drug suppliers, wholesalers and transporters barter with impunity.

* * *

"I'm not going to take the state narcotics job," I promised Gale that night at the kitchen table. And although she didn't say it, her eyes told me that our marriage would not have survived it. I suppose in my heart, I knew it too. I gave her my word that I would never work another undercover assignment again.

When I had been out of the unit for a while, my head began to clear and I was finally able to gain the perspective I had lost. I came to realize that nothing, especially a job, could possibly take the place of my wife and daughters. I would never again forget the importance of family over all else in my life.

Like the captain who had tried to warn me, I too was able to redeem my career after such an unceremonious ouster. The police department promoted me to sergeant a year later, and I eventually rose through the ranks to lieutenant and then captain. In a final sardonic irony, the first assignment offered to me after becoming a sergeant was to run the narcotics unit. Besides having given Gale my word, by that time the smoke had cleared and I wouldn't have taken the position even if I could. It would have been like offering a bartender job to a reformed alcoholic—it simply wouldn't have worked for us on any level.

My growing pains and adolescent rebellion had played out late in life. I was 26 years old, married, and had two young daughters. The values I had built over a lifetime of doing the right thing were eroded by self-indulgence, and eventually collapsed under the tremendous weight of my ego. I had masked my conduct behind the pretext of career, work assignment, and the undercover persona—Phil Soto. And I had become so convincing in the role, that I was even able to hide the truth from myself.

Some of life's lessons are learned through the wisdom of others, and some are learned by witnessing failure. The most profound lessons are learned through experience. For me it was suffering the humiliation of self-destruction. In the process, I had not only failed myself, but I had failed my friends, my bosses, my department, and my family. Most importantly, I failed the wife who had stood by me and endured more than any spouse should ever have to.

Made in the USA
Lexington, KY
09 May 2011